OLYMPIA
PROVISIONS

CURED MEATS AND TALES

OLYMPIA PROVISIONS

FROM AN

AMERICAN CHARCUTERIE

ELIAS
CAIRO

and

MEREDITH
ERICKSON

PHOTOGRAPHY BY ERIC WOLFINGER

TEN SPEED PRESS

Berkeley

Contents

So Damn Greek It Hurts

My sister Michelle has always bailed me out.

Like the time I moved to Greece to cook without first discussing with the management how much they were going to pay me. I worked for the entire summer before finding out I was only getting paid room and board. So I had to call Michelle to buy me a ticket back to Switzerland, where I had moved from our hometown of Sandy, Utah, to do a four-year *stage* in Wildhaus, a tiny mountain village that has an amazing, one-of-a-kind food culture.

Or when I was preparing to leave Switzerland and the Swiss put the fear of god into me about going back to the U.S. ("I hope you enjoy this *appenzeller* because you're never going to eat handmade cheese again. Or drink good beer. Or eat good sausage!") Michelle told me to come to Portland, vowing that their prophecies wouldn't become reality. She had moved to Portland during my time abroad, and having never visited the city, I braced for a wasteland of vapid food. I readied myself to never eat chocolate again, to be cool with Denny's, to see the world through Costco blue-colored glasses.

She picked me up at the airport, and perhaps sensing my apprehension, took me straight to the Portland State University farmers' market. There I saw mâche, Tillamook cheese, Oregon truffles, cherries

Athens via Portland: a regular Sunday afternoon with Olympia Provisions co-owners Tyler Gaston, Michelle Cairo, and Elias Cairo.

from the Gorge, smoked fish from the Nez Perce reservation, and giant salmon fresh from the Columbia. It was then, after experiencing the inspiring Wild West ethos of Portland, that I told Michelle about my dream of making meat in the Old World traditions I'd learned in Switzerland. And Michelle understood the vision because, well, it was in our blood.

Our dad didn't move to America until he was in his late twenties. He grew up in a tiny Greek village in the mountains where there was no choice but to do everything for yourself. And so he was a natural entrepreneur: a farmer, beekeeper, distiller, and butcher. He brought this ethos with him, and we grew up on three-quarters of an acre outside of Salt Lake City—an exotic Greek island in a sea of Mormon suburbia.

Dad had a Greek column built outside on the porch. The lawn was a Greek oasis of whitewashed furniture, sundials, and a large fountain of Venus pouring water out of her *bota* bag. Indoors we had a bright blue carpet—yes, to mimic the color of the Mediterranean—and all-white furniture (covered in plastic, obviously). Covering one wall was a painting of the Parthenon; just above it was the Greek key stenciled as a border around the room. So damn Greek it hurt.

The backyard was a fully functioning farm. You name it, we had it: lambs, ducks, geese, chickens, a hundred-plus pigeons (which we raced and ate), beehives, pine trees, and a garden bursting at the seams. Hungry? Find something in the backyard. Scrape your knee? Pour grappa from Dad's still on it. Need glue? Go cut into the pine tree and mix the sap with sand to make it pliable. Oh, you were planning on buying it? Are you lazy or just stupid?

On Sunday afternoons, while our Mormon neighbors began their workweek, our lawn was awash with drunken Greeks dancing around a lamb on a spit. I would be the one playing clarinet, as my dad forced me to take lessons so I could play tunes from *Zorba* with a bouzouki band. My parents once were called to the principal's office at school because we stunk of garlic so badly that the other kids' parents complained.

Michelle was mortified . . . by all of it, really. She hated the animals, hated the backyard, hated the Cadillac Brougham, and hated doing chores on a Saturday morning, like digging a potato cellar for my dad. The only refuge she had was the roof of the shed, her little oasis away from the animals, where she could suntan naked with our cousins in preparation for one of her beauty pageants.

When not in the backyard, we were at one of my parents' two restaurants: Queen One and Queen Two. They were typical Greek-American diners with specials like lamb's leg gyros, fresh spanakopita, and *pastitsio* (Greek lasagna). Of course, Mom kept the pie case stuffed not only with American pies, but also with baklava and *galaktompoureko*

Growing up Cairo.

Michelle Cairo, age 12, killing it at the Miss America Pageant.

(custard pie). On weekends I would often sneak over and fish fresh *loukoumades* (honey dumplings) from right out of the fryer.

Some of my best childhood memories are of meeting customers, standing on a stool so I could reach the griddle to make grilled cheese, and playing Battleship in the dish pit with old wooden salad bowls. And, of course, eating like a king. My mom baked bread pretty much every morning. We spooned gobs of honey from the beehives onto the bread before our swimming lessons in the summer, and we picked salad ingredients from the garden every afternoon. To this day, both my sister and I are happiest eating from our own gardens.

At dinner, it was normal to have three types of meat on the table: huge steaks from the restaurants and lamb and chicken from the yard. Entire weekends were devoted to making meats, eating, and family. What I'm saying is that I grew up with what people now call DIY; most Old World folks like my dad just called it "life." And so that foundation, my desire to make meat, was built in. Later in life, a four-year trip to Switzerland sealed it. But more on that later.

A Window into a Meat Shop

At present—with the exception of my dad, who died in 1991—my whole family now works at Olympia Provisions. If you came to visit our headquarters on Portland's Produce Row, you would see my brother, Bill, working in packaging; my mom loading up her trunk for the coastal farmers' markets; and Alexis, my niece, working the phones in our sales department. And of course Michelle is here, running the entire business (and running after me about our margins).

Adjacent to the office is our new meat plant: 38,000 square feet of meat-making heaven that we built in 2013. Here, on any given day, Handsome Joe is at the center sausage table pushing fresh Northwest pork through the grinder, Paulie is pulling 1,000 pounds of sweetheart ham from the smoker (a machine made down the road in Clackamas, Oregon), and Mike is in the dry box (5,000 square feet, set at 58°F (14°C) and 83 percent relative humidity) methodically spacing strings of salumi, each cased in natural hog intestine and dusted in natural white mold. Paulie fires up the oven with pâté and then returns to grinding fresh nutmeg—yes, we formulate our own recipes and in each we use freshly ground spices. And in the packaging room, our plant manager Josh is yelling out orders of what retailers from Alaska to Florida need, and how fast.

Co-owner Tyler Gaston is reviewing how last night at the restaurants went, while simultaneously preparing the käsekrainer cart for that day's farmers' market.

In our fabrication shop—pretty much everyone's favorite part of the new plant—the other co-owners, Marty Schwartz and Nate Tilden, are ordering, measuring, or welding steel, preparing to build new meat racks or repair something in one of our two restaurants.

Me? I'm at my bowl chopper or stuffer waiting for the next problem to pop up, or ensuring the plant is as clean as a hospital, or waiting for the daily once-over from the United States Department of Agriculture (USDA) agent. My usual week consists of about thirty hours of stuffing sausage, plus grinding, portioning, and cleaning, and another thirty hours of administrative and USDA paperwork. Most of it is done in a massive cold room on a wet floor, eight hours a day of standing. I'm not asking for sympathy: it's my heaven.

The Pursuit of a Beautiful Thing

I never thought I would work in a kitchen. Even in Switzerland I knew that cooking wasn't my calling. After arriving in Portland, I worked in the kitchen at Castagna, an amazing little restaurant and café owned and operated by Monique Sui. She allowed me to buy all of the best ingredients that I could find in the Pacific Northwest, and I was able to really get to know some of the great farmers, foragers, and fisherman here. It made me love Oregon even more for what it had to offer, and I stayed for six years, but my focus sharpened after hours, spent reading meat safety books and the Code of Federal Regulations from the USDA.

Making charcuterie is not cooking: you're producing something, repeating the same motion in the same way with the same ingredients in hopes of perfectly rendering the same product over and over and over. Thousands per day. Yes, this also is true for restaurant chefs: they have to put forth an effort to make dishes perfect as well. The difference is that once I release a product, it can never change, not one bit. I have to ensure that the millions of pounds I make of it are all perfectly identical. Chefs can create a dish, and once they are sick of making it, they can take it off the menu. They are also able to create new dishes every time they get inspired, which I miss and envy. Over the course of a year, I make one, or maybe two, new products. If I do make a new product, it has to be amazing. What keeps me going in the day-to-day is the fact that I am always getting better, finding small efficiencies that make the process easier and the product better. I make 8,000 pounds of salami per day, and there hasn't been one time when I've thought, "Well, that tastes absolutely perfect. I can quit now." I'm not a master, and I never will be. It's the pursuit of it that I love: making a glorious thing with base elements of pork, fine sea salt, and technique.

Take our Saucisson d'Arles (page 140), for example. It's utter simplicity—just pork and salt, really—but making it perfectly, again and again, is much more impressive than, say, making something like Coppa di Testa (headcheese) (page 33) once. Because to make simple charcuterie well, you have to have full control of every level of the process. To make charcuterie at home, rather than at the industrial level, is to make it simply. And when you make it simply, you cannot hide any flaws. And that's a beautiful thing.

Olympia Provisions: The Book

Olympia Provisions is a unique animal: two simple and honest restaurants that serve the kind of food and drink most people want to have every night (at least I hope so), plus a fast-growing charcuterie business. I wanted to write a book at this point in the life of our business to reveal the people behind the product and to show that we are a family that cares about what we do. I have been working at realizing this dream most of my life—not to take over the world with meat, necessarily, but to live in a world where meat, and smart meat making, reign.

I thought a lot about how to organize this book and ended up with a structure that mirrors our business. Part 1 presents our charcuterie recipes. The chapters run from simple to more complicated, beginning with slow-cooking pâtés and making fresh sausages—recipes that don't require a lot of equipment or know-how—and finishing with fermenting and dry-curing sausages, recipes that need more specialized equipment, ingredients, techniques, and skills. It's a curriculum of sorts. Quite a few of these recipes—like those for Capicola (page 38), Salami Cotto (page 92), and Nduja (spreadable salami)(page 153)—aren't available in other English-language charcuterie books. And many of the recipes out there are more difficult than they need to be. Mortadella (page 88), for example, should always be made in a grinder rather than a processor, in my opinion. And while it's true that making meat is a bit more involved than baking bread or brewing beer, it's really not dangerous if you follow some relatively simple safety rules (which we'll cover starting on page 12).

I also wanted to showcase our restaurants, so Part 2 features recipes from both of our locations. We are open all day, and both the mood and the food change as the day goes on. We start with brunch and lunch, then move on to happy hour and dinner. I've included plenty of recipes that utilize the meat we teach you to make in Part 1—but if you're a novice cook and the idea of making charcuterie is intimidating, you can always go online and order the meat directly from us to make these recipes.

Along the way I'll share some stories, particularly a dive into the time and place it all started for me (Switzerland in the late nineties). I've also included the people who inspired my love of traditionally made products and food, and explained the origins of the OP love for pairing wine and meat.

PART
1

OP
CHARCUTERIE

Currently in America there seems to be a renewed desire for charcuterie products, as well as a heightened interest in the craft itself. Charcuterie, in the simplest sense, is the process of preserving meat for a longer shelf life. In many cases, the *charcutiére's* craft involves utilizing all of the animal, turning some of the less desired parts into the most delicious of treats.

Preserving meat with salt dates back to about 3000 BCE. At that time, people were just trying to keep their meat from going bad before they could eat it all. However, being the industrious creatures that we are, humans eventually started to cook, smoke, and cure meat as well as salt it. Before long, we got very good at preserving meat in a lot of creative ways, and we started to love and crave it. I have often thought about the people who discovered the techniques I use to make my living today, and those who kept trying to perfect the techniques to make cured meat more enjoyable and appealing, longer lasting, and safer. Who were the first people to slow-cook in fat, a technique that keeps out spoilage-causing oxygen and makes meat unutterably moist? Or the first person to hand-chop meat, add fat and spices, and then poach it slowly so you end up with pâté? Who discovered that apple-wood smoke is sweet and hardwood smoke is bitter, but if you use them together to smoke meats, mold won't grow on those meats. One of my favorite imaginings is about the lucky person who accidentally dried meat with salt that contained nitrate and thus discovered the means of keeping meat beautifully pink during curing. And who was the absolute madman who figured out that you can ferment a sausage, cover it in mold, then dry it—and its flavor will blow your mind? I often wonder how far from those original products mine have come. I am sure many of the techniques I use today were developed through a good mixture of necessity and dumb luck. However, I love thinking about the people who, like me, kept trying to make the product better in the hopes of making it as close to perfect as possible.

In the chapters that follow, we'll begin with the most simple charcuterie methods (slow-cooking, pâtés, and fresh sausages), and walk you through each process to provide a foundation on which to build to the more technical and tricky ones (smoking, curing, and fermenting).

Despite what you may have heard, "quick charcuterie" is a contradiction in terms. It doesn't exist. Like traveling by train, making great charcuterie takes patience—and like Amtrak, it can be a little smelly. There is no easy way, nor a perfect way, to create charcuterie.

It takes quality, technique, and time. When I see a flaw in one of our products, I feel as though I've been served an overcooked egg at brunch or am dealing with a server who doesn't know the wine he's pouring—a little bit of me dies inside. I work really hard at what I produce, and I would never cut a corner for any reason. So when I am trying as hard as possible and the product does not come out perfect, I can only try harder to perfect it. It is exhausting to be consistent.

I am very lucky to live in the Northwest where I am able to work with Hutterite hog farmers who treat their pigs with kindness and respect. Down the road from the farms is the slaughterhouse, a third-generation, family-owned operation. This is by no means the cheap way to make meat, but it's the right way. The big meat industry in America is all about speed and margin. I want to make an honest product by methods that never force me to compromise quality or ethics for margin or speed. And although I produce on a large scale, my basic techniques for making meat at home are the same. To make the recipes here work for home kitchens, I've done the figuring for you; just follow the recipes and a few rules and you will have a new lifetime hobby. Some of the recipes that follow require very little hands-on action followed by, say, a 3-week cure. The beauty is in the slowness of the process. The fascination is in watching the chemistry over time, and the changes that occur.

Although it may seem like the following information on percentages, safety, quality, nitrite, and nitrate isn't fun stuff, it is imperative for your home meat-making that you adhere to the advice. It's kind of like me running through my daily checklist with the USDA: At the beginning, the meeting was something I dreaded, and so I engaged with it in a rather half-assed way. But ultimately, spending that time with the USDA agent every morning settled into a checks-and-balance system that helped me make a safe and wholesome product. By engaging with the process in a deep way, I began to understand every little nuance of my business, and that, of course, improved my skill level and, by proxy, my charcuterie. The same is possible for you.

General Meat-Making Safety Steps

Regardless of what type of charcuterie you are making, there are six crucial elements you must keep in mind. They are (1) cleanliness, (2) raw product temperature, (3) cooked product temperature, (4) cooling, (5) calibration, and (6) correct measurement.

CLEANLINESS

Everything involved in the process of making meat must be clean. Hands, surfaces, grinder blades, stuffer attachments, knives—absolutely everything. There is a myth I hear in the halls of the meat world about not cleaning a smoker or a dry box because the filth will add to the flavor, or to what folks call *terroir*. I call it lazy. If you want to have complete control of what you are making, you need to start with a completely sterile environment. One small pathogen in or on any of your product, and someone is getting sick.

All surfaces that may come into contact with the meat should be washed with soapy water, then rinsed with clean water. It should then be sanitized with a bleach and water mixture—I use 2 teaspoons (10 ml) of bleach to every 1 gallon (4 liters) of water. It is impossible to get the environment and equipment too clean. So when in doubt, clean it again.

RAW PRODUCT TEMPERATURE

Raw meat should never, ever exceed 44°F (7°C) until you are cooking it or starting the fermentation process. In practical terms, this means you have to work in an organized way, often in small batches, to ensure you keep the temperature down. When you are not actually handling the meat, keep it in the refrigerator. Whenever possible, work on a cutting board that has been chilled in the freezer for at least 30 minutes. And when you're grinding meat, it should land in a bowl placed nestled in another bowl filled with ice.

COOKED PRODUCT TEMPERATURE

Every product needs to be cooked to an internal temperature of 155°F (68°C), with fermented and dry-cured products being the only exception. If after cooking to this temperature, your product is not perfect, there was a problem in technique or formulation. Undercooked meat products, like college kids on spring break, are ideal breeding grounds for bacteria.

To test internal temperatures, I like to use an adjustable thermometer that can be calibrated easily. It is important to calibrate your thermometer to make sure the temperature reading you are getting is correct.

To measure the internal temperature of any given product, place the thermometer into the thickest part of the product. The temperature on the outside of a product can be extremely different than the temperature in the middle.

COOLING

Because it is really easy for pathogens to go crazy when the temperature of your meat is in the danger zone, between 40°F and 100°F (4°C to 38°C), it is important to chill the finished product as quickly as possible. You should be able to cool your heated product (no matter how hot it is to begin with) to below 39°F (4°C) within 5 hours. An ice bath is your friend. The deep freezer, too. And don't worry: in each of the recipes that follow, I will tell you the best method for cooling the product.

CALIBRATION

Although you won't need specialized technical equipment for every charcuterie recipe in this book, when a recipe does call for tools like a thermometer, pH meter, or water activity meter, you need to calibrate these tools each time you use them. This might sound a bit difficult at first, but after you've calibrated a machine once, you will know that it is easy as can be. All of the equipment used to make charcuterie will come with a how-to-calibrate booklet when you buy it, so read it. And make sure you know how to use each piece of equipment before beginning.

Although I am a true believer in "getting a feeling" for some things in meat making—like achieving a good bind, casing well, and perfecting seasoning—factors like exact temperature, pH, and water activity are not among those things. Always check the numbers, every time, carefully.

CORRECT MEASUREMENT

As I said earlier, charcuterie is not cooking. And so, unlike cooking, it's not possible to be spontaneous or flexible with measurements. That's why, in all of the charcuterie chapters, I've included measurements in grams for all small quantities, even those less than 2 tablespoons. This type of precision is the only way to guarantee accuracy.

I know these six elements make it seem like charcuterie making involves a lot of rules. You may not love rules; I myself hate them. But just think about how good it will feel to bask in the compliments you'll receive for being a great meat maker—and knowing for sure that you are not going to make anyone sick.

Nitrate and Nitrite

Nitrate (NO_3) and nitrite (NO_2) are ionic compounds made up of the common elements nitrogen (N) and oxygen (O). Nitrate and nitrite are all around us—in the air we breathe, the water we drink, and the soil in which we grow our vegetables. Nitrate is the more common of the two. We consume nitrate and transform it into nitrite; in fact, we produce 75 to 80 percent of all the nitrite in our bodies. The nitrite we consume in a normal diet turns into nitric oxide in the stomach, which serves a variety of natural functions in the body.

Sodium nitrate ($NaNO3$) and sodium nitrite ($NaNO2$), which are stable and readily available forms of nitrate and nitrite, are applied to meat to prevent pathogens from proliferating and for enhancing both color and flavor.

The pathogen we as meat makers are most concerned about is *Clostridium botulinum*, the bacterium that causes botulism. Not only is it lethal, it is also heat resistant and acid tolerant, and can survive without oxygen. One thing that can hinder the growth of this pesky pathogen (among others) is nitrite. Long story short: adding nitrite to meat is a great way to guard against multiplying pathogens.

Nitrite also oxidizes when it comes into contact with oxygen, producing nitric oxide, which binds to the iron found in the myoglobin in meat, turning the meat that beautiful pink color that is often associated with cured meats. Nitrite also creates a flavor that is characteristic of cured meats.

In some of the recipes in this book, I add nitrate and nitrite in the form of curing salt #1 and curing salt #2 (commonly sold as Insta Cure #1 or #2, or Prague powder #1 or #2). Curing salt #1 is a mixture of sodium (regular salt) and nitrite. Curing salt #2 is a mixture of sodium, nitrate, and nitrite. Curing salt #1 is used more often in meat processing than curing salt #2 because it's faster acting. Only nitrite can bond with iron in meat, which means curing salt #1—with its readily available nitrite—can start working right away. Conversely, the nitrate in curing salt #2 must oxidize one of its oxygen elements before it can bond to the iron in meat in the form of nitrite. We use curing salt #2 on longer curing products, for example Lomo (page 124), Coppa (page 123), and Salami (see chapter 6) (basically, fermented and/or dry-cured products).

With curing salt #2, sodium is the transport vessel that moves the nitrite to the myoglobin to start working right away. Once the meat is mixed with salt, it starts to pull moisture out of the meat. This moisture is called active water weight—that is, the water that is suspended in the meat. As soon as the nitrite comes into contact with the meat, it begins to work its magic: preserving the meat, killing any lurking botulism bacteria, and stopping oxidation from happening. But during this magic, sodium chloride from sea salt begins to affect nitrite and slowly but surely halts its productivity. In meats that need longer cures, a little back-up nitrate is needed, which is more resistant to sodium chloride. Nitrate is like the cleanup hitter—the Reggie Jackson of meat making—hitting all the salt spots that nitrite missed. The nitrate will take a bit of time to lose its extra oxygen element and turn into nitrite, bonding to the deeper myoglobin found in the meat. It works as a sleeper cell of sorts, plotting its attack against any pesky pathogens.

Curing salt is not always easy to find, especially in Europe. A good resource is SausageMaker.com, a one-stop shop for curing salt and everything else your meat-making heart desires.

Nitrite has definitely caught a bad rap. In the 1960s, we had a bacon and ham boom, and the meat makers of the era tried to fill the demand fast. They pumped an ungodly amount of nitrite into their meat so it would turn pink and develop its cured flavor as quickly as possible. This left way too much nitrite in the meat. And when you have a lot of excess nitrite in meat and then add high heat (for example, frying it in a hot pan), you can produce a poison called nitrosamine. This was found to be carcinogenic in large doses. What happened next is what I call the Fox News phenomenon—a fact or two ripped out of context for scare value. The FDA released a report saying that nitrite in large amounts is dangerous when cooked at high temperatures. What we heard was that all nitrite was dangerous.

Fast forward to today, and meat makers are taking advantage of nitrite fear by producing "naturally cured meat." These producers use the nitrate found in vegetables for curing. News flash (real news this time): this nitrate is the exact same nitrate (and precursor to nitrite) it has always been. It's just that we're able to call a product "nitrite-free" due to a labeling loophole.

In the end, nitrite isn't dangerous when used in proper amounts. At right are some facts that may put your mind at ease.

Nitrate and Nitrite Facts

FACT: *Spinach, beets, lettuce, and cabbage all have at least 400 times more nitrate, pound for pound, than bacon and hot dogs.*

FACT: Clostridium botulinum *produces botulism, a paralytic illness. That's bad. The nitrite in cured meat prevents* Clostridium botulinum *from growing. That's good.*

FACT: *It is 100 percent illegal to cure meat without the addition of nitrite.*

FACT: *Nitrite gives cured meats a unique flavor, and preserves that beautiful pink tone. A smoked pig belly that doesn't contain nitrite is an unappealing gray color. Add nitrite and you have bacon.*

Charcuterie Tools and Equipment

You don't need a lot of fancy equipment and supplies to make charcuterie, but there are a few items, some essential, that will probably be unfamiliar to you. In most cases, these specialized tools will make your charcuterie making easier and ensure that your final product is safe and delicious. Any and all charcuterie materials—thermometers, casings, grinders, stuffers, smokers, smoking accessories, nets, seasoning, spices, scales—can be found at SausageMaker.com.

DIGITAL SCALE

You will need a digital scale that is accurate up to .5 gram. It's also ideal if the scale can work in both grams and ounces, and if you can zero it out after placing a bowl or other vessel on the scale.

DRY BOX

To make fermented meats you will need a room or chamber that maintains 58°F (14°C) and 83 percent relative humidity, with a very slow airflow. More on this on page 118–19.

FERMENTATION CHAMBER

To make fermented meats you will need a room or chamber that can be held at 73°F (23°C) and 95 percent relative humidity, with very little or no airflow. More on this on page 132.

GRINDER

There is something really rewarding about making a simple sausage or pâté using a hand-grinder. But if I have a good amount of product to make or am trying to make an emulsification, I like the ease of using an electric grinder. A KitchenAid mixer with a grinder attachment is a good starting place. It can handle a decent amount of meat. However, if you plan on making most of the recipes in this book, any one-horsepower grinder with a steel grinder head is the way to go.

KNIVES

You can do most of the tasks required in the charcuterie chapters of this book with two knives: a deboning knife and a sausage-making knife.

The Victorinox 6-inch (15-cm) deboning knife has a nice point on the tip and not too much flex. It will help you easily get the meat off the bones and is great for removing sinew and unwanted fat.

A sausage-making knife isn't absolutely necessary, but it will make your life a bit easier. It looks like a small paring knife but has thin needlelike points on the opposite edge of the blade. You use this end to puncture your casing if you get any air in it during sausage making.

> CHARCUTERIE IS NOT THE TIME TO BE FAST AND LOOSE WITH INGREDIENTS; YOU HAVE TO GET THE SCIENCE DOWN BEFORE MOVING TO THE ART ASPECT OF THE CRAFT.

PÂTÉ MOLDS AND SLOW-COOKING VESSELS

I love a solid, good-looking pan with a tight-fitting lid for making pâtés and slow-cooking meats. Le Creuset is my go-to brand; they aren't cheap and they make you look fancy, but they are also just damn fine cooking vessels.

pH METER

A pH meter measures the pH level of your product and provides the only way to know for sure whether or not you are making a safe fermented product. If you are making fermented meats, such as salami, this is a small investment to make for serious peace of mind. I use one from Hanna Instruments that is easy to calibrate and simple to read.

SMOKER

You can smoke most of the meats in this book using a Weber grill or any charcoal grill with a lid. But if you plan on smoking more than once or twice a year, buy an electric smoker with a heating pad that will burn your chips without you having to stoke the coals. My smoker of choice is the Little Chief.

STUFFER

Although it's possible to stuff sausages using a grinder, I personally don't like to; it takes a bit of time to get the feel for it. For these recipes, I would use a stand-up piston stuffer with a hand crank and a capacity of up to 3½ pounds (1.6 kg) of meat. Far and away the best stuffer of this size is made by a German company called Dick.

THERMOMETER

Buy one that you can calibrate easily. At home, I use a standard thermometer with an adjustable dial. I calibrate it by making an ice and water slurry, then setting the proper temperature as necessary. To calibrate your thermometer, in a large pot, mix ice and water in equal parts, then place the thermometer into the ice slurry; it should read 32°F (0°C). If it doesn't, adjust your thermometer until it displays the correct temperature when stuck in the ice bath.

WATER ACTIVITY METER

This piece of equipment will let you know you are making a safe dry-cured or fermented product. A water activity meter measures the unbound water content of your product, and the more unbound water you remove from a dry-cured or fermented sausage, the better your chances of reducing spoilage. The industry standard is the Pawkit made by Decagon. This amazing meter will last for a lifetime of meat making. It is only used for dry-cured items.

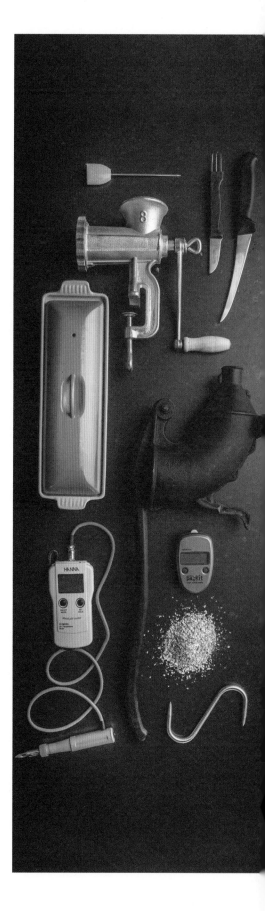

About Percentage Charts

I cannot tell you how many times a respected chef has told me that he or she "kinda weighs out" nitrite or nitrate. You know from the earlier discussion (see pages 14–15) not only how important it is to use nitrate, but also how essential it is to use the proper amount. Charcuterie is not the time to be fast and loose with ingredients; you have to get the science down before moving to the art aspect of the craft, where you add your own touches to a recipe. The rewards and the risks are very clear: doubling the amount of nitrite you add to a recipe can produce nitrosamine and give someone a case of lethal food poisoning. On the other hand, not adding enough nitrite can allow pathogens to multiply and you end up with botulism. Not fun.

In Part 1 of this book, we cover a different charcuterie technique in each chapter (slow-cooking, smoking, dry-curing, and so on). At the start of each chapter, we describe the traditional, or more basic, methods of each technique, and we also include a percentage chart for the more advanced sausage-making fiends. My hope is that once you learn a few of the charcuterie basics, you will get into the meat-making groove enough to eventually be able to work solely from the percentage charts. Percentage cooking is commonly referred to as using "baker's percentages." Bakers use percentages to scale recipes up or down depending on how much volume they want to produce. Meat makers do the same thing, using percentage charts to increase or decrease the amount of ingredients in a recipe depending on how much meat we have to work with.

The charts serve two purposes. The first is that it helps you get a handle on ratios. Good charcuterie is all about balance: salt and savory, protein and fat, spices and herbs. Knowing the proper ratio of salt to meat (and fat) is essential to achieving quality, flavor, texture, and safety, and the best way to learn those ratios is to study percentage charts.

The second purpose is that using percentages allows you to utilize all the meat you have, without waste. Let's say, for example, that you are buying a whole pork shoulder, or in the extreme case, butchering a whole pig. You would have to be psychic to know how much trim you will have to make rillettes, or how much salt is needed for a piece of coppa. I have been taking apart animals for most of my life and, I'm telling you, it's impossible to eyeball the exact weight of any cut on any animal. I'll give one hundred bucks to the person who looks at a leg of pig and knows the exact weight of the resulting ham to the gram.

All of the percentage charts in this book are ones I developed in my plant by doing thousands and thousands of test batches using a try-then-adjust method. If a finished product needed a bit more salt, I would increase the percentage of salt just a bit. Too spicy? The percentage of red pepper flakes would go down. Once I was completely happy with a product, I locked in the percentages, never to be changed again. (Ever.)

These charts give me the ability to process any amount of meat—and scale any recipe—by telling me the exact amount of the basic ingredients I should use for each product. If I'm making Coppa di Testa (page 33) with a 4-pound pig head one day and a 5-pound pig head the following week, the percentage charts help me ensure that both of the resulting products are consistently delicious and safe. You can see how percentage charts give you flexibility: each recipe can be adjusted to the exact weight of meat you have on hand.

How does this benefit you at home? Let's say you are one of the ambitious cooks who wants to make Capicola (page 38) from an entire pork shoulder. You buy the shoulder, then cut out the coppa (which is the cut used for Capicola). When you weigh it, you discover that it weighs a half pound less (not all pigs are created equal) than what the recipe calls for. You say to yourself, this book sucks and so does OP. But wait: not so fast. Because I have given you the base percentage required of salt as it relates to your protein, all you need to do is adjust the amount called for in the recipe to the correct percentage to get the amount needed for the weight of your coppa. Now you also have the ability to use up the rest of that shoulder in another meaty product, like rillettes, for example. Just chop up the rest of the shoulder, place it on the scale, and use the percentage of salt for rillettes (see page 26).

When you are cooking a dish, you can taste as you go and add more salt, some fat, a bit more pepper, and so on. But when you are making something that has to cure for months before you can taste the end result, you need to be exact in formulating the recipe from the get-go.

One particular word of caution: Make sure you maintain the exact percentages for the nitrite and nitrate (curing salt #1 and #2) to ensure you are making a safe product. The spices and other elements are more flexible, but nitrate and nitrite are not.

Let's break down a percentage chart to show how they work, starting with the one for Slow Roasted (see page 22).

You start with the weight of the meat. The weight is the baseline, the 100 percent everything else is measured in relation to. For all the charts, the meat components together add up to 100 percent. To make it simple, say you start with exactly 10 pounds (4.53 kg) of meat. Let's say the percentage for salt is 2 percent. You'd need 10 x .02 or .2 pounds salt, or 3.2 ounces (90.6 g). If you are a serious baker, you are familiar with using this kind of math to scale recipes up or down.

Now let's take a more real-world example. In the chart that follows on page 22, the left column contains the ingredients for making Capicola as described in the recipe on page 38. As you can see, it calls

THE SPICES AND OTHER ELEMENTS ARE MORE FLEXIBLE, BUT NITRATE AND NITRITE ARE NOT.

How to Scale Using Percentage Charts

The percentage charts are ingredient ratios by weight, with the meat serving as the baseline weight. They're especially useful for scaling recipes, allowing you to get consistent recipe results no matter how much meat you have. All the meat portions add up to 100 percent.

SLOW ROASTED

*Meat	100%
*Salt	2.5%
Sugar	1.3%
*Curing salt #1	0.2%
Rub	1.5%
Spices	0.3%

* Ingredients marked with an asterisk should be converted as precisely as possible. Ingredients not marked with an asterisk can be tweaked depending on your preferences, and depending on the recipe.

The Capicola recipe (page 38) calls for 3 pounds of meat, or pork coppa. Say you only have 2½ pounds of coppa. Here is how to use the percentage chart to make sure that you scale safely and accurately. I cannot stress enough that if you are using the percentage charts you should use a calculator and scale and not use tablespoons and teaspoons for measuring your ingredients.

1 Convert the weight of your meat into grams by multiplying the pounds (in this case 2.5) by 453.6. **2.5 x 453.6 = 1,134 grams**

2 To find the amount of salt needed, multiply your meat grams number (in this case 1,134) by the salt percentage in the chart (in this case .025). **1134 x .025 = 28.4 grams salt**

3 To find the amount of sugar needed, multiply your meat grams number (in this case 1,134) by the sugar percentage in the chart (in this case .013). **1134 x .013 = 14.7 grams sugar**

4 To find the amount of curing salt needed, multiply your meat grams number (in this case 1,134) by the curing salt percentage in the chart (in this case .002). **1134 x .002 = 2.3 grams curing salt**

5 To find the amount of the rub needed, multiply your meat grams number (in this case, 1, 134) by the rub percentage in the chart (in this case .015). **1134 x .015 = 17 grams rub**

6 To find the amount of spices needed, which for Capicola is just the red pepper flakes under the "Cure" heading, multiply your meat grams number (in this case, 1, 134) by the spice percentage in the chart (in this case .003). **1134 x .003 = 3.4 grams spices**

ORIGINAL RECIPE FOR 3 POUNDS OF PORK	ALTERED RECIPE FOR 2½ POUNDS OF PORK
3 pounds (1.4 kg) pork coppa	1,134 g pork coppa
2 tablespoons plus 1 teaspoon (35 g) fine sea salt	28.4 g fine sea salt
2 tablespoons (20 g) sugar	14.7 g sugar
1 teaspoon (4 g) curing salt #1	2.3 g curing salt #1
Rub, consisting of red pepper flakes, peppercorns, coriander seeds, fennel seeds, and aniseed for Classic Rub (18.8 g)	17 g rub
Spices, consisting of red pepper flakes in the Cure (4 g)	3.4 g spices

for 3 pounds (1.4 kg) of pork coppa. However, if you have a 2½-pound (1.1-kg) piece of pork coppa and want to adjust the recipe accordingly, you'll use the Slow Roasted percentage chart (left) to figure out the exact amounts you'll need of the rest of the capicola ingredients. These charts are most important for the charcuterie portions of the recipes, but they also include things like rubs. You should also scale the rubs and other components, but they are more forgiving and can be rounded.

When working with the recipes, stay within the parameters of the percentage charts to make nicely seasoned meat. Once you learn how to work in this fashion, you can adjust the flavors of the meat to your own palate. Do not adjust the nitrite or nitrate levels (curing salt #1 and #2), as these ingredients need to stay at the percentages listed in the recipes for safety. In the charts, ingredients that need more precise conversions are indicated with an asterisk.

Reading all this, you have probably figured something out by now: you need to weigh the ingredients for your charcuterie. This is the truth. You need a good digital kitchen scale that measures to the hundredth of a gram, at least. Weighing is the only way you will get the percentages right—the percentage of curing salt to meat, which is essential for safety, and the percentages of salt, fat, and spices to meat, which are essential for flavor. In this book, I've provided volume measurement conversions for many dry ingredients, like salt and spices, because cooks in the U.S. are accustomed to working with teaspoons and tablespoons and cups, and including these measurements makes the recipes more accessible. But in charcuterie, even more than in baking, precise weighing of your ingredients (and, in the case of dry-curing without a water activity meter, of your product) is the only way to go. So use the spoon and cup measures to orient yourself, and by all means use them in the recipes for dishes in Part 2, but when you are making a cured product—one that uses curing salt—weigh your meat to the gram and stick to the percentages.

* * *

The recipes collected in the first part of this book are only a sample of our wares at ole OP. I chose them because they are all really delicious. I also chose quite a few of them because I could not find the recipes anywhere else, and because they are such a joy to make— and often dead easy. These also represent a unique way of making charcuterie—my way, arrived at over years of testing, tinkering, and producing. In my humble opinion, each is the best way to make a perfect product of its kind.

CHAPTER 1 | *Slow-Cooked Meats*

Clockwise from top right: Pork Rillettes (page 27), Duck Confit (page 31), Pork Rillons (page 27), Pork Rillettes, Coppa di Testa (page 33), Capicola (page 38), Duck Rillettes (page 31) at center.

Often I am asked to teach classes on charcuterie and, in almost every case, people want to make prosciutto or salami first. I get it; they are amazing products. But learning how to make dry-cured salami without prior meat-making experience is like learning how to ski on a black diamond run. So start with something that you can enjoy right away and that will allow you to enjoy the whole process: start with rilletes.

The beauty of slow-cooked meats is the ease; they cook at a low temperature, nice and even. In this chapter you'll learn a key technique for slow-cooked meat: cooking with animal fat and preserving the meat under a lid of fat. This is one of the best ways to preserve meat and to make it unbelievably delicious. And all you will need for these recipes is a knife, an oven, and a pan.

The percentage charts are ingredient ratios by weight, with the meat serving as the baseline weight. They're especially useful for scaling recipes, allowing you to get consistent recipe results no matter how much meat you have. For more information on how to use them, see page 22.

COOKED IN FAT (CONFIT)

Confit is meat cooked in fat and often preserved under a cap of fat. For confit recipes in this chapter, you can try Pork Rillettes and Rillons (page 27), Duck Confit and Rillettes (page 31), and Coppa di Testa (page 33).

*Meat	100%
Salt	2%
*Curing salt #1	0.2%
Spices	3%
*Cooking fat	23%

SLOW ROASTED

Slow-roasted meats are exactly what they sound like. For a slow roasted recipe, try Capicola (page 38).

*Meat	100%
*Salt	2.5%
Sugar	1.3%
*Curing salt #1	0.2%
Rub	1.5%
Spices	0.3%

* Ingredients marked with an asterisk need to be converted precisely.

Quality Tips

Master three key components of slow-cooking—(1) marinating, (2)cooking temperature, and (3) preserving—and you'll be golden.

Marinating: At the shop, we call marinating "letting the cure set." Grind the spices using a dedicated coffee grinder or a mortar and pestle as close as possible to the time you set your marinade. Use fresh onions, garlic, and herbs. And, to ensure the marinade or cure will reach the middle of the meat, wrap the meat in marinade with plastic wrap and let it sit for at least 2 days in the refrigerator before you cook it.

Cooking Temperature: This cooking method is called "low and slow" for a reason, so use a gentle hand. A nice, slow pace means the meat cooks evenly, the center simultaneous with the outside. In the charcuterie world, we chill out and enjoy a refreshing beverage while the meat cooks. I cook, smoke, and poach everything I make at temperatures lower than 300°F (148°C)—there's no need, in any phase of my production, for a temperature that's any higher. I hate to see meat boil or even simmer in my shop. It's like watching kids get yelled at in a park—just awkward for everyone.

Preserving: The key to preserving confit and other slow preparations is keeping the meat sealed in fat. This keeps oxygen out and flavor in.

PORK RILLETTES AND RILLONS

One of the beauties of making charcuterie is that you can use the whole animal—from the muscle to the trim to the fat—to create something delicious. In the case of rillettes and rillons, you use the animal's own fat to tenderize and preserve the meat. Rillettes and rillons use the same cooking technique; however, for rillettes, the meat is chopped fine and ends up a bit like pâté, with a smooth texture, while for rillons, larger chunks of meat are tossed in sugar and crisped in a pan.

Rillettes are said to be the first "butter" in the world—smeared on stale bread to make it palatable. When I was a kid, my parents would heat up a small amount of rillettes, spread it on thick-cut country toast, and place a fried egg on top. They served it with a dandelion salad dressed in lemon and oil; this was the breakfast of champions in the Cairo household. Rillons, once you have crisped them up in a pan, are best enjoyed with a simple radish salad and some great bread.

If you are able to get lard that has been freshly rendered by your butcher, please do. It will give you the best porky flavor.

NOTES: CURING SALT #1 IS OPTIONAL IN THIS RECIPE. IT WILL AID IN COLOR AND PRESERVATION BUT IS BY NO MEANS NECESSARY. THIS IS A 3-DAY RECIPE WITH 2 HOURS OF HANDS-ON TIME.

1 Using a mortar and pestle, coarsely grind the cloves, coriander, and white and black peppers. In a large bowl, combine the ground spices with the sea salt, curing salt, fresh ginger, garlic, thyme, nutmeg, ground ginger, cinnamon, and wine and mix well with a fork.

2 Add the cubed pork to the bowl and, with clean hands, mix the pork and rub until the pork is well coated. Cover the bowl with plastic wrap and refrigerate for 3 days. By day 3, the meat should have a great smell of clean spice and garlic; it should have a slight pink color to it if you used the curing salt.

3 Remove the pork from the fridge and let it come to room temperature, about 30 minutes. Preheat the oven to 275°F (135°C).

4 Melt the lard in a small pot over low heat, warming it until it is completely translucent and begins to bubble. This should take no more than 5 minutes.

5 Transfer the pork to a Dutch oven and carefully pour the melted lard over it. Be sure that the meat is totally covered. If there is not enough lard, add a bit of olive oil so that the meat is totally covered. Cover the pot and cook in oven for about 3 hours, or until the pork is fork tender but not dry and "cottony." Start

CONTINUED

MAKES ONE 4 BY 12-INCH (10 BY 30 CM) TERRINE OR 2½ POUNDS (1.1 KG) OF RILLETTES OR RILLONS; SERVES 8 TO 10

6 whole cloves

2 teaspoons (10 g) ground coriander

½ teaspoon (2 g) ground white pepper

1 teaspoon (5 g) ground black pepper

2 tablespoons (30 g) fine sea salt

½ teaspoon (2 g) curing salt #1 (optional)

1½ tablespoons (17 g) chopped fresh ginger

2½ tablespoons (36 g) chopped garlic

1½ tablespoons (18 g) chopped fresh thyme

½ teaspoon (2 g) freshly grated nutmeg

Pinch of ground ginger

¾ teaspoon (2 g) ground cinnamon

¼ cup (60 ml) dry white wine

3 pounds (1.4 kg) boneless pork shoulder, cut into 1-inch (2.5 cm) cubes

11 ounces (312 g) good-quality lard

Olive oil (optional)

1 cup (220 g) sugar (if making rillons)

checking for doneness after 2½ hours so as not to overcook the pork. Remove from the oven and allow the pork to rest in the fat for 1 hour.

6   Using a slotted spoon, transfer the pork from the fat to a bowl. Reserve all the fat and liquid and set aside to cool. Separate the fat from the cooking liquid as you would if you were skimming fat off of a stock: press the bowl of a ladle into the liquid until the lip breaks the surface and the fat flows into the ladle, being very careful not to stir together the fat and the liquid. Reserve the skimmed lard in a separate bowl and set aside at room temperature. You will be able to tell that you are into the cooking liquid when you see the darker color liquid on the bottom of the pot. At this point, choose whether you are making rillettes or rillons: If you're making rillons continue with steps 7, 8, and 9. If you're making rillettes, skip to step 10.

7   To finish the rillons, place the pork in a large bowl and, working very gently, sprinkle the sugar in a steady flow while stirring with a rubber spatula. You are trying to cover all sides of the rillons with sugar while keeping them as intact as possible.

8   Heat a large nonstick pan over medium heat. Pour a small amount of the reserved lard into the pan and fry the sugar-covered rillons in batches to prevent crowding, until nice and crispy on all sides, about 2 minutes. Wipe out the pan with a paper towel and add fresh lard before each batch. Serve the rillons hot from the pan.

9   To store any leftover rillons, fried or unfried, cover them completely with leftover lard, with all of the meat submerged in fat. Discard the cooking liquid. The rillons will keep, refrigerated, for up to 1 month.

10 To finish the rillettes, put the pork on a cutting board and chop coarsely. You are looking for an uneven texture. Transfer to a bowl.

11 To the chopped pork, add one-third of the reserved lard and a third of the cooking liquid stirring until well incorporated. Taste the pork; it should be well salted and very succulent. If not, add more salt to taste. Press down on the meat with a slotted spoon. Liquid should ooze a bit, and the meat should begin to bind. Place the meat in a 4 by 12-inch (10 by 30 cm) terrine mold or in a casserole, jar, or any other vessel you would like. Press down gently to slightly compact the meat. Refrigerate for 1 hour.

12 In a saucepan over medium heat, melt the remaining reserved lard until liquid. Remove the rillettes from the refrigerator and pour the melted lard over the rillettes until they are covered by at least ¼ inch (6 mm). Cover the terrine or other vessel (or not, it doesn't really matter as you have your fatty protective layer) and refrigerate for up to 1 month. (You can eat the rillettes right away while still warm; however, the flavors will become much more incorporated and mellow if you let them rest for a day or two.) Remove from the refrigerator about 1½ hours before serving; the rillettes are best at room temperature.

DUCK CONFIT AND RILLETTES

Slow-cooking meat in its own fat is grand, but the truly great quality of this recipe has to be the flavor from the fresh garlic, ginger, and sweet spices—in other words, the rub.

I've created a choose-your-own-adventure below: one path will lead you to a warm duck confit, the other to succulent rillettes topped with crackled duck skin. There is no right way, only different moods. Confit for dinner, rillettes for lunch?

NOTES: CURING SALT #1 IS OPTIONAL IN THIS RECIPE. IT WILL AID IN COLOR AND PRESERVATION BUT IS BY NO MEANS NECESSARY. THIS IS A 3-DAY RECIPE WITH 5 HOURS OF HANDS-ON TIME.

1 To prepare the rub, grind the shallot, chopped garlic, ginger, allspice, cloves, coriander, black pepper, thyme, and parsley using a mortar and pestle or dedicated coffee grinder until the texture is like coarse ground pepper, about 3 minutes. Add the sea salt and curing salt and mix to combine well. Transfer to a large bowl.

2 Add the duck legs to the bowl and, using your hands, coat and rub the duck with the rub. Cover the bowl with a lid or plastic wrap and refrigerate for 2 days.

3 If possible, remove the legs from the fridge and let them come to room temperature, about 30 minutes. Preheat the oven to 300°F (148°C).

4 Remove the duck legs and set them aside on a dish to drain. Place the legs in a Dutch oven or casserole, skin side up. In a heavy pot over low heat, warm the duck fat until it melts and becomes almost translucent. This should take about 5 minutes. Very carefully pour the hot fat over the legs; they should be completely covered. Nestle the garlic head into the fat, making sure it is submerged as well.

5 Cover the pot and place in the oven. After 2 hours, check for doneness by poking one leg with a skewer. It should slide out of the meat with very little resistance. If it doesn't, place the pot back in the oven and cook for another 15 minutes or so, until the skewer slides out easily. Remove from the oven, uncover, and allow to cool for 1 hour. If you are not going to proceed to confit or rillettes right away, place the pot, covered, in the refrigerator, where it can stay for up to 1 month.

6 Remove the pot from the refrigerator 1 hour before cooking to allow the fat to soften.

CONTINUED

MAKES 6 SERVINGS OF CONFIT OR ONE 4 BY 12-INCH (10 BY 30 CM) TERRINE OF RILLETTES; SERVES 8 TO 10

2 teaspoons (9 g) finely chopped shallot

2 teaspoons (9 g) finely chopped garlic, plus 1 head garlic, root end chopped off

2½ teaspoons (11 g) finely chopped fresh ginger

Pinch of ground allspice

Pinch of ground cloves

Pinch of ground coriander

Pinch of ground black pepper

Pinch of chopped fresh thyme

Pinch of chopped fresh parsley

1½ tablespoons (22 g) fine sea salt

½ teaspoon (2 g) curing salt #1 (optional)

6 duck legs, about 3 pounds (1.4 kg) total

2 cups (450 g) duck fat

TO SERVE (OPTIONAL)

Chicories Salad (page 213; if serving confit)

Baguette slices (if making rillettes)

Cornichons (if making rillettes)

7   Place a nonstick pan over low heat. Using a slotted spoon, remove one of the legs from the fat and let the fat drain off for a second. Place the leg, skin side down, in the hot pan. Allow to sizzle, without moving, until the skin is golden, about 5 minutes, then flip and cook for 4 minutes on the other side. Remove to a paper towel–lined plate. Repeat with the remaining legs.

8   If you are serving the confit legs, place them on plates and serve with the chicories salad. You can use the leftover fat for roasting potatoes or vegetables.

9   If you are making rillettes, let the legs cool for 5 minutes after browning. Carefully remove the skin from the legs and reserve in the refrigerator to make the duck cracker. Pull the bones out of the legs; they should come out easily. Put the meat on a cutting board and give it a coarse chop with a sharp knife. You are looking for an uneven texture. Place the meat in a bowl and add about 1 cup (225 g) of the cooking fat from the confit; give the mixture a good stir and taste. It should be moist but not too greasy and have plenty of salt. Place the meat in a 4 by 12-inch (10 by 30 cm) terrine mold or in a casserole, jar, or any other vessel you would like. Press down gently to slightly compact the meat. Refrigerate for 1 hour.

10   In a saucepan over medium heat, melt the remaining cooking fat until liquid. Remove the rillettes from the refrigerator and pour the melted fat over them until they are covered by at least ¼ inch (6 mm). Cover the terrine or other vessel (or not, it doesn't really matter since you have your fatty protective layer) and refrigerate for up to 1 month. (You can eat the rillettes right away while still warm; however, the flavors will become much more incorporated and mellow if you let them rest for a day or two.) Remove from the refrigerator about 1½ hours before serving; the rillettes are best at room temperature.

11   To make the duck cracker, remove the reserved duck skin from the refrigerator and let it come to room temperature, about 10 minutes. Carefully scrape excess fat from both sides of the skin and place the skin in a small heavy pot. Set over medium heat and render for about 5 minutes, until crisp like a delicate, gossamer piece of bacon. Take care not to burn the skin. (Alternatively, lay the skin pieces in a single layer on a parchment paper–lined baking sheet and render them in a 300°F (148°C) oven until crisp, about 10 minutes.) Drain on paper towels and allow to cool.

12   Serve the rillettes with baguette slices, cornichons, and the duck cracker.

COPPA DI TESTA

To those who think coppa di testa is too difficult for the home cook, I would say you're half correct. Yes, you're flipping a pig's face inside out and rolling it into a tight sleeping bag in this recipe. But clearly this doesn't deter quite a few of you, as the class I teach about making coppa di testa at the annual Feast Portland food festival is always the first to sell out, period. This preparation is the one that routinely brings the ooohs and aaahs. And it's definitely doable, especially if you get your butcher to debone and clean the head for you and to give you the skull to use in the stock.

Our coppa is not a typical headcheese, which is to say, it's not brined or bound with aspic in a terrine. In our method (inspired by similar coppa I've seen at the Austrian markets in the Alps), you slice the meat thinly so that a mixed texture of cartilage and jowl fat is on display (both aesthetically and in terms of flavor). I like to eat thin slices of coppa di testa on crostini with a drizzle of olive oil, some crunchy salt, and a squeeze of lemon. You could also serve this with a mix of fennel, mint, parsley, and lemon—or anything bright and acidic, really.

NOTE: THIS IS A 2-DAY RECIPE, WITH 5 HOURS OF HANDS-ON TIME.

1   If your butcher has deboned and cleaned your pig's head, proceed to step 2. To debone the head, start with the head chin-up facing away from you. I use a stiff 6-inch deboning knife. Slice the chin, starting at the neck cutting up towards the chin and eventually through the lips, and work your way around the skull, trying not to make extra cuts through the skin as you get the skull detached from the skin and flesh (if you do cut through the skin, it's not the end of the world—it just may be a bit more difficult to tie up). Work all the way around the head until the skull is fully removed from the skin. Then lay the face skin side down on the work surface and remove all of the glands in the jowl area (they should look like purplish rounds of fat), as well as any bits of bone you may have missed. (see photos, following pages, for reference). Place the deboned head in the fridge to chill while you get the stock started.

2   Place the pig's skull in a stockpot that is large enough to hold it. Cover completely with water. Slowly bring the water to a simmer over low heat, skimming off and discarding any scum that may come to the surface. Add the carrot, celery, and onion and keep at a very low simmer for at least 4 hours, or up to 6 hours. Skim every 20 minutes or so. Place the whole pot in the refrigerator and allow to chill overnight.

CONTINUED

MAKES 20 SNACK-SIZE PORTIONS

1 pig's head, 4 to 5 pounds (2 kg) when deboned

1 large carrot, peeled and cut into matchsticks

2 stalks celery, cut into matchsticks

1 onion, quartered

Fine sea salt

¾ teaspoon (3 g) black peppercorns

¾ teaspoon (3 g) coriander seeds

1 teaspoon (4 g) curing salt #1

¾ teaspoon (3 g) orange zest

½ teaspoon (2 g) chopped fresh rosemary

1 tablespoon (16 g) minced garlic

Making Coppa Di Testa.

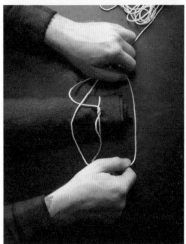

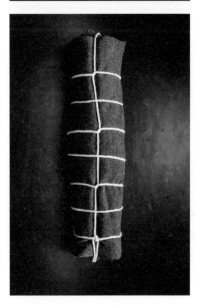

3   Weigh the boneless and cleaned pig's head and measure out, as precisely as possible, 2 teaspoons (8 g) of fine sea salt per pound (455 g) of weight. Using a mortar and pestle, grind the pepper corns and coriander seeds. Then add the fine sea salt, curing salt, orange zest, rosemary, and garlic, and mix well.

4   Sprinkle one third of the cure mixture into a casserole dish and place the pig's face in the dish, meat side up (skin side down). Add the rest of the cure mixture to the face and massage really well, making sure to cover the entire face and get the cure into all the nooks and crannies.

5   Set out your twine so it is on hand once you start rolling the face. Pull the ears through the eye holes so that the ears are on the inside of the face. Place the face, meat side up, on the work surface with its snout pointing away from you and, starting at one side of the face, near the cheek, roll it up as tightly as you can, trying to keep the ear tucked inside the face.

6   Hold onto the roll to keep it as tight as possible. Place the face on a work surface, with the snout facing away from you. To begin, tie the twine tightly around the face using one end of your twine, about 1 inch from the snout. Next, take the ball of twine and pull it toward you with your right hand. Place your right thumb on the twine to hold it in place once you have measure out 1 inch, then use your left hand to take the twine at a 90-degree angle to your left and wrap it underneath and around the face. Bring the twine back up, cross it over in between your right hand and the snout, and then pull it back toward you tight. Your twine should make a taut cross on the face. Take your right hand, pull the twine toward you again, and keep repeating the procedure at 1-inch intervals. When you are within 2 inches of the end of the face, securely tie off the twine (see photos, left, for reference). Place the rolled face back in the the casserole dish, cover with plastic wrap, and refrigerate for 24 hours.

7   Remove the casserole dish from the fridge and allow the pig's face to come to room temperature, about 30 minutes. Preheat the oven to 250°F (121°C). Take the face out of the casserole and place it in a large pot with a tight-fitting lid. Your chosen vessel must be large enough to hold the rolled face fully submerged in stock.

8   Take the stock out of the refrigerator and slowly heat it on the stovetop until liquefied. Pour the warm stock through a fine-mesh strainer over the face until it is completely covered; you will need about 1½ gallons (5.7 liters). Cover the pot, put it in the oven, and forget about it for at least 3 hours. After 3 hours, check to see if the face is still submerged. If not, you need to add a bit more stock

(or water if you're out of stock). Cook for about 1 hour longer, then stab the meat with a wooden skewer: it's done when you can pull out the skewer without any resistance.

9   Remove the pot from the oven and immediately place it—face, broth, and all—in the refrigerator. (You may have to remove one or two shelves in your fridge to accommodate it.) Refrigerate for 5 to 6 hours.

10 Remove the coppa from the stock and, using your hands, scrape the excess broth off of the face (it will be gelatinous when it's cold). Keep the stock to serve on its own as a broth, or use it to cook beans or polenta.

11 Starting at the snout and working your way back, slice the coppa as thin as you possibly can—it's best sliced as thinly as paper, either on a slicer or with a really sharp knife and a skilled hand. (You might take it to your butcher and have him slice it for you— say you'll pay in coppa di testa and he will surely oblige.) Wrapped tightly in plastic wrap, the unsliced coppa di testa will keep in the fridge for up to 1 month.

CAPICOLA

MAKES ONE 2½-POUND (1.1-KG) CAPICOLA, ENOUGH FOR 4 GOOD-SIZE SANDWICHES OR 8 AVERAGE SANDWICHES

Choose one rub from the three listed below: Classic, Sweet, or Herb.

CURE

3 pounds (1.4 kg) pork coppa (see Notes, right)

2 tablespoons plus 1 teaspoon (35 g) fine sea salt

2 tablespoons (20 g) sugar

1 teaspoon (4 g) crushed red pepper flakes

1 teaspoon (4 g) curing salt #1

CLASSIC RUB

1 teaspoon (4 g) crushed red pepper flakes

2 teaspoons (10 g) black peppercorns

½ teaspoon (1.6 g) coriander seeds

½ teaspoon (1.6 g) fennel seeds

½ teaspoon (1.6 g) aniseed

SWEET RUB

1 teaspoon (4 g) coriander seeds

1 teaspoon (1 g) fennel seeds

1 teaspoon (5 g) black peppercorns

½ teaspoon (2 g) crushed red pepper flakes

HERB RUB

1 teaspoon (5 g) black peppercorns

1 teaspoon (4 g) chopped fresh thyme

1 teaspoon (4 g) chopped fresh rosemary

1 teaspoon (4.5 g) chopped garlic

Capicola to Italians, capocollo to Americans, capicolla to Canadians, "gabagoul" to Tony Soprano—whatever you call it, capicola is made from the neck of the pig, coppa, prized for its perfect ratio of 30 percent fat to 70 percent lean, making the meat moist and tender. At OP, it's cured for 10 days, then coated in black pepper, fennel seed, coriander, and anise and slow-roasted to produce a tender ham. (We have also included two other options if you want to mix it up.) If you can roast beef, you can pull this off with no trouble at all.

Yes, but what to do with it? Well, one can't make a proper Italian sub (or, I'd say, any proper lunchbox sandwich) without capicola. I use it in our OP Cured Meats Sandwich (page 219). You can also find it, tossed like mini Frisbees, on the Apizza Amore served at Apizza Scholls, our favorite Portland pizzeria.

NOTES: THIS IS A 10-DAY CURE WITH 4 HOURS OF HANDS-ON TIME. ASK A GOOD BUTCHER FOR THE COPPA, WHICH WILL NEED TO BE CUSTOM CUT FROM A WHOLE SHOULDER.

Special Equipment: You will need a size 16 ham net for this recipe. Ask your butcher for one or buy one online at SausageMaker.com.

1   To make the cure, grind the fine sea salt, sugar, red pepper, and curing salt using a mortar and pestle.

2   Place the pork in a large bowl and massage the cure into the pork, really coating it and working it into the cracks and crannies. Wrap tightly in plastic wrap (or put into a big zipper-top bag), place on a dish, and refrigerate for 5 days. Then flip it over so that the top side is down and refrigerate for another 5 days.

3   After 10 days of curing, remove the coppa from the refrigerator and unwrap it. Rinse under cold water until all particles of salt and spice have been removed. Allow it to dry while you prep your rub.

4   Prepare the rub of your choice by combining all the ingredients in a mortar and grinding with the pestle for about 2 minutes. You're looking for a coarse texture, not too fine. Pour the rub into a large bowl and add the meat, turning to coat it well.

5   Preheat the oven to 250°F (121°C). Place a roasting pan filled halfway with water in the middle rack of the oven to create humidity. Put the meat into the ham net and tie the net closed on both ends. Place the meat in a roasting pan and cook for 1 hour on the top rack. Turn the meat over and cook for 1 hour longer. Check the internal temperature: you want it to reach 155°F (68°C). When

the capicola done, it should be evenly roasted and smell so wildly good that you can't wait to slice and dig in. But not yet! Instead, remove it from the oven, transfer to a plate, and refrigerate, uncovered, for 3 to 4 hours, until the capicola's internal temp is below 39°F (4°C). Remove the capicola from the refrigerator, slice thinly, and serve, either solo or atop a sandwich or pizza. Wrapped tightly in plastic wrap, the unsliced capicola will keep for 3 weeks in the refrigerator.

Harvesting a coppa for Capicola.

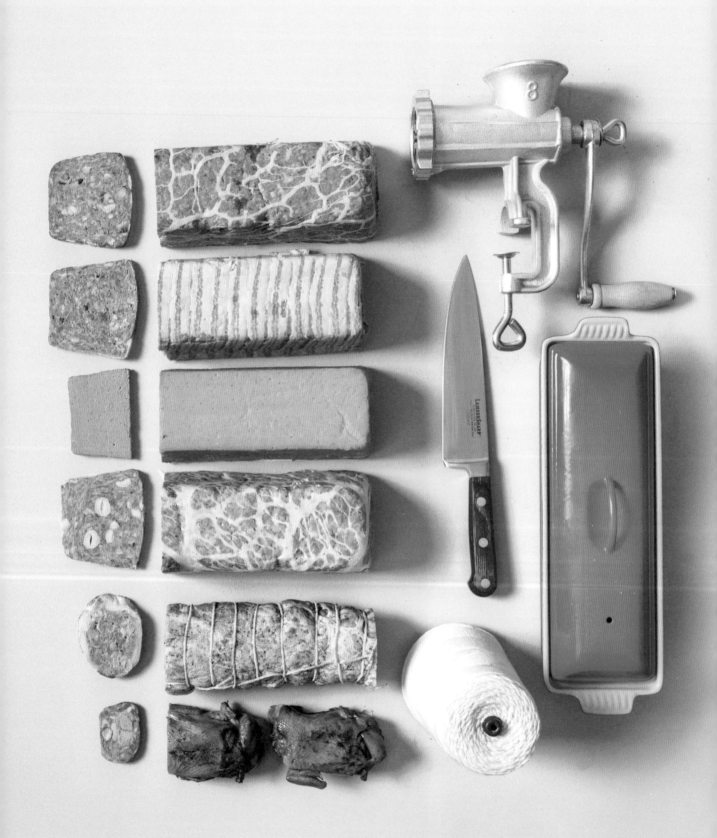

CHAPTER 2

Pâté and Forcemeat

M aking pâté at home is one of the true pleasures of cooking: once you've learned the basics, you can begin adding your own touches—more booze, different spicing, or creative garnishes. The possibilities are endless. The trick is to get those basics down pat so you can consistently make good pâté (see Quality Tips, page 44), because, honestly, it's just cold meat loaf with a fancy name.

Like the majority of charcuterie, pâté was created to use up the excess product—offal, trim, fat—from a day of slaughter. In its most rustic form, the offcuts for pâté were just hacked at with a knife until they were of proper size, then were mixed with stale bread and fat of some sort. But give cooks time, and we will make anything fancier and better tasting. The use of a grinder and a bain-marie and the addition of some onion, spices, herbs, and liqueur make this hacked-up meatloaf into the most lovely of treats. Make it a few days in advance and all you have to do when company comes is slice it; place it prettily on a platter; and add some mustard, pickles, and crusty bread.

This may be the first time that you have made something called farce or forcemeat, ground or pureed meat bound with some kind of fat and salt. Forcemeat can be pâté before it is formed, or sausage before it is stuffed, and it is also the ground meat that you stuff into any of the animals in this chapter.

From top: Pork Pistachio Pâté (page 45), green peppercorn pâté, Pork Liver Mousse (page 50), honey hazelnut pâté, Rabbit Ballotine (page 58), Quail en Gelée (page 53).

The percentage charts are ingredient ratios by weight, with the meat serving as the baseline weight. They're especially useful for scaling recipes, allowing you to get consistent recipe results no matter how much meat you have. All the meat portions together add up to 100 percent. Garnish includes ingredients folded in at the end such as nuts and dried fruit. For more information on how to use them, see page 22.

RUSTIC PÂTÉ

This is a country pâté with a coarse texture that is sliced. Examples are Pork Pistachio Pâté (page 45), Pheasant and Prune Pâté (page 47), Rabbit, Apricot, and Tarragon Pâté (page 56).

*Lean meat	60%
*Fat	20%
*Liver	20%
*Salt	3%
*Curing salt #1	0.2%
Sugar	3%
Wine, spirits	1.5%
Onion, shallot	3%
Spices	3%
Bread for panade	2.5%
Liquid for panade	2.5%
Garnish	4%

FINELY GROUND PÂTÉ

This is a whipped or pureed pâté that is spread. An example is Pork Liver Mousse (page 50).

*Liver	75%
*Lard	25%
*Salt	2.5%
*Curing salt #1	0.3%
Spices	2%
Port	3%
Cream	9%

* Ingredients marked with an asterisk need to be converted precisely.

Quality Tips

Before you start getting all creative with your pâté, take the time to execute a few of the classics. To make pâté at home, master four key techniques: (1) grinding, (2) mixing, (3) cooking, and (4) pressing.

Grinding: For a nice coarse country pâté, like many in this chapter, grind the meat only once to ensure good contrast between the lean meat and the fat. If you make pâté only occasionally, you'll be happy with just an old-fashioned hand-grinder with a ¼-inch (6-mm) die and a ⅛-inch (3-mm) die. If you plan to make quite a few charcuterie recipes, such as coarse pâté, sausage, baloney, or salami, it may behoove you to get an electric grinder with a bit of power behind it. The KitchenAid with a grinder attachment will work for light use, but I suggest buying a grinder that has at least a ½-horsepower and grinds 10 pounds a minute on average. This will help you keep your meat ice cold, which is good for food safety and getting a good bind.

Mixing: Panade (a mixture of bread and milk) is your pâté pal. (If you've ever added bread crumbs and eggs to a meatloaf, you've used a very basic panade.) The right amount of panade works as a texture aid, making your pâté light but not crumbly, and also adds a richness to the flavor. Because the panade helps bind the pâté, you don't have to mix as vigorously as you do other forcemeat; the short mixing time helps keep the texture really light.

Cooking: When making pâté, cook the meat in a water bath for a nice, gentle heat. An overcooked pâté can be as grainy as a sandbox—no one wants that. A gently cooked pâté will be smooth and evenly silky: think of spreadable liver pâté.

Pressing: To make a perfectly square pâté, like you might see in a Burgundian meat case, add a bit of weight to the terrine as the pâté cools. Cut a piece of cardboard to the size of the opening of the terrine mold and lay it on top of the foil-covered pâté. Then set a pound (453 g) or so of weight on it—a can of beans from your cupboard will do, placed on its side (anything heavier will squeeze out some of the delicious fat or gelée inside). The distributed weight forces the pâté into the corners of the mold and compresses it into that desirable square shape.

PORK PISTACHIO PÂTÉ

Pork pistachio pâté is a gateway pâté: once you make this delicious but accessible gem, you won't want to stop. Soon enough you'll be hocking your TV for pork shoulder and cashing convenience checks for pork liver and pistachios. In terms of technique, this is the easiest pâté we make; the most difficult part is assembling the extensive list of spices. This is a country-style pâté, which is to say the texture is coarse, not whipped or pureed—you'll slice it, not spread it.

NOTE: THIS IS A 2-DAY RECIPE, WITH 4 HOURS OF HANDS-ON TIME.

Special Equipment: You will need a grinder.

1 Place the pork shoulder and liver in a bowl and transfer to the freezer. Let chill for 45 minutes, or until a calibrated thermometer inserted into the center of the mixture reads 32°F (0°C). If your freezer is big enough, also chill the meat grinder and all its parts, as well as the bowl and paddle attachment of a stand mixer.

2 To make the panade, in a bowl, mix together the bread and milk using your hands. Allow the bread to soak up the milk and become nice and soggy. Refrigerate for 45 minutes.

3 In a small sauté pan over low heat, warm the olive oil and sauté the garlic, shallot, and onion until they begin to pick up color, about 8 minutes. Add the thyme, parsley, and port and cook until the liquid is reduced by half, about 5 minutes. Transfer the mixture to a bowl, refrigerate for 5 minutes, and then mix into the panade. Return the panade to the fridge.

4 Using a mortar and pestle, grind together the sugar, black pepper, white pepper, coriander, cloves, cinnamon, sea salt, curing salt, nutmeg, and ginger. Remove the pork shoulder and liver from the freezer and add the spice mixture to the bowl. Mix well, using your hands to coat all the meat. Place the bowl in the refrigerator to keep cold while you set up the grinder.

5 Assemble the grinder with a large, coarse die and, working quickly and in batches to keep the meat mixture cold, grind the mixture into the chilled stand-mixer bowl. Using the chilled paddle attachment, mix the meat for 3 minutes on low speed, until well blended and the mix of spices appears even but you can still see clear definition between meat and fat. Stir in the pistachios, then cover the bowl with plastic wrap and refrigerate for 24 hours to let the curing salt work its magic.

CONTINUED

3 pounds (1.4 kg) boneless pork shoulder, cut into 1-inch (2.5 cm) cubes

8 ounces (225 g) pork liver, cut into 1-inch (2.5 cm) cubes

3 slices of white bread (60 g), crusts removed and cut into 1-inch (2.5 cm) cubes

¼ cup (60 ml) whole milk

2 tablespoons (30 g) olive oil

1 tablespoon (18 g) chopped garlic

2 tablespoons (20 g) minced shallot

3 tablespoons (30 g) minced onion

Pinch of fresh thyme

1 tablespoon (3.5 g) chopped fresh parsley

2 tablespoons (30 ml) port

½ teaspoon (3 g) sugar

¼ teaspoon (1 g) ground black pepper

Pinch of ground white pepper

Pinch of ground coriander

Pinch of ground cloves

Pinch of ground cinnamon

2½ tablespoons (37 g) fine sea salt

½ teaspoon (2 g) curing salt #1

Pinch of freshly grated nutmeg

Pinch of ground ginger

⅔ cup (125 g) whole shelled pistachios

9 or 10 thin slices of pancetta (about 2.3 ounces/66 g total)

TO SERVE

Crusty bread

Whole-grain mustard

Frisée salad

Cornichons

6   The next day, preheat the oven to 300°F (148°C). Fill a medium pot with water and bring to a simmer. Have ready a 4 by 12-inch (10 by 30 cm) terrine mold. Cut a piece of waxed paper the same length as the terrine mold and about three times the width (so that it will cover the bottom and reach up both long sides). Cut a piece of cardboard slightly smaller than the width and length of the terrine, so it will fit inside the terrine's mouth.

7   Set the waxed paper on a work surface and cover it with the pancetta in a single layer, overlapping the slices just a little. Pick the paper up and flip it into the terrine, pancetta side down. Remove the waxed paper, leaving the pancetta in the terrine, and adjust the slices as needed so there are no gaps among them.

8   Remove the forcemeat from the refrigerator. Using your hands, form it into a tightly packed ball. Press the ball into the terrine, making sure it gets fully into all the edges and corners. Smooth the top of the forcemeat, and fold any overhanging pancetta over the top. Then, to force out any air around the pâté, pound the terrine down on a sturdy work surface. Really work it—ten solid smacks should do it. Cover the terrine with aluminum foil. By this time the water should be simmering.

9   Make a bain-marie: Place the terrine mold in the center of a large roasting pan or deep casserole dish. Carefully pour simmering water into the roasting pan until it comes two-thirds of the way up the terrine. Cover the bain-marie with aluminum foil and transfer to the oven. After 1½ hours, place a calibrated thermometer in the middle of the pâté. You're looking for an internal temperature of 155°F (68°C); if it's not there yet, put the terrine back in the oven and check the temperature every 15 minutes. Carefully remove the bain-marie from the oven.

10   Remove the terrine from the roasting pan and very carefully pour out the hot water. Fill the now-empty pan two-thirds full with ice and nestle the terrine into it. You now need a weight, something to press the pâté into the perfect shape: a large can of beans or soup will do. Place the piece of cardboard you have prepared on top of the aluminum foil covering the terrine, add the weight, and refrigerate for 2 to 3 hours.

11   Remove from the refrigerator and check the internal temperature; it should be 39°F (4°C) or lower. If it is, and you're ready to serve, invert the mold onto a serving platter; the pâté should gently slide out.

12   Slice the pâté and serve with crusty bread, whole-grain mustard, frisée, and cornichons. Wrap the remaining pâté with plastic wrap and store it in the fridge for up to 2 weeks.

PHEASANT AND PRUNE PÂTÉ

On PheasantsForever.org, I learned that Oregon's Willamette Valley was the first place in America to have ring-neck pheasants (which are native to Asia though they have been introduced around the globe). Judge O. N. Denny brought them here in 1881, declaring the valley the most beautiful place in the United States to encounter such birds.

In this pâté of tender pheasant, wine-soaked prunes, and warm spices, you'll find the perfect autumn combination. This is a refined country-style pâté, which is to say the texture is coarse but the ingredients are sophisticated. As an alternative to cooking a big bird at Thanksgiving, I really enjoy making this pâté a centerpiece to the meal, served with nuts, crusty bread, and, of course, a nice Oregon Pinot Noir.

NOTE: THIS IS A 2-DAY RECIPE, WITH 4 HOURS OF HANDS-ON TIME.

Special Equipment: You will need a grinder.

1   Put the pheasant, fatback, and liver in a bowl and transfer to the freezer. Let chill for 45 minutes, or until a calibrated thermometer reads 32°F (0°C). If your freezer is big enough, also chill the meat grinder and all its parts, as well as the bowl and paddle attachment of a stand mixer.

2   To make the panade, in a bowl mix together the bread and milk using your hands. Allow the bread to soak up the milk and become nice and soggy. Refrigerate for 45 minutes.

3   In a small sauté pan over low heat, warm the olive oil and sauté the onion, shallot, and garlic until completely tender, about 5 minutes. Remove from the heat and set aside.

4   In a small pot over medium heat, bring the port to a simmer. Add the diced prunes and simmer until just heated through, 1 to 2 minutes. Transfer to a bowl and refrigerate until needed.

5   In a large bowl, mix together the sea salt, curing salt, thyme, black pepper, ginger, cinnamon, cayenne, cloves, nutmeg, coriander, white pepper, and sugar. Add the cooked onion mixture, the cold panade, and the chilled pheasant. Mix to combine thoroughly. Place the bowl in the refrigerator to keep cold while you set up the grinder.

6   Assemble the grinder with a large, coarse die and, working quickly and in batches to keep the meat cold, grind the mixture into the chilled stand-mixer bowl. Then put one-half of the ground meat mixture through a second time. Fit the mixer with the chilled

CONTINUED

MAKES ONE 4 BY 12-INCH (10 BY 30 CM) TERRINE

2¼ pounds (1 kg) pheasant meat, cut into 1-inch (2.5 cm) pieces

10½ ounces (300 g) pork fatback, diced

8½ ounces (240 g) chicken liver, diced

3 slices (60 g) white bread, crusts removed and diced into 1-inch (2.5 cm) cubes

¼ cup (60 ml) whole milk

1 tablespoon (15 ml) olive oil

2 tablespoons (30 g) diced onion

1½ tablespoons (20 g) diced shallot

1½ tablespoons (20 g) chopped garlic

1 cup (240 ml) port

½ cup (110 g) diced prunes

2½ tablespoons (37 g) fine sea salt

½ teaspoon (2 g) curing salt #1

20 sprigs thyme leaves, chopped

¼ teaspoon (2.5 g) ground black pepper

Pinch of ground ginger

Pinch of ground cinnamon

Pinch of cayenne

Pinch of ground cloves

Pinch of freshly grated nutmeg

Pinch of ground coriander

Pinch of ground white pepper

Pinch of sugar

TO SERVE

Crusty bread

Walnuts

Frisée salad

paddle attachment and mix for 2 minutes on low speed. Add the prunes and port and mix for 1 minute longer.

7   Pack the forcemeat into a 4 by 12-inch (10 by 30 cm) terrine mold, making sure it gets into all the edges and corners. Smooth the top of the forcemeat. Then, to force out any air around the pâté, pound the terrine down on a sturdy work surface. Really work it— ten solid smacks should do it. Cover the terrine with aluminum foil and refrigerate for 24 hours to let the curing salt work its magic.

8   The next day, preheat the oven to 300°F (148°C) and bring a medium pot of water to a simmer. Cut a piece of cardboard slightly smaller than the width and length of the terrine, so it will fit inside the terrine's mouth.

9   Make a bain-marie: Place the terrine in the center of a large roasting pan or deep casserole dish. Carefully pour simmering water into the roasting pan until it comes two-thirds of the way up the terrine. Cover the bain-marie with foil and transfer to the oven. After 1½ hours, place a calibrated thermometer in the middle of the pâté. You're looking an internal temperature of 155°F (68°C); if it's not there yet, put the terrine back in the oven and check the temperature every 15 minutes. When it's done, carefully remove the bain-marie from the oven.

10 Remove the terrine from the roasting pan and very carefully pour out the hot water. Fill the now-empty pan two-thirds full with ice and nestle the terrine into it. You now need a weight, something to press the pâté into the perfect shape: a large can of beans or soup will do. Place the piece of cardboard you have prepared on top of the aluminum foil covering the terrine, add the weight, and refrigerate for 2 to 3 hours.

11 Remove from the refrigerator and check the temperature. It should be 39°F (4°C) or lower. If it is, and you're ready to serve it, flip the mold over onto a serving platter, and the pâté should gently slide out.

12 Thinly slice the pâté and serve with crusty bread, walnuts, and a frisée salad. Wrap what you don't eat in plastic wrap; it will keep for up to 2 weeks in the fridge.

PORK LIVER MOUSSE

MAKES ONE 4 BY 12-INCH (10 BY 30 CM) TERRINE

3 pounds (1.4 kg) pork liver, cubed

¾ teaspoon (4 g) ground black pepper

¾ teaspoon (4 g) ground coriander

¼ teaspoon (2 g) crushed red pepper flakes

2 tablespoons (30 g) fine sea salt

¾ teaspoon (3 g) curing salt #1

¼ cup (60 ml) port

1 pound (455 g) lard

3 eggs

1 cup (240 ml) heavy cream

TO SERVE

Good-quality extra virgin olive oil

A few turns of black pepper

Maldon salt

Crusty bread

Olives

Pickles

When I first opened Olympia Provisions, I worried that I would have trouble selling my pork liver pâté, because the other liver pâtés—foie gras, chicken liver, and so on—are usually more sought after. Luckily, the year we released it, our pork liver won a Good Food Award (a sort of James Beard award for responsible artisan producers). It has since become our best-selling pâté. It's lighter than a standard pâté, and we serve it on almost every charcuterie board we make, coated with olive oil and sprinkled with crunchy salt.

NOTE: THIS IS A 3-DAY RECIPE, WITH 3 HOURS OF HANDS-ON TIME.

1 Place the cubed liver in a Dutch oven with a tight-fitting lid. Using a mortar and pestle, coarsely grind the black pepper, coriander, and red pepper flakes. Then add the sea salt and curing salt and mix a minute more; the mixture should remain coarse. Using your hands, mix the spices with the liver until well incorporated, making sure not to leave any spice mix at the bottom of the dish. Add the port and mix again. Cover with plastic wrap and the lid and refrigerate for 48 hours.

2 Preheat the oven to 300°F (148°C). Prepare an ice bath and set a large bowl in it. Transfer the liver to a food processor and blend for 3 to 4 minutes, until smooth and creamy. Using a spatula, force the liver through a fine-mesh sieve into the bowl; this is extremely tedious and will take some time.

3 In a heavy pot over low heat, heat the lard until it is liquid, about 3 minutes. Remove from the heat. Break the eggs in a bowl and whip with a whisk for 3 to 4 minutes—whisk, whisk, whisk until frothy. Slowly whisk in the cream and whisk for 1 minute longer, then pour the mixture into the liver. Add the melted lard to the liver as well and mix well.

4 Line a 4 by 12-inch (10 by 30 cm) terrine mold with plastic wrap. I do this by wetting the interior of the mold, and then placing inside a piece of plastic wrap long enough that 3 inches overhang on all sides. Pour the liver mixture into the mold and fold the plastic overhang to cover the top of the pâté.

5 Bring a medium pot of water to a simmer. Make a bain-marie: Place the terrine in the center of a large roasting pan or deep casserole dish. Carefully pour simmering water into the roasting pan until it comes two-thirds of the way up the terrine. Cover the bain-marie with foil and transfer to the oven. After 1½ hours, place a calibrated thermometer in the middle of the pâté.

You're looking for an internal temperature of 155°F (68°C); if it's not there yet, put the terrine back in the oven and check the temperature every 15 minutes. When it's done, carefully remove the bain-marie from the oven.

6   Remove the terrine from the roasting pan and very carefully pour out the hot water. Fill the now-empty pan with ice, place the terrine back in the pan, and carefully transfer the pan to the refrigerator. Let chill for 2 hours, or until the internal temperature is 39°F (4°C).

7   Peel open the plastic wrap from the surface of the pâté. Invert the mold onto a cutting board and, holding the plastic against the cutting board, remove the mold. Carefully peel off the plastic wrap and slice the pâté into ¼-inch (6-mm) slices.

8   To serve, coat the slices with your best olive oil, freshly ground black pepper, and Maldon salt. Devour with good crusty bread. Wrap what you don't eat in plastic wrap; it will keep for up to 2 weeks in the fridge.

QUAIL EN GELÉE

Quail marinated in Cognac, stuffed with pork pistachio forcemeat and foie gras, coated in Sauternes gelée, and served cold: this is the more elegant side of Olympia Provisions. This recipe sounds like it would be way more difficult to make than it actually is. In fact, it's a pure joy to create, because just a little bit of effort yields something that is so damn classy. In my fantasy world, I would make and sell these little charms in custom ceramic ramekins.

You can buy semi-boneless quail at most butcher shops; the birds will have all the bones removed except for the wings and legs. And any decent Cognac will do for this recipe. As for the Sauternes, you only need ½ cup (120 ml) for the gelée, but you should be drinking Sauternes as you work, or at least have a little glass with the quail. For the pork pistachio forcemeat, set aside 5½ ounces (155 g) from the Pork Pistachio Pâté (page 45). You can buy deveined foie gras online at DArtagnan.com.

NOTE: THIS IS A 12-HOUR RECIPE, WITH 4 HOURS OF HANDS-ON TIME.

1 Put the quail in a shallow vessel and pour over 2 tablespoons (30 ml) of the Cognac. In a bowl, mix together the foie gras and the remaining Cognac. Cover both with plastic wrap and refrigerate for 3 to 4 hours.

2 Preheat the oven to 350°F (176°C).

3 Using a slotted spoon, remove the foie gras from the Cognac and transfer it to a separate bowl. Add 1 teaspoon (5 g) of sea salt to the foie gras and mix with your hands until well combined. Divide the foie gras into four equal portions and roll each into a cylinder the size of a fat thumb (see photo, page 54). Set aside.

4 Lay one quail breast-side down on a work service. Sprinkle salt and pepper all over the quail, rubbing it into the skin and cavity. Remove the pork forcemeat from the refrigerator. Take a quarter of the pork forcemeat meat and line the cavity with it, pressing it down. Place a foie gras cylinder in the middle and fold the forcemeat around the log, like you're making a foie taco. On one side of the quail, pull the skin up and out to get a bit of slack, then wrap the quail meat around the foie; hold it in place with your finger while you pull and fold the other side up and over. The skin should stick together, holding the quail closed with the forcemeat and foie inside. Flip the quail into a small, individual ramekin, breast side up. Now, using a sharp knife, cut two holes in the skin

CONTINUED

SERVES 4

4 semi-boneless quail

¼ cup (60 ml) Cognac

6 ounces (170 g) foie gras, deveined and crumbled

Fine sea salt

5½ ounces (155 g) chilled Pork Pistachio forcemeat (see page 45)

1 teaspoon (5 g) ground black pepper

½ cup (120 ml) water

½ cup (120 ml) Sauternes

1 (¼-ounce/7-g) packet gelatin

TO SERVE

Maldon salt

Hard-boiled eggs

Pickled beets

Parsley

between the legs and the breast. Crossing the quails legs, poke each leg through the holes. Tuck the legs into the ramekin. Repeat with the other three quail. Sprinkle the quail with salt.

5   Place the ramekins on a baking sheet and bake until golden and the internal temperature is 140°F (60°C), about 25 minutes. Remove the ramekins from the oven and transfer to a plate. Refrigerate for 1½ hours or for up to overnight.

6   Remove the quail from the refrigerator and let come to room temperature, 30 or 45 minutes.

7   In a saucepan over medium heat, combine the water and Sauternes and heat until barely simmering. Remove from the heat and allow to cool for 1 minute. Using a whisk, stir in the gelatin, working very quickly so it doesn't clump up. Add a pinch of sea salt. Pour two-thirds of the gelée onto a serving platter with a high edge. Turn the ramekins over to remove the quail. Slice the quail on a bias and arrange the slices on the gelée. Pour the rest of the gelée on top of the quail. Allow the gelée to set, about 10 minutes. Sprinkle with crunchy salt and serve.

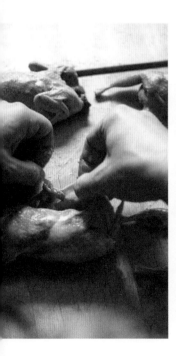

RABBIT, APRICOT, AND TARRAGON PÂTÉ

**MAKES ONE 4 BY 12-INCH
(10 BY 30 CM) TERRINE**

2¼ pounds (1 kg) boned rabbit leg
    meat, cubed

12 ounces (340 g) pork fatback, diced

4 ounces (100 g) pork liver, diced

1 slice (20 g) white bread, crusts
    removed and cut into 1-inch
    (2.5 cm) cubes

¼ cup (60 ml) whole milk

¼ cup (60 ml) chicken stock

1 tablespoon (15 ml) olive oil

1 tablespoon (15 g) chopped garlic

2 tablespoons (36 g) diced shallot

1 tablespoon (10 g) chopped
    fresh thyme

2 tablespoons (30 ml) dry white wine

Pinch of ground ginger

½ teaspoon (7 g) aniseed

½ teaspoon (7 g) fennel seeds

1 teaspoon (5 g) ground black pepper

½ teaspoon (2.5 g) ground white
    pepper

2 tablespoons (30 g) fine sea salt

½ teaspoon (2 g) curing salt #1

1 teaspoon (5 g) sugar

2 tablespoons (6 g) chopped
    fresh tarragon

1 cup (170 g) diced dried apricots

Although we don't currently sell rabbit pâté at Olympia Provisions, we hope to add it to our product list in the future. Meanwhile, make this pâté for yourself, like I do.

If you have a really nice butcher, he or she will grind the rabbit and mix it with the fatback for you, so all you have to do is add the spices and run with it. Good rabbit should have a natural, herby flavor, like wild sage (the hippie kind that you burn, not the kind you eat). Adding tarragon to this pâté brightens up the flavor with a hint of anise. The apricot lightens it further, making this terrine perfect for spring and summer. Rabbit is a very delicate flavor, so I like to pair it with simple, light vegetables that won't overpower—in this case, a carrot salad.

NOTE: THIS RECIPE TAKES 1 DAY, WITH 3 HOURS HANDS-ON TIME.

Special Equipment: You will need a grinder.

1   Put the rabbit meat, fatback, and liver in a large bowl and transfer to the freezer. Let chill for 20 minutes, or until a calibrated thermometer inserted into the center of the mixture reads 32°F (0°C), about 30 minutes. If your freezer is big enough, also chill the meat grinder and all its parts, as well as the metal bowl and paddle attachment of a stand mixer.

2   To make the panade, mix the bread, milk, and stock together using your hands. Allow the bread to soak up the liquid and become nice and soggy. Transfer to the fridge and chill for 45 minutes.

3   In a small sauté pan over medium heat, warm the olive oil. Sweat the garlic, shallot, and thyme until lightly brown and completely tender, about 8 minutes. Add the wine and reduce by almost half, about 5 minutes. Transfer the pan with its contents to the fridge to cool.

4   Using a mortar and pestle, grind together the ginger, aniseed, fennel seed, black pepper, and white pepper until you have a fine powder.

5   In the chilled bowl of your stand mixer, combine the spices with the garlic, shallots, and thyme. Add the cold rabbit meat, fatback, and liver. Add the panade, sea salt, curing salt, sugar, and tarragon and mix with a wooden spoon until all of the ingredients are nicely incorporated, about 2 minutes. Put the bowl in the freezer while you set up the grinder.

6 Assemble the grinder with a fine (⅛-inch/3-mm) die and, working quickly and in batches to keep the meat mixture cold, grind the mixture into the chilled bowl. Fit the mixer with the chilled paddle attachment and mix on low for 1 minute, until all of the ingredients are evenly distributed. Fold in the dried apricots. This is your forcemeat. At this point you can continue making it into pâté, or you can use it to make Rabbit Ballotine (page 58).

7 Pack the forcemeat into a 4 by 12-inch (10 by 30 cm) terrine mold, making sure it gets into all the edges and corners. Smooth the top of the forcemeat; then, to force out any air around the pâté, thump the terrine down on a sturdy work surface. Cover the terrine with aluminum foil and refrigerate for 24 hours to let the curing salt work its magic.

8 The next day, preheat the oven to 300°F (148°C). Cut a piece of cardboard slightly smaller than the width and length of the terrine, so it will fit inside the terrine's mouth.

9 Bring a medium pot of water to a simmer. Make a bain-marie: Place the terrine in the center of a large roasting pan or deep casserole dish. Carefully pour simmering water into the roasting pan until it comes two-thirds of the way up the terrine. Cover the bain-marie with aluminum foil and transfer to the oven. After 1½ hours, place a calibrated thermometer in the middle of the pâté. You're looking for an internal temperature of 155°F (68°C); if it's not there yet, put the terrine back in the oven and check the temperature every 15 minutes. When it's done, carefully remove the bain-marie from the oven.

10 Remove the terrine from the roasting pan and very carefully pour out the hot water. Fill the pan two-thirds full with ice and nestle the terrine into it. You now need a weight, something to press the pâté into the perfect shape: a large can of beans or soup will do. Place the piece of cardboard you have prepared on top of the aluminum foil covering the terrine, add the weight, and refrigerate for 2 to 3 hours.

11 Remove the terrine from the refrigerator and check the temperature; it should be 39°F (4°C) or lower. If it is, and you're ready to serve, invert the mold onto a serving platter; the pâté should gently slide out.

12 Slice the pâté ½ inch (1.3 cm) thick and serve. Wrap what you don't eat in plastic wrap; it will keep for up to 2 weeks in the fridge.

RABBIT BALLOTINE

SERVES 8 AMERICANS
OR 24 PARISIANS

1 piece (18-inch-/45 cm-square)
    pork caul fat

1 (3-pound/1.4 kg) rabbit, skinned,
    cleaned, and deboned, with head
    and feet removed

2 pounds (910 g) uncooked Rabbit,
    Apricot, and Tarragon forcemeat
    (steps 1 through 6, pages 56–57)

Fine sea salt

1 (¼-ounce/7-g) packet gelatin

⅔ cup (150 ml) Cognac

⅓ cup (90 ml) chicken stock

TO SERVE

Pickles

Crusty bread

Whole-grain mustard

Pickled beets

Parsley

Pickled cauliflower

When we first opened our restaurant, Olympia Provisions Southeast, it took a couple of months to complete the USDA paperwork necessary to open the meat production plant. And so I ended up working at the restaurant full-time, making pâtés, confit, and other classics like this ballotine, a deboned rabbit stuffed with forcemeat to hold its form.

I know this recipe, which combines forcemeat, a deboned rabbit, and caul fat, is quite involved, but mastering these techniques will pay dividends for life. If you're having friends or family over, it's a brilliant move to have this work of art complete and ready for slicing so you can get on with having a great time.

For this recipe, you will need pork caul fat, the lacy net of fat that surrounds and holds an animal's stomach and other organs. Any good butcher should be able to get it for you. You also need something classy to serve the ballotine on, preferably a silver platter with a lip so the gelée stays put when you pour it in.

NOTE: THIS RECIPE TAKES 5 HOURS, WITH 3 HOURS HANDS-ON TIME.

1   Preheat the oven to 350°F (176°C). Lay out the caul fat on a flat surface and place the rabbit in the middle. Pound the rabbit with a rolling pin until it is ½ inch (1.3-cm) thick; cover up any holes using small chunks of leg meat. Place the forcemeat in a sort of log down the center of the rabbit and compress it with your hands (see photos, page 61). Fold one side of the rabbit over the forcemeat, then fold the other side over so that the edges of the rabbit meat overlap and enclose the forcemeat. Starting from a long side, wrap the caul fat around the rabbit, and then roll the rabbit toward the other side. The rabbit should be wrapped in a double layer of caul fat and the caul fat should extend about 1 inch (2.5 cm) past the ends of the rabbit; trim off any excess. Tuck the ends of the caul fat under the roll so that the forcemeat will not come out.

2   Starting at the far end of the rabbit, truss the meat using the method used for the Coppa di Testa on page 36.

3   Place the rabbit in a roasting pan and sprinkle it with 1 tablespoon (15 g) of salt. Roast the ballotine for 1½ hours, until it has reached an internal temperature of 150°F (65°C), the caul fat is melted and golden. Remove from the oven and allow to rest for 15 minutes, then transfer to the refrigerator to chill for 2 hours, or up to overnight.

CONTINUED

4   Remove the ballotine from the fridge and use scissors to snip the twine. Keeping the seam side down, slice crosswise into ¼-inch (6-mm) medallions. If you're not ready to serve, wrap the slices in plastic wrap and refrigerate.

5   When you're ready to serve, make the gelée. In a small saucepan over medium heat, combine the water and Cognac and heat until barely simmering. Remove from the heat and allow to cool for 1 minute. Whisk in the gelatin, working very quickly so it doesn't clump up. Add a pinch of salt and very carefully pour the gelée onto the serving platter until it forms a layer about ¼ inch (6 mm) thick. Allow the gelée to cool and set, about 10 minutes. Place the ballotine slices on the platter, on top of the gelée. Serve with your favorite pickles, crusty bread, and whole-grain mustard alongside.

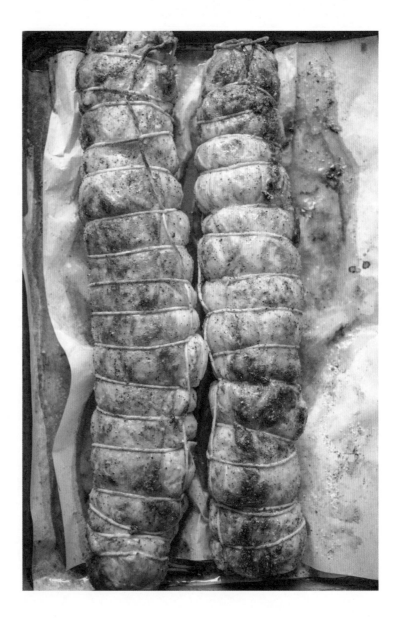

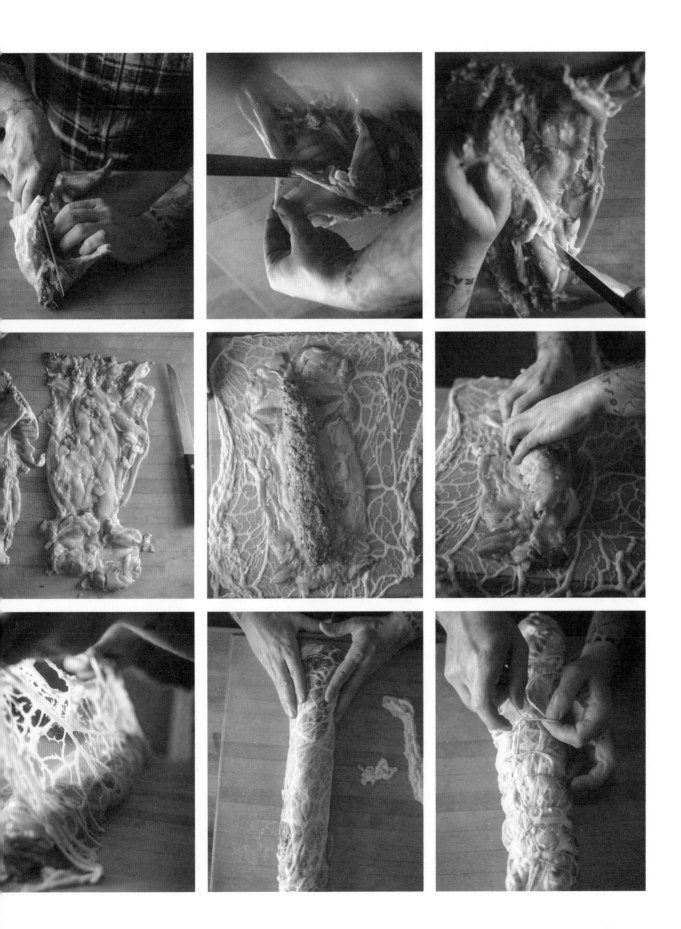

SERVES 12 TO 16

6 pounds (2.7 kg) Italian Sausage
with Lacinato Kale uncooked
forcemeat (see Variation page 84),
chilled

1 (25-pound/11.3 kg) whole suckling
pig. Once deboned, but with
head, feet, and skin intact, it
will consist of roughly:
> 14 lb (6.3 kg) deboned pig loins,
head, and feet intact
> 4½ lb (2.0 kg) trim meat,
for sausage*
> 1½ lb (680 g) fat*, for sausage

½ cup (100 g) fine sea salt, plus
5 tablespoons for salting the cavity

* The trim meat and fat from
the suckling pig should be used
to make the Italian Sausage with
Lacinato Kale forcemeat. They will
replace the pork shoulder in the
doubled recipe on page 84. You will
still need fatback.

Nothing says "feast" like a whole roasted pig as a centerpiece. We made this porchetta one spring day for a group of our favorite European winemakers (see page 240). It's not an easy feat to impress a discerning bunch of Europeans with American charcuterie served in an industrial warehouse in the middle of Portland. But (they said) they loved it, so I'm including the recipe here. It makes a whole suckling pig, cleaned and mostly boned out, with skin, head, and feet intact, and stuffed with a forcemeat made of its own leg and shoulder meat, sausage seasonings, and braised kale. The pig is tied up and roasted, then cut into round slices of herby forcemeat and roasted pork loin wrapped in crispy golden skin.

To be perfectly honest, this is one recipe that may be a challenge to pull off in a home kitchen. You'll be able to do it if you have access to a kitchen with a really large, commercial range or a (big) outdoor fire pit. This is what you're looking at: you'll ask your butcher to debone a suckling pig, and you'll make a forcemeat from the animal's shoulder and leg meat (see page 84). Then you'll stuff the forcemeat into the animal, tie it up nicely, poke it all over with a knife, and roast it.

At OP, we butcher the pig ourselves, but a good relationship with a great butcher is really all a home cook—or even a chef—needs to make great charcuterie. Ask your butcher to remove all of the bones except the head and feet from a suckling pig, leaving the skin and pig in one complete piece. Ask that the loin be kept on the skin and any trim from the legs and shoulders be reserved. If you are interested in learning home butchery, some great books that cover it are *Whole Beast Butchery* by Ryan Farr and *The Butcher's Guide to Well-Raised Meat* by Joshua and Jessica Applestone.

CONTINUED

Special Equipment: You'll need a huge roasting pan and a commercial-size oven. Have on hand an entire roll of butcher's twine.

1   Preheat the oven to 350°F (176°C). Bring 1 gallon (4 liters) of water to a boil in a large pot. Remove the forcemeat from the refrigerator.

2   Place the pig on the work surface, skin side down. Sprinkle the salt all over the meat, and rub it in with your hands, getting it into all of the nooks and crannies. Take out your roll of twine. Place the pig on top of the twine, skin down, and snout pointing away from you. Scoop the sausage onto the pig in a line down the middle, packing it into a fat log shape. Fold the sides of the pig up over the forcemeat so they overlap by a few inches. If there is too much forcemeat for this to happen, remove some. Starting at the tail end (the end closest to you), tie up the pig using the method for the Coppa di Testa (see page 36).

3   Poke the pig all over with a small sharp knife, making sure to puncture the skin without going so deep that you stab the forcemeat. This allows the fat to come out of the pig, crisping up the skin as it roasts. Put the pig in a large roasting pan or over your clean sink and very carefully pour the boiling water over it. This tightens up the skin and also opens up the holes you just poked in it.

4   Transfer the pig to a huge industrial-size roasting pan. Roast for 1 hour, then check the internal temperature by inserting a calibrated thermometer through the skin and into the forcemeat. At this point, the internal temperature should be hovering around 100°F (38°C). Crank the oven to 500°F (260°C) to let the crisping begin. Disable your smoke alarms and open the windows—the oven will begin to smoke. You may feel scared, but I promise it will be worth it. After 20 minutes, check the internal temperature; once it reaches 150°F (65°C), remove the pig from the oven. Allow to cool for 15 minutes.

5   Place the golden, crispy, beautiful pig on a large cutting board (or on layers and layers of parchment paper) and bring it to the table so it can be admired before you carve it. Beginning at the tail end and working toward the head, cut 1-inch (2.5 cm) slices. I find a really sharp serrated knife works best. Serve hot or warm.

Preparing Porchetta.

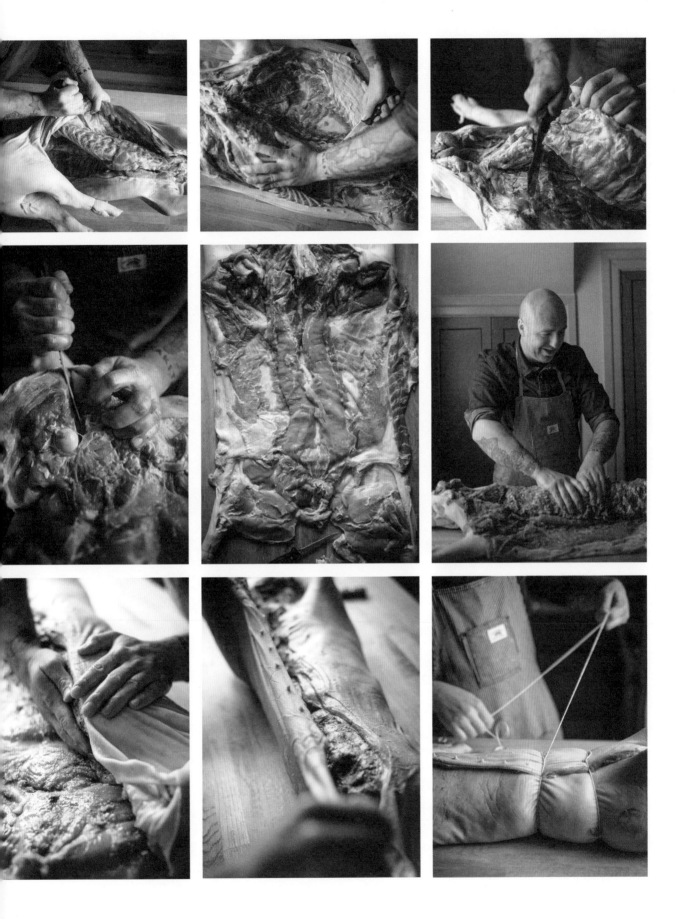

CHAPTER 3

Fresh Sausage

I have often wondered about the first person to come up with the idea of stuffing the intestines of an animal with the animal itself. Obviously this person was a true genius, and undoubtedly resourceful, but maybe also a bit warped.

I loved making sausage before I loved eating sausage. As a kid, I would watch my dad make loukanika in the kitchen—listening to Greek records; smoking cigarettes; and grinding, mixing, and stuffing the animals (that he had just killed) into some sort of cheap intestine. It wasn't until later in my life, when I tried a god-awful dry, crumbly, tasteless sausage that I realized there must be more to sausage making than I knew. My dad made it look easy.

To make sausage at OP, I have access to an industrial bowl chopper, a VEMAG Robot 800 (industrial sausage stuffer), a massive refrigerator, and a kick-ass staff. However, the sausage recipes that follow reflect how I would make sausage at home without all the professional tools and equipment. You'll need a grinder, a stuffer, and (ideally) a stand mixer to make these recipes.

Many grinders, both manual and electric, come with a stuffer attachment. Toss this into the trash ASAP and purchase a small, hand-crank stuffer with a capacity of at least 5 pounds (2.3 kg). This allows you to really pack your meat tightly and fill the casings in a more consistent manner, without air pockets. Having a good electric mixer with a paddle attachment will allow you to mix all of your ingredients evenly and help form a nice bind between the lean and fat meat.

Grab your *Zorba the Greek* soundtrack and light a cigarette: we're about to make sausage.

From the top, then going left to right: Breakfast Sausage patties (page 81), Breakfast Sausage links (page 81), chorizo, Bratwurst (page 80), Salami Cotto (page 92), Mortadella (page 88).

I will give you two different percentage charts for sausage. One is for product that is supposed to be consumed cold, like baloney or mortadella—deli meat, if you will. The other is for the classic sausages intended to be eaten hot, like bratwurst or breakfast links. All the meat portions add up to 100 percent. Garnish includes ingredients folded in at the end, such as nuts and dried fruit. For more information on how to use them, see page 22.

SAUSAGE CONSUMED COLD

Sausage consumed cold is just what it sounds like. Examples are Mortadella (page 88) and Salami Cotto (page 92).

*Pork shoulder	64%
*Fat	36%
*Salt	2.7%
*Curing salt #1	0.2%
*Milk powder	2.6%
Ice	15%
Garnish	7%

SAUSAGE CONSUMED WARM

This is what we think of as conventional sausage. Examples are Our Basic Sausage (page 73), Parsley Pecorino Sausage (page 77), Bratwurst (page 80), Breakfast Sausage (page 81), and Italian Sausage with Lacinato Kale (page 84).

*Meat	70%
*Fat	30%
*Salt	1.5%
Spices	1 to 1.5%
Ice	7%
*Milk Powder	4%

* Ingredients marked with an asterisk need to be converted precisely.

Quality Tips

The trick to making delicious, high-quality sausage is in the details: how you grind, mix, stuff, and cook, and the quality of the casings that hold everything in place. Always keep your meat cold and your grinding blades sharp, and remember practice makes perfect.

Grinding: Sharp meat grinder blades are paramount. Get them sharpened often. Ask your butcher who does his, then do it as needed. The sharper the blades, the less friction. Less friction will keep the grinding temperature down, which in turn guarantees a better bind. Having a good bind leads to a better texture or mouthfeel. In technical, meat-nerd speak, you want to develop the myosin in the meat. Myosin is a protein that, in ground meat like sausages, wraps itself around fat particles, stabilizing the meat so that when it's cooked, the fat stays put inside its little myosin pillowcases rather than oozing or melting out.

A properly sharpened grinder will also ensure that you get good separation of fat and lean meat. When you look at cotto, for example, you should see real distinction between the fat particles and the lean meat. A dull blade will smash the two together, resulting in a big, slimy mess that doesn't stick (hold the emulsion). This leads to fat running out of the sausage when you cook it, leaving you with a casing full of lean ground meat, the ultimate sign of a poorly made sausage!

Finally, if you are going to be using two different dies (the things with holes that determine the coarseness of the grind), you should always use the same plate with the same blade. That way if you have a ding in your plate, the blade will only wear out in that one spot.

Temperature: As you grind, keep your grinder blades, plates, and, most importantly, the meat and fat mixture very cold. If the mixture gets warm, the fat will start to melt and become soft and greasy. The emulsion you're trying to make of fat, water, and protein will break down, wrecking your sausage batter. If your equipment is warm, it will warm the product, and then the only positive you'll have is a happy dog (who cleans up your mistakes). Ice added to the meat and fat helps keep the temperature down, ensuring the fat doesn't melt.

Mixing: After you grind, mix the other ingredients—the seasonings—into the meat. One main goal of mixing is to make sure all of your ingredients are evenly distributed throughout the batter. If you don't distribute the salt well, for example, you will end up with an unevenly seasoned product. The other main goal of mixing is getting the fat covered in myosin (see Grinding, above) without the fat getting so warm that it starts to melt. For the same reason, it's important to keep all parts of the mixing process as cold as possible: the bowl and the paddle of your stand mixer, or whatever you decide to mix with. Mix your meat over an ice bath or, if possible, in a refrigerated room.

After mixing, make a small patty and fry it up in a pan over low heat until it is cooked through. Then test it for seasoning and flavor and make adjustments as needed. If you adjust the seasonings, make a second sample patty; you want to be sure the finished product is what you want. If the final product is going to be consumed cold, like mortadella, allow it to cool before you try it.

Casings: When working with real animal casings (rather than synthetic ones), try to soak the casings in tepid water for 2 hours before you plan on using them. This will remove any salt (most natural casings are packed in salt to preserve them). Ideally, synthetic casings should be soaked in warm water for at least 4 hours before use to make them more pliable. I use natural casing whenever possible. They add flavor to the sausage, but the trade-off is that they are more fragile and a bit frustrating to work with.

Stuffing: When it comes to stuffing, water is your friend! The horn (the tube that you place your casing on while you're stuffing it), table, and casing should all be as wet as possible. This helps everything slide nicely and smoothly so you can concentrate on stuffing the sausage evenly and tightly. Right before you attach the casing to the horn of your stuffer, fill the casing with a bit of cold water for a final flushing, then empty it and proceed. You will most likely need to rewet casing and equipment as you go, so keep a bowl of water nearby.

Cooking: You do know that every time you boil a sausage, an angel dies, right? Okay, maybe not, but really, don't boil your damn sausage. If you poach them in water nice and slow, to an internal temperature of no more than 155°F (68°C), your sausages will cook evenly throughout. If you boil them, they will most likely burst out of their casings before they are even warm in the middle. So think poaching, not boiling.

OUR BASIC SAUSAGE

Sausage making at home is more or less this routine: grind, mix, stuff, cook, enjoy. This is a very basic recipe so you won't get lost in lots of ingredients and can learn and enjoy the process. Read the Quality Tips at the beginning of this chapter, too, if you haven't already. Most of the other recipes in this chapter will refer to this recipe for the techniques. If you have a nice butcher who likes you or who is just good at his job, you could ask him to grind together your cold shoulder and fatback.

NOTE: THIS RECIPE TAKES 2 HOURS, WITH 1.5 HOURS HANDS-ON TIME.

Special Equipment: You will need a grinder and stuffer.

1   Rinse out your casing by placing one end under the water tap and filling it with about ½ cup (120 ml) water. Run this water through the casing by pulling up on the end that you filled up, until the water comes out the other end of the casing. It will come out a bit cloudy. This is totally normal, as you are removing salt on the inside of the casing. Place the rinsed casing in a bowl of clean warm water to soak.

2   To make the spice mixture, using a mortar and pestle, grind together the ingredients until coarsely combined. Set aside. If your butcher has ground your pork shoulder and fatback for you, skip ahead to step 5.

3   If grinding the meat yourself, put the pork shoulder in the freezer for about 45 minutes, or until a calibrated thermometer inserted into the meat reads 32°F (0°C). If your freezer is big enough, also chill the meat grinder and all its parts, as well as the metal bowl and paddle attachment of a stand mixer and the hopper of your stuffer.

4   In a large bowl, mix together the chilled pork shoulder, the fatback, and the crushed ice. Fill a second large bowl with ice cubes to make an ice bath. Remove the grinder parts from the freezer and assemble the grinder with a ¼-inch (6-mm) die. Set up the grinder so the mixing bowl sits atop the ice bath. Working quickly and in batches to keep the meat mixture cold, grind the mixture, then put half of it through a second time. How will you know if you're on the right track? You should be able to see very clear definition—specks of white fat among the lean meat.

5   Transfer the ground meat mixture to the chilled stand-mixer bowl. Add the spice mixture. Mix with the chilled paddle attachment for 3 to 4 minutes. Here you're looking for what we call "legs" in

CONTINUED

MAKES 9 TO 12 LINKS,
ABOUT 3 POUNDS (1.4 KG)

1 (4-foot/1.2-m) length
    (1¼-inch/32-mm) natural
    hog casing

SPICE MIXTURE

1½ tablespoons (18 g) kosher salt

1½ teaspoons (7 g) ground black
    pepper

1½ teaspoons (7 g) chopped garlic

2¼ pounds (1 kg) pork shoulder, diced
    into ½-inch (1.3-cm) chunks

12 ounces (340 g) fatback, diced
    into ½-inch (1.3-cm) chunks
    and frozen

2 cups (225 g) crushed ice, plus
    additional ice cubes for an ice bath

1 tablespoon (12 g) kosher salt,
    for poaching

Oil, for frying

the meat batter (see image, page 73): Take a clump of the mixture and pull it apart. You should see small threadlike pieces trying to hold on to each other. You also need to make sure you can see separation between the fat and the lean meat. If they are all mashed together, the mixture is most likely smeared and broken and you should turn it into some kind of ragù because you'll need to start over.

6   Pinch off about a tablespoon of the meat batter and press it into a patty. Refrigerate the bowl of batter. In a small skillet over low heat, fry the patty in a bit of oil until cooked through, about 5 minutes. Taste it for seasoning. Tweak the seasoning if needed, adding salt or any spices and mixing the batter well (and always taking care to keep it cold), and then fry up another test patty. When the meat is seasoned to your liking, divide the batter into two balls and give each a few good slams against your work surface to get all the air out. Refrigerate the balls in the fridge while you prepare the stuffer.

7   Before setting up your stuffer, if possible place the hopper (the part that the meat will go in) in the fridge or the deep freezer so that it will be nice and cold. When assembling, take a second and make sure that everything is clean and that all parts are on tightly so that nothing will come lose and make a mess. If you are stuffing from your grinder, you will need to remove the blades and dies and place the horn on the end. Get all of the surfaces that the casing will be touching (the horn and the table) really wet with water so that it will slide and not tear. When linking sausages, water is your ally, so keep a bowl of fresh, clean water close by. If you have a stainless steel or other smooth tabletop, pour about ¼ cup (60 ml) of water on the surface so that the casing will slide with ease and not tear.

8   Take the balls of meat batter out of the refrigerator and put one in the hopper of the stuffer. Remove the casing from the water and slide one end onto the horn of the stuffer or grinder. Tie a knot on the other end. Slide the open end over the horn, making sure the tied end is pressed snuggly against the horn. As you work the stuffer, avoid creating any air gaps and take care to fill the casing full enough, but don't fill it so full so that you won't have enough room to link the sausages. Once you have all the meat in the casing, tie the end and cut off any excess casing. Examine the stuffed casing: if you see any air gaps, pierce the casing lightly with the back of a sausage knife or the tip of a sharp knife.

9   To form the links, start at whichever end of the casing you like. With your dominant hand, measure a hand's length from the end

of the casing and, using your index finger and your thumb, pinch the casing and twist the sausage two full rotations. The initial sausage should feel nice and tight. Measure another hand's length from the spot you just pinched and pinch again. This time, rotate the sausage two full rotations in the opposite direction from the last twist. As you twist the sausage in the opposite direction, you will feel the last sausage you twisted getting tighter. Repeat this process for the entire length of the casing: pinch and twist one way, then pinch and twist the other way. This technique ensures that you do not untwist the link that you just made.

10   In a large pot over medium heat, bring 1 gallon (4 liters) of water and the kosher salt to a simmer. Add the sausages and poach—don't boil—for about 30 minutes, or until the internal temperature reaches 155°F (68°C) when tested with a calibrated meat thermometer.

11   If you're saving the poached sausages to eat later, let them cool for 2 minutes in ice water, then store in the refrigerator wrapped in plastic for up to 1 week, or in the freezer for 2 months. If you are going to eat the sausages right away, warm a bit of oil in a frying pan over medium heat. Snip apart the sausages and cook for about 3 minutes on each side, until golden brown and screaming "Try me now!"

PARSLEY PECORINO SAUSAGE

The first time I tasted a sausage like this, I had just finished climbing in the Dolomites with my buddy Eric Moore. We were on our way back to the Alpenrose, where we worked, and stopped in the village of Bellinzona, just short of the Italian-Swiss border. In an amazing restaurant there, the name of which I unfortunately cannot recall, we enjoyed a meal of poached sausage speckled with parsley and hints of nutty pecorino, served in a nonna's tomato sauce atop the most tender polenta. I modeled this sausage after that dish. It's so refreshing and light, you'll forget you're eating sausage.

NOTE: THIS RECIPE TAKES 2 HOURS, WITH 1.5 HOURS OF HANDS-ON TIME.

Special Equipment: You will need a grinder and stuffer.

1   Using the ingredients listed at right, follow steps 1 through 4 of Our Basic Sausage (page 73) to prepare the casing, make the spice mixture, and grind together the pork shoulder, fatback, and the crushed ice.

2   In the chilled stand-mixer bowl, combine the ground meat mixture with the spice mixture, parsley, and cheese and mix as directed in step 5.

3   Follow steps 6 through 11 to test the seasoning of the meat batter, fill the casing, and cook the sausages. After poaching, these sausages will keep in the refrigerator wrapped in plastic for up 1 week, or in the freezer for up to 1 month.

**MAKES 9 TO 12 LINKS,
ABOUT 3 POUNDS (1.4 KG)**

1 (4-foot/1.2-m) length
   (1¼-inch/32-mm) natural
   hog casing

SPICE MIXTURE

1½ tablespoons (18 g) kosher salt

1½ teaspoons (7 g) ground black
   pepper

1½ teaspoons (7 g) chopped garlic

2¼ pounds (1 kg) boneless pork
   shoulder, diced into ½-inch
   (1.3-cm) chunks

12 ounces (340 g) fatback, diced into
   ½-inch (1.3-cm) chunks and frozen

2 cups (225 g) crushed ice, plus
   additional ice cubes for an ice bath

A handful (about 20 g) flat-leaf
   parsley leaves

3 ounces (85 g) grated Pecorino
   Romano cheese

1 tablespoon (12 g) kosher salt,
   for poaching

Oil, for frying

Grind, stuff, link.

BRATWURST

1 (4-foot/1.2-m) length (1¼-inch/
32-mm) natural hog casing

SPICE MIXTURE

1½ tablespoons (18 g) fine sea salt

¼ cup (55 g) milk powder

1¾ teaspoons (8 g) ground white
pepper

¾ teaspoon (3 g) ground black pepper

½ teaspoon (2 g) ground ginger

¾ teaspoon (3 g) mustard powder

¼ teaspoon (1 g) freshly grated
nutmeg

2¼ pounds (1 kg) boneless pork
shoulder, diced into ½-inch
(1.3-cm) chunks

12 ounces (340 g) fatback, diced
into ½-inch (1.3-cm) chunks
and frozen

2 cups (225 g) crushed ice, plus
additional ice cubes for an ice bath

1 tablespoon (12 g) kosher salt,
for poaching

Oil, for frying

People often make brats with both veal and pork or with eggs and cream. Tsk, tsk. Let's address these violations. First, I find brats made with the addition of veal to be a waste of baby cow. Pork is already a superior product, so don't be wasteful. Second, eggs and cream are usually added to achieve lightness in flavor and texture. But if you stick with my technique, you won't need these additives and you'll get better flavor. A bratwurst should be so light yet rich that it leaves you confused: How did I devour that so fast? Why do I want another? Serve them with Sauerkraut (page 212) on the side.

NOTE: THIS RECIPES TAKES 2 HOURS, WITH 1.5 HOURS OF HANDS-ON TIME.

Special Equipment: You will need a grinder and stuffer.

1 Using the ingredients listed at left, follow steps 1 through 11 of Our Basic Sausage (page 73) to make and cook the sausages. After poaching, these sausages will keep in the refrigerator wrapped in plastic for up 1 week, or in the freezer for up to 1 month.

BREAKFAST SAUSAGE

Mike Boyd is a god in the sausage world, and his phone number is on my speed dial for many a reason. He is a retired meat equipment salesperson who knows more about meat making than all of us next-generation meat makers combined. Mike once told me a story about a farmer who had a bunch of really old sows down in Texas. The man asked Mike how he could make a sausage out of their meat, and what kind of spices he could use to cover up, well, the taste of old sow: "Something for breakfast, maybe." Mike suggested the farmer add a lot of sage, maple syrup, and lemon. That farmer's name was Jimmy Dean.

This is my take on the breakfast sausage, and Mike has approved it. The good student will notice that it's the same recipe as our Bratwurst (opposite), but with maple syrup and sage added. As we love to say in OP world: this is the most important sausage of your day!

This is just as great made into patties as it is twisted into casings.

NOTE: THIS RECIPES TAKES 2 HOURS WITH 1.5 HOURS HANDS-ON TIME.

Special Equipment: You will need a grinder and stuffer.

1   Using the ingredients listed at right, follow steps 1 through 4 of Our Basic Sausage (page 73) to prepare the casing, make the spice mixture, and grind together the pork shoulder, fatback, and half of the ice.

2   In the chilled stand-mixer bowl, combine the ground meat mixture with the spice mixture and maple syrup and mix as directed in step 5.

3   Follow steps 6 through 11 to test the seasoning of the meat batter, fill the casing, and cook the sausages. After poaching, these sausages will keep in the refrigerator wrapped in plastic for up 1 week, or in the freezer for up to 1 month.

MAKES 9 TO 12 LINKS, ABOUT 3 POUNDS (1.4 KG)

1 (6-foot/1.8-m) length (¾-inch/20-mm) natural lamb casing

SPICE MIXTURE

1½ tablespoons (18 g) fine sea salt

¼ cup (55 g) milk powder

1¾ teaspoons (8 g) ground white pepper

¾ teaspoon (3 g) ground black pepper

½ teaspoon (2 g) ground ginger

¾ teaspoon (3 g) mustard powder

¼ teaspoon (1 g) freshly grated nutmeg

1¾ teaspoons (7 g) chopped fresh sage

2¼ pounds (1 kg) boneless pork shoulder, diced into ½-inch (1.3-cm) chunks

12 ounces (340 g) fatback, diced into ½-inch (1.3-cm) chunks and frozen

¼ cup (50 g) maple syrup

2 cups (225 g) crushed ice, plus additional ice cubes for an ice bath

1 tablespoon (12 g) kosher salt, for poaching

Oil, for frying

ITALIAN SAUSAGE WITH LACINATO KALE

**MAKES 9 TO 12 LINKS,
ABOUT 3 POUNDS (1.4 KG)**

BRAISED KALE

1 pound (455 g) lacinato kale

1 tablespoon (15 ml) olive oil

1 teaspoon (5 g) chopped garlic

½ teaspoon (2.5 g) crushed red
  pepper flakes

1 cup (240 ml) water

Kosher salt

1 (4-foot/1.2-m) length
  (1¼-inch/32-mm) natural
  hog casing

SPICE MIXTURE

1½ tablespoons (22 g) fine sea salt

1½ teaspoons (7 g) ground coriander

1½ teaspoon (7 g) ground black pepper

1 teaspoon (4 g) fennel seeds

1 teaspoon (4 g) crushed red
  pepper flakes

1 teaspoon (3 g) dried oregano

¾ teaspoon (3 g) chopped garlic

2¼ pounds (1 kg) boneless pork
  shoulder, diced into ½-inch
  (1.3-cm) chunks

12 ounces (340 g) fatback, diced into
  ½-inch (1.3-cm) chunks and frozen

2 cups (225 g) crushed ice, plus
  additional ice cubes for an ice bath

1 tablespoon (12 g) kosher salt,
  for poaching

Oil, for frying

This recipe is ideal for anyone who grows huge amounts of kale in the garden and is trying hard not to waste it. Like Italian grandmothers, we braise the kale and mix it with our favorite simple sausage recipe, making us the heroes of our families and the envy of all Italian villagers. Without the kale, this is our basic Italian sausage. This is also the same sausage I use to stuff my Porchetta (page 62); see Variation, below.

NOTE: THIS RECIPES TAKES 2 HOURS WITH 1.5 HOURS HANDS-ON TIME.

Special Equipment: You will need a grinder and stuffer.

1   To make the braised kale, strip away and discard the stems from the kale leaves. Wash, dry, and coarsely chop the leaves. In a medium pot over medium heat, warm the olive oil. Add the garlic and red pepper flakes and cook, stirring constantly, until soft, about 1 minute. Add the kale, the water, and a good pinch of kosher salt. Stir well, cover, and cook until the kale is very tender and has no bite left (so that it will meld with the texture of the sausage), about 5 minutes. Taste the kale and for salt, transfer to a bowl, and refrigerate until needed.

2   Using the ingredients listed at left, follow steps 1 through 4 of Our Basic Sausage (page 73) to prepare the casing, make the spice mixture, and grind together the pork shoulder, fatback, and the crushed ice.

3   In the chilled stand-mixer bowl, combine the ground meat mixture with the spice mixture and braised kale and mix as directed in step 5.

4   Follow steps 6 through 11 to test the seasoning of the meat batter, fill the casing, and cook the sausages. After poaching, these sausages will keep in the refrigerator wrapped in plastic for up 1 week, or in the freezer for up to 1 month.

Variation: To make this sausage to use for Porchetta (page 62), use the meat and fat from the 25-lb suckling pig to replace the pork shoulder and simply double the recipe. You will still need fatback. Follow Our Basic Sausage recipe only through step 6; do not stuff the sausage.

Baloney and Its Many Faces

Baloney, or bologna, is a meat emulsion—a stable puree of protein, fat, and water with a completely uniform color and texture. Here, lean meat is pretty much pulverized to extract as much myosin as possible. (Remember, myosin is the protein that encases fat particles, keeping the fat from leaking out of a sausage product.)

At OP, we use a commercial (read: industrial) bowl chopper to first grind up the lean meat, developing the myosin, and then we chop in the fat. It's similar to making mayonnaise in a food processor, where you start with the egg yolk and dribble in the oil to make an emulsion.

Fortunately, you don't need a commercial chopper the size of a Honda to make great mortadella or baloney or weisswurst. Many books will tell you to use a food processor to make emulsified meats at home. However, I prefer to run the meat through a motorized grinder over and over again, as I find that using a food processor can result in a complete mess and a terrible texture because you can only process ½ pound (225 g) at once and the food processor whips air into the meat. (I'm not saying you can't use a hand grinder, but you may end up with a less-than-perfect grind, along with huge forearms.)

MORTADELLA

MAKES ONE 3-POUND (1.4-KG)
SAUSAGE; SERVES 10 TO 12 AS
AN APPETIZER

1 (18-inch/45.7 cm) length (5-inch/
13 cm) collagen casing

21 ounces (600 g) fatback, cut into
½-inch (1.3-cm) squares, plus
3 ounces (90 g) fatback, cut into
½-inch (1.3-cm) chunks

2 pounds (910 g) boneless pork
shoulder, cut into ½-inch
(1.3-cm) chunks

½ teaspoon (2 g) freshly grated
nutmeg

¼ teaspoon (1 g) ground cinnamon

¼ teaspoon (1 g) cayenne

¼ teaspoon (1 g) ground coriander

2 teaspoons (10 g) chopped garlic

2½ tablespoons (37 g) fine sea salt

2 cups (225 g) crushed ice, plus
additional ice cubes for ice baths

¾ teaspoon (3 g) curing salt #1

1 tablespoon plus ½ teaspoon (18 g)
sugar

2 tablespoons plus 2 teaspoons (38 g)
milk powder

1 tablespoon (15 g) black peppercorns

2 tablespoons (12 g) whole shelled
pistachios

Oil, for frying

¼ cup (48 g) kosher salt, for poaching

Mortadella is the king of sausage. These fatties can stretch up to 6 feet (1.8 m) long and weigh up to 300 pounds (135 kg). But with the slice of a blade, mortadella's aspect changes completely, from a big brutish stump of meat product to airy, pink-silk handkerchiefs, resting daintily on a charcuterie board.

Mortadella should have amazing depth of flavor, with fresh garlic and a balance of sweet and savory spices. Breaking up the airy meat should be the crunch of a rich pistachio or the heat of a peppercorn. A greasy mortadella is a sad mortadella. A great mortadella makes you thirsty for a great Lambrusco. You should be proud to show off this accomplishment! Make a mortadella sandwich with white bread, raw onion, and mayo, like when you were young, and wonder why baloney got such a bad name.

NOTES: THIS IS A 2-DAY RECIPE WITH 3 HOURS OF HANDS-ON TIME. YOU CAN FIND SYNTHETIC CASINGS AT YOUR BUTCHER OR AT SAUSAGEMAKER.COM.

Special Equipment: You will need a grinder and stuffer.

1   Fill the casing with warm water and dump out the water. Place the casing in a bowl with clean, warm water. Put the fatback and pork shoulder in the freezer on a sheet pan and let chill until the internal temperature reads 32°F (0°C), about 20 minutes. If it's possible to fit the meat grinder, its parts, the hopper, and the paddle attachment of a mixer in the freezer, include them as well. Combine the nutmeg, cinnamon, cayenne, coriander, and garlic in a mortar and grind to a paste with the pestle. Set aside.

2   Fill a small pot with water and bring to a boil. Add 3 ounces (90 g) of the fatback from the freezer and cut into nice ½-inch (1.3-cm) squares and blanch for 10 seconds, then drain. Lay out the pieces of fatback on a baking sheet and transfer to the freezer. Keep separate from other fatback. This fat will be the garnish in the final sausage.

3   When the remaining fatback and the meat are fully chilled, remove them from the freezer and mix together in a large bowl with half of the crushed ice. Fill another large bowl halfway with ice cubes to make an ice bath; set the bowl of your stand mixer in the ice. Remove the grinder parts from the freezer and assemble the grinder with a large (¼-inch/6-mm) die. Position the chilled stand-mixer bowl, still in its ice bath, so that it catches the meat as it is ground. Push the meat and ice mixture through the grinder twice. Check the internal temperature with a calibrated thermometer: it should not exceed 39°F (4°C).

CONTINUED

4   Change the grinder die to the smallest one you have—a ⅛-inch (3-mm) die works perfectly. (If you do not have a smaller die, continue to use the ¼-inch/6-mm die.) Add the last half of the crushed ice to the meat, then run the mixture through the grinder two more times. (If using a ¼-inch/6-mm die, run the mixture through the grinder four more times, for a total of six times.) Make sure your meat mixture never exceeds 39°F (4°C). You are looking for a mass that is uniform in color and texture and that is as cold as possible.

5   Add the spice and garlic mixture, sea salt, curing salt, sugar, milk powder, peppercorns, pistachios, and blanched fatback to the ground-meat mixture. Fit the stand mixer with the paddle attachment and mix on low speed until all of the ingredients are fully incorporated, about 2 minutes.

6   Pinch off a little of the mixture and form it into a patty. Put the rest of the meat batter back in the fridge to keep it cold. In a small skillet over medium heat, fry the test patty in a little oil, and taste for salt and to see if the texture is correct: you're looking for the best fried baloney you have ever tasted. If it is low on salt or seasoning, grind additional seasonings, add more, and mix for another minute. If the texture is bad or grainy, you will have to start over. There is no saving it now.

7   When you are setting up your stuffer, if possible place the hopper (the part that the meat goes into) in the fridge or the freezer so that it will be nice and cold. While assembling, take a second and make sure that everything is clean and that all parts are on tightly so nothing will come lose and make a mess. If you are stuffing from your grinder, you will need to remove the blades and dies and place the horn on the end. Once you have it all ready to go, you should get all of the surfaces that the casing will be touching (the horn and the table) really wet with water so that the casing will slide and not tear. Most synthetic casings will be tied at one end. Pour out any water that might be in the casing. Place the casing onto the largest casing horn that you have. Slide the open end over the horn, making sure that the tied end is pressed snuggly to the end of the horn.

8   Take half the meat batter out of the fridge and beat it with your hand to get out all of the air. Place it in the hopper of your sausage stuffer. Using your fist, firmly press the meat down to the bottom of the hopper, trying to push any remaining air out of it. Fill the casing at a steady pace. If you see that you have air trapped in the

sausage, when you are done stuffing, use a pin or the spikes of a sausage knife to pierce the casing and work the air out with your hands. Knot the end.

9   Fill a pot large enough to hold the sausage about two-thirds full with water and add the kosher salt. Bring to a simmer over medium heat. Prepare a fresh ice bath. Once the water has come to a simmer, add the sausage and, adjusting the heat as necessary to keep the water at a gentle simmer, poach until the internal temperature reads 150°F (65°C), about 45 minutes. It's important that the water never reach a boil. When the temperature sweet spot has been reached, remove the sausage from the pot and immediately place in the ice bath for 5 minutes. Remove from ice bath, pat dry, and transfer to the refrigerator to chill for 1 hour, or for up to 2 days.

10 To serve, remove the casing from the sausage by cutting off the tip of one of the knotted ends with a sharp knife. Then make a shallow cut down the length of the sausage and peel back the casing. Slice the mortadella very, very thinly—as close to paper-thin as you can get it. If you can't slice it thinly enough with a knife, take it to your butcher and ask him to slice it. The unsliced mortadella will keep for up to 3 weeks, refrigerated.

SALAMI COTTO

MAKES ONE 3-POUND (1.4-KG) SAUSAGE; SERVES 10 TO 12

1 (18-inch/45.7 cm) length (5-inch/13 cm) collagen casing

3 pounds (1.4 kg) boneless pork shoulder, cut into 1-inch (2.5-cm) cubes

2½ ounces (70 g) pork fatback, cut into 1-inch (2.5-cm) cubes

2½ tablespoons (37 g) fine sea salt

Pinch of curing salt #1

1 teaspoon (8 g) fennel seeds

1 teaspoon (5 g) crushed red pepper flakes

½ teaspoon (2.5 g) chopped garlic

Pinch of chopped fresh rosemary

10 whole coriander seeds

¾ cup (100 g) crushed ice, plus additional ice cubes for an ice bath

1 tablespoon (15 g) black peppercorns, freshly ground

Oil, for frying

Within the charcuterie world, folks are extra-crazy secretive about their recipes for cotto—even though (or maybe because) it is so simple. In truth, to make superior cotto, you only have to pay proper attention to the Four Cs: coarse-grind, cure, casing, and cooking.

NOTES: THIS IS A 2-DAY RECIPE WITH 3 HOURS OF HANDS-ON TIME. YOU CAN FIND SYNTHETIC CASINGS AT YOUR BUTCHER OR AT SAUSAGEMAKER.COM.

Special Equipment: You will need a grinder and stuffer.

1   Fill the casing with warm water, then dump the water out. Place the casing in a bowl filled with clean, warm water. Put the pork shoulder and fatback in the freezer and let chill until the internal temperature reads 32°F (0°C), about 20 minutes. If it's possible to fit the meat grinder, its parts, the hopper and the paddle attachment of a mixer, include them as well. Using a mortar and pestle, grind together the sea salt, curing salt, fennel seed, red pepper flakes, garlic, rosemary, and coriander seeds. Set aside.

2   When the shoulder meat and the fatback are fully chilled, remove them from the freezer and mix together in a large bowl with half of the crushed ice. Fill another large bowl halfway with ice cubes to make an ice bath; set the bowl of your stand mixer in the ice. Remove the grinder parts from the freezer and assemble the grinder with a large (⅓-inch/8-mm) die. Position the chilled stand-mixer bowl, still in its ice bath, so that it catches the meat as it is ground. Push the meat and ice mixture through the grinder just once. The results should look like raw burger meat with large, distinct chunks of white fat. Check the internal temperature with a calibrated thermometer: it should not exceed 39°F (4°C).

3   Add the ground spices and ground peppercorns to the meat mixture. Fit the mixer with the paddle attachment and mix on low speed until all of the ingredients are fully incorporated, about 4 minutes.

4   Pinch off a little of the mixture and form it into a patty. Put the rest of the meat batter back in the fridge to keep it cold. In a small skillet over medium heat, fry the test patty in a little oil, and taste for salt and to see if the texture is correct: you're looking for the best fried baloney you have ever tasted. If it is low on salt or seasoning, grind additional seasonings, add more, and mix for another minute. If the texture is bad or grainy, you will have to start over. There is no saving it now.

5   When you are setting up your stuffer, if possible place the hopper (the part that the meat goes into) in the fridge or the freezer so

that it will be nice and cold. While assembling, take a second and make sure that everything is clean and that all parts are on tightly so nothing will come lose and make a mess. If you are stuffing from your grinder, you will need to remove the blades and dies and place the horn on the end. Once you have it all ready to go, you should get all of the surfaces that the casing will be touching (the horn and the table) really wet with water so that the casing will slide and not tear. Most synthetic casings will be tied at one end. Pour out any water that might be in the casing. Place the casing onto the largest casing horn that you have. Slide the open end over the horn, making sure that the tied end is pressed snuggly to the end of the horn.

6   Divide the meat batter into three portions, each about the size of a softball. Using your hands, pack each for about a minute; you're trying to get all of the air out of the meat. Load the stuffer's hopper with the first ball and, with your fist, pack down the meat batter as tightly as possible. Repeat until all of the batter is in the hopper.

7   Stuff the casing at a steady pace, being diligent about keeping air out of the sausage. If you see some air in the sausage when you are done stuffing, prick the casing with a pin or the spikes of a sausage knife and work the air out with your hands. When all of the meat is stuffed into the casing, tie off the end with butchers twine and a simple knot. Refrigerate the sausage for 24 hours to ensure that the spices have time to infuse, and that the cure has set.

8   Preheat the oven to 250°F (121°C). Fill a roasting pan of halfway with hot water and place on the middle rack of the oven; you're adding humidity so that your salami will cook more evenly. Place the sausage on a rimmed baking sheet and on the top rack. Cook for 30 minutes, and then flip the sausage so that the side that was against the pan is now facing up. Cook until the internal temperature of the sausage is 150°F (65°C), checking the temperature every 30 minutes; it should take about 2 hours. When the temperature hits the sweet spot, immediately transfer the sausage to the freezer to get it as cold as possible, as quickly as possible; keep it there for at least 20 minutes.

9   When you're ready to serve the sausage, remove the casing by cutting off the tip with a sharp knife. Then make a shallow cut down the length of the sausage and peel back the casing. Slice the salami very, very thinly—if you can't slice it thinly enough with a knife, take it to your butcher and ask him to slice it for you. The unsliced salami will keep for up to 3 weeks refrigerated, wrapped in plastic.

CHAPTER 4

The Smokehouse

Top row, from left: Bacon on a Grill (page 108), andouille, OP Frankfurter (page 101). Middle row, from left: Käsekrainer (page 98), kielbasa, Sweetheart Ham (page 111). Bottom Row: OP Peperettes (page 113).

Way back in the days before refrigeration, some very attentive genius noticed meat that encountered a lot of smoke did not form mold or go rancid nearly as fast as unsmoked meats. (The reason is that smoke contains some compounds that kill microbes on the meat's surface and others that delay oxidation in surface fats, which is what causes rancidity.) Around the same time, that genius and her buddies noticed that smoky meat was crazy good eating, too. Something deep and primal inside of us gets all fired up when we taste smoke in meat. So even though we don't need it to preserve meat anymore, we still crave it. Smoke is about flavor.

I have seen so many different takes on smokers that the only thing I can say for sure about smoking is that it's not rocket science. You need a heat source to burn your wood, a cross draft to pull the smoke over the meat, and a way to capture the smoke so that it envelops the meat. When I make the recipes in this chapter at home, I primarily use a regular charcoal grill with a lid. If you only plan on smoking just a few projects a year, this set-up is fine. If you start doing smoking on a regular basis, spring for a smoker with an electric burner plate so you don't have to keep stoking your fire to keep your wood burning.

The percentage charts are ingredient ratios by weight, with the meat serving as the baseline weight. They're especially useful for scaling recipes, allowing you to get consistent recipe results no matter how much meat you have. All meat components add up to 100 percent. For more information on how to use them, see page 22.

WHOLE CUTS OF UNBRINED MEAT

The example in this chapter is Bacon on a Grill (page 108).

*Meat	100%
*Salt	2.5%
Sugar	1.3%
*Curing salt #1	0.2%
Spices	2%

WHOLE CUTS OF WET-BRINED MEAT

The example in this chapter is Sweetheart Ham (page 111).

*Meat	100%
*Water	67%
*Salt	3.3%
Sugar	7%
*Curing salt #1	1.5%
Spices	6%

SMOKED SAUSAGE

The examples in this chapter are Käsekrainer (page 98), OP Frankfurter (page 101), and OP Pepperettes (page 113).

*Meat	70%
*Fat	30%
*Salt	1.5%
*Curing Salt #1	0.2%
Ice	7%
*Milk powder	4%
Spices	1.5%

* Ingredients marked with an asterisk need to be converted precisely.

Quality Tips

There are a few key components that determine the quality of your smoked meats: choice wood, clean smoke, dry meat, and cooking time.

Wood: Wood from a tree that bears sweet fruit—like cherry, apple, peach, or pear—produces sweet smoke. Sweet smoke is the mellowest and allows you to have a more delicate hand with smoking, producing flavors that are not overpowering. Hardwoods—like maple, hickory, and alder—give meat a smoky, bold flavor. For balanced flavor, combine a sweet wood with a hardwood. For most OP smoked meats, I smoke with two-thirds apple and one-third hickory.

Smoke: If you're smoking on a grill, soak the chips in water for about 10 minutes before using. This enables them to smolder rather than burn too hot and fast. The key to creating good smoke is to make sure your wood chips get enough fresh air as they burn. You are looking for beautiful smoke, as white as a cloud. Black smoke pluming out of your smoker means the vents are plugged with ash, and you'll be left with a metallic flavor on your meat. Before you start, make sure the grill vents are clean and clear. You will need to allow enough air to keep the smoke white and the fire going. On a standard grill, this is three open holes, each about 1 inch (2.5 cm) wide.

Dry Meat: Never put wet meat in the smoker. Instead, allow the meat to air dry for at least 1 hour before putting it in the smoker. If you just stuffed the sausage or rinsed your bacon, allow it to dry on a rack or hanging in your fridge. A dry surface (which, with raw meat, means a sticky, tacky surface) allows the smoke particles to stick to it evenly. A wet surface means an uneven smoke color and taste.

Cooking: The recipes in this chapter employ hot smoking—that is, the products are smoked and cooked at the same time. Hot smoking is all about my two favorite words: slow and low. You often need to smoke your meat for only about half of the cooking time—a little bit of smoke goes far. During the smoking stage, you typically want your grill temperature to be as low as possible, but once you are happy with the color, you can increase the heat incrementally—50°F (27°C) every half hour is my rule of thumb—until the meat's internal temperature is 155°F (68°C). The slow approach ensures that the meat cooks evenly and that the outside doesn't dry out before the center is done.

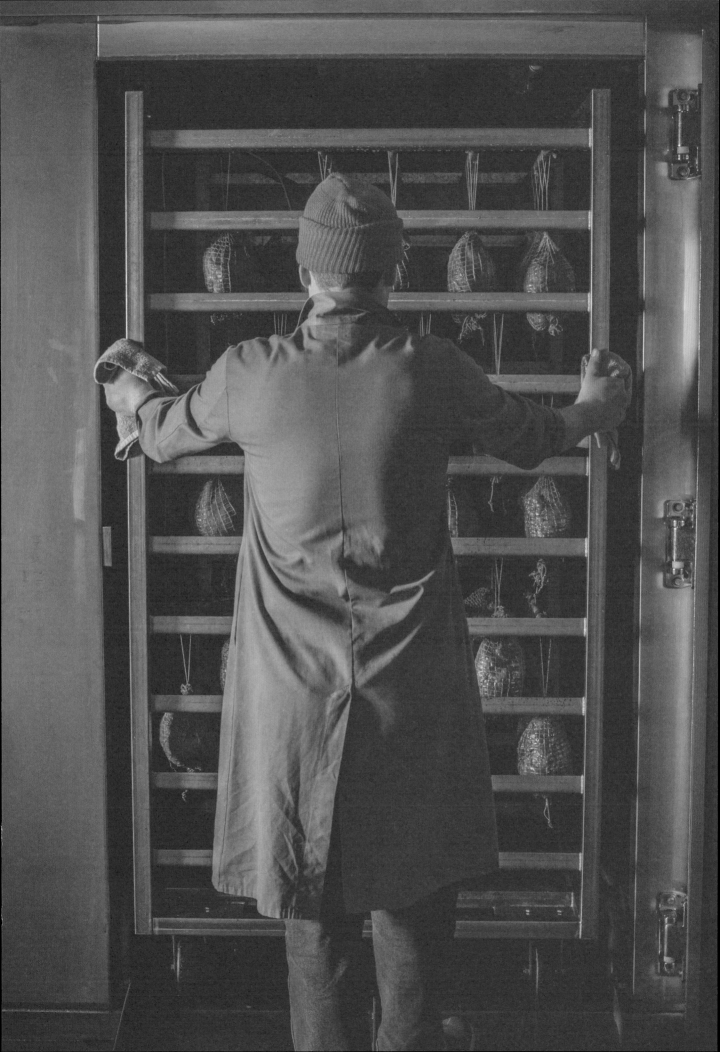

KÄSEKRAINER

MAKES ABOUT 11 SAUSAGE LINKS, EACH ABOUT 5 OUNCES (150 G)

1 (4-foot/1.4-m) length (1⅓-inch/35-mm) hog casing

2½ pounds (1.1 kg) boneless pork shoulder, cut into 1-inch (2.5-cm) cubes

1 pound (455 g) fatback, frozen and cut into ½-inch (1.3-cm) cubes

2 cups (225 g) crushed ice, plus additional ice cubes for an ice bath

2 tablespoons (30 g) fine sea salt

¾ teaspoon (4 g) sugar

¾ teaspoon (3 g) curing salt #1

4½ tablespoons (66 g) milk powder

2½ teaspoons (13 g) chopped garlic

1 teaspoon (10 g) ground black pepper

12 ounces (340 g) Emmentaler cheese, cut in ¼-inch (6-mm) cubes

Oil, for frying

Beer, for poaching (optional)

2 tablespoons (24 g) kosher salt, for poaching

Kaiser rolls

Käsekrainer is a smoked pork sausage injected with Emmentaler cheese. When I was working in Switzerland, I would go to St. Gallen to buy Käsekrainer from a tiny cart. The owner served them in toasted buns, heaped with sauerkraut. I would eat them while sucking down a Halden Gut (a Swiss lager), swearing I would never move back to America. Once I did come back, I kept telling my OP partners about that damn cart. Finally, we made one of our own (see photo, opposite).

I like Käsekrainer fried crispy and served with sliced apples and potatoes. At OP, we serve them on buns with apple slaw and mustard.

NOTE: THIS RECIPES TAKES 6 HOURS, WITH 3 HOURS HANDS-ON TIME.

Special Equipment: You will need a grinder, stuffer, a grill or smoker, 2 pounds (910 g) of apple wood chips, 1 pound (455 g) of hickory wood chips, and a bag of charcoal. Any type of charcoal without added lighter fluid will work.

1　Rinse out your casing by placing one end under the water tap and filling it with about ½ cup (120 ml) of water. Run this water through the casing by pulling up on the end that you filled up, until water comes out the other end of the casing. It will come out a bit cloudy. This is totally normal, as you are removing salt on the inside of the casing. Place the rinsed casing in a bowl of clean warm water to soak.

2　Put all of the parts of your stuffer and meat grinder (including the blades and grinder head), as well as your stand-mixer bowl and paddle attachment, in the freezer to chill. Put the pork shoulder and fatback in the freezer and let chill for about 30 minutes, or until the meat reaches an internal temperature of 32°F (0°C).

3　In a large bowl, mix together the chilled pork shoulder, fatback, and crushed ice. Set up the grinder with the largest die you have (I use a ¼-inch/6-mm die). Fill another large bowl halfway with ice cubes and set it under the grinder. Nestle the chilled stand-mixer bowl in the ice and grind the meat mixture into it. Check the temperature of the ground meat to make sure it is below 35°F (2°C). If it isn't, place the meat in the freezer to bring the temperature down. If the meat is below 35°F (2°C), or when it drops to that temperature, run it through the grinder a second time. You are looking for good definition between the fat and the lean meat. The mixture should not look emulsified, and it should have the texture of finely ground beef, like for hamburger.

4   Place the sea salt, sugar, curing salt, milk powder, garlic, pepper, and cheese in the mixer bowl with the ground meat. Mix for 3 minutes with the chilled paddle attachment on medium speed. Here you're looking for what we call "legs" in the lean meat: Take a clump of the mixture and pull it apart. You should see small threadlike pieces of the meat trying to hold onto each other.

5   Pinch off a little bit of the meat batter and press it into a patty. Put the bowl of meat batter in the fridge. In a small skillet over medium heat, fry the test patty in a little oil and taste it for seasoning. Tweak the seasoning if needed, mixing the batter well (and taking care to keep it cold), and fry up another test patty.

6   Before setting up your stuffer, if possible, place the hopper (the part that the meat goes into) in the fridge or the freezer so that it will be nice and cold. When assembling, take a second and make sure that everything is clean and that all parts are on tightly so that nothing will come lose and make a mess. If you are stuffing from your grinder, you will need to remove the blades and dies

CONTINUED

and place the horn on the end. Get all of the surfaces that the casing will be touching (the horn and the table) really wet with water so that the casing will slide and not tear; if you have a stainless steel or other smooth tabletop, pour about ¼ cup (60 ml) of water on the surface. Using your hands, a spatula, or a wooden spoon, take the meat batter and press it into the hopper of the stuffer. Stuff and link into 6-inch (15 cm) sausages as described in step 9 of Our Basic Sausage (pages 74–75).

7   To dry the links, you can either transfer them to a baking sheet and place them in the refrigerator, or you can tie them with butcher's twine and hang them from a meat hook in the refrigerator. Refrigerate for a minimum of 3 hours.

8   When you are ready to smoke the sausages, soak two large handfuls of apple wood chips and one large handful of hickory wood chips in water to cover for 10 minutes. Light the charcoal and start the grill or smoker at the lowest temperature you can; ideally you'll want to start smoking at about 70°F (21°C). Once the heat is nice and even, drain the wood chips and sprinkle about ½ cup (55 g) in an even layer over the coals. Once you see white, billowy smoke, add the sausages and cover with the lid. You want to see a nice steady flow of white smoke coming out of your grill or smoker. After 30 minutes, add another ½ cup (55 g) of chips, but if you see the smoke slowing down, add chips more frequently. After 1 hour, the sausages should have a nice tan look to them. Add more coals or turn up your smoker and add another ½ cup (55 g) of chips. If you can check the temperature, for this second hour, you should try to hold the temperature to about 180°F to 200°F (82°C to 93°C) by adding more hot coals. Continue smoking for another hour, until the sausages are golden, with a very beautiful, even color. Preheat the oven to 350°F (176°C) in case the sausages need to finish cooking in the oven. Insert a calibrated thermometer into a sausage; the internal temperature should be 155°F (68°C). If it isn't, transfer the sausages to a baking sheet, place in the oven, and cook until they reach the proper temperature. Near the end of cooking, prepare a large ice bath. When the sausages are done, immediately place them in the ice bath and cool for 15 minutes. Remove the links.

9   Store the sausages in the refrigerator in a plastic bag; they will keep for up to 3 weeks. To serve, in a large pot, bring plenty of water (or equal parts of water and beer) to a simmer over medium heat, and add the kosher salt. Add the sausages and simmer for 3 minutes—do not boil. Meanwhile, heat 1 tablespoon of oil in a skillet over medium heat. Transfer the sausages from the water to the skillet and crisp for 2 minutes. Serve with kaiser rolls.

OP FRANKFURTER (THE O.G. FOOT-LONG)

When I was a kid, eating a hot dog was truly a spiritual experience. The frank hung out of the bun a solid inch at both ends, and when you bit into it, it snapped in your mouth. The flavors were real smoke and fresh garlic. At some point in the last thirty years, though, the hot dog has become a bun-fitting, casing-free mockery of what a frankfurter should be. When I set out to make the first OP frankfurter, I wanted to make the frankfurter I remembered loving as a kid—the real O.G. foot-long—with two extra inches of pure meat enjoyment and a casing with a snap. I love it oh so much when I walk into the dining room at OP and see a kid destroying a frank.

NOTES: HOT DOGS, LIKE BALONEY, ARE MEAT EMULSION PRODUCTS, SO YOU'LL BE GRINDING THE MEAT REPEATEDLY FOR MAXIMUM MYOSIN DEVELOPMENT (SEE PAGE 70) AND WORKING TO KEEP THE INGREDIENTS AND EQUIPMENT COLD SO THE EMULSION DOESN'T BREAK. THIS RECIPE TAKES 5 HOURS WITH 3 HOURS HANDS-ON TIME.

Special Equipment: You will need a grinder, stuffer, a grill or smoker, 2 pounds (910 g) of apple wood chips, 1 pound (455 g) of hickory wood chips, and a bag of charcoal. Any type of charcoal without added lighter fluid will work.

1   Rinse out your casing by placing one end under the water tap and filling it with roughly ½ cup (120 ml) of water. Run this water through the casing by pulling up on the end that you filled up, until water comes out the other side of the casing. It will come out a bit cloudy. This is totally normal, as you are removing salt on the inside of the casing. Place the rinsed casing in a bowl of clean warm water to soak.

2   Using a mortar and pestle, grind the mustard powder, chile powder, paprika, white pepper, coriander, oregano, and chopped garlic to a fine paste. Set aside.

3   Put all of the parts of your stuffer and meat grinder (including the blades and grinder head), as well as your stand-mixer bowl and paddle attachment, in the freezer to chill. Put the pork shoulder and fatback in the freezer and let chill for about 30 minutes, or until the meat reaches an internal temperature of 32°F (0°C).

4   In a large bowl, mix together the chilled pork shoulder and fatback and half of the crushed ice. Set up the grinder with the largest die you have (I use a ¼-inch/6-mm die). Fill another large bowl halfway with ice cubes and set it under the grinder. Nestle the

CONTINUED

MAKES 12 (12-INCH/30 CM) FRANKS

1 (6-foot/1.8-m) length (¾-inch/18-mm) lamb casing

¾ teaspoon (3 g) mustard powder

1 teaspoon (5 g) chili powder

1 teaspoon (5 g) sweet paprika

1½ teaspoons (6 g) ground white pepper

1 teaspoon (5 g) ground coriander

¾ teaspoon (3 g) dried oregano

1 tablespoon (18 g) chopped garlic

2¼ pounds (1 kg) boneless pork shoulder, cut into 1-inch (2.5-cm) cubes

1 pound (455 g) fatback, frozen and cut into ½-inch (1.3-cm) cubes

2 cups (225 g) crushed ice, plus additional ice cubes for an ice bath

1½ tablespoons (22 g) fine sea salt

2 teaspoons (11 g) sugar

½ teaspoon (2 g) curing salt #1

¼ cup (60 g) milk powder

Oil, for frying

Victor Deras, the mad genius behind OP's frankfurter specials (see following pages).

chilled stand-mixer bowl in the ice and grind the meat mixture into it. Check the temperature of the ground meat to make sure it is below 35°F (2°C). If it isn't, place the meat in the freezer to bring the temperature down. If the meat is below 35°F (2°C), or when it drops to that temperature, run it through the grinder a second time. Do not allow the temperature to exceed 39°F (4°C).

5   Change to the smallest die you have—a ⅛-inch/3-mm die is perfect. (If you do not have a smaller die, continue to use the ¼-inch (6-mm) die.) Add the remaining crushed ice, then run the meat mixture through the grinder two more times. (If using a ¼-inch/6-mm die, run the mixture through the grinder four more times, for a total of six times.) Make sure your meat does not exceed 39°F (4°C). You are looking for a mass that is uniform in color and texture and that is as cold as possible.

6   Add the spice mix, sea salt, sugar, curing salt, and milk powder to the mixing bowl. With the chilled paddle attachment, mix on low speed until all of the ingredients have fully been incorporated, about 2 minutes.

7   Pinch off a little bit of the meat batter and press it into a patty. Put the bowl of meat batter in the fridge. In a small skillet over medium heat, fry the test patty in a little oil and taste it for salt. It should taste, well, like a hot dog (but without any smoke). Tweak the seasoning if needed, mixing the batter well (and always taking care to keep it cold), and fry up another test patty.

8   Before setting up your stuffer, if possible place the hopper (the part that the meat goes into) in the fridge or the freezer so that it will be nice and cold. When assembling, take a second and make sure that everything is clean and that all parts are on tightly so that nothing will come lose and make a mess. If you are stuffing from your grinder, you will need to remove the blades and dies and place the horn on the end. Get all of the surfaces that the casing will be touching (the horn and the table) really wet with water so that the casing will slide and not tear; if you have a stainless steel or other smooth tabletop, pour about ¼ cup (60 ml) of water on the surface. Using your hands, a spatula, or a wooden spoon, press the meat batter into the hopper of the stuffer. Stuff and link into 12-inch (30 cm) frankfurters (or feel free to make smaller wieners if you like), as described in step 9 of Our Basic Sausage (pages 74–75).

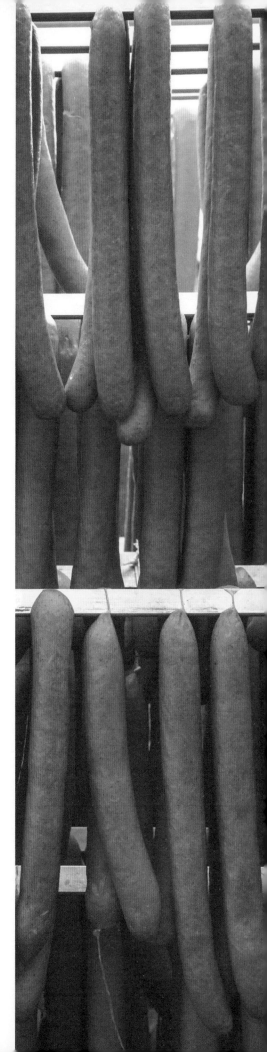

9 To dry the links, you can either transfer them to a baking sheet and place them in the refrigerator, or you can tie them with butcher's twine and hang them from a meat hook in the refrigerator.

10 Soak two large handfuls of apple wood chips and one large handful of hickory wood chips in water to cover for 10 minutes. When the franks are chilled, light your charcoal and start the grill or smoker at the lowest temperature you can; you'll want to start smoking at about 70°F (21°C). Once the heat is nice and even, drain the wood chips and sprinkle about ½ cup (55 g) in an even layer over the coals. Add the sausages and cover with the lid. You want to see a nice steady flow of white smoke coming out of your grill or smoker. After 30 minutes, add another ½ cup (55 g) of chips, but if you see the smoke slowing down, add chips more frequently. After 1 hour, the sausages should have a nice tan look to them. This is proof that the smoke is starting to stick. Add more coals or turn up your smoker and add another ½ cup (55 g) of chips. If you can check the temperature of your grill or smoker, for this second hour, you should try to hold the temperature at 150°F (65°C) with a nice flow of smoke the entire time. Keep sprinkling on chips as needed to ensure that you get a steady stream of smoke. If you run out of soaked chips, soak more in water for 10 minutes before using. After 2 hours, your sausages should have a nice, smoky brown color, and the internal temperature should be around 140°F (60°C). You may need to add a bit more charcoal or turn the heat up to get your finish temperature of 150°F (65°C). If you're not there yet, bump up the smoker's heat to 200°F (93°C) and check the temperature again in 15 minutes.

11 You are obligated by the law of sausage-making to bite into a frank as soon as they're out of the smoker, and to try not to flinch when the casing snaps in your mouth. I've included more than enough ways to top a frank (see pages 104–5), but try one with nothing at all, or with a tube of Thomy German mustard. The frankfurters will keep in the refrigerator for up to 3 weeks, wrapped tightly in plastic wrap. Grill them as needed.

OP'S FRANKFURTER SPECIALS

1 REUBEN 2 HOUND 3 GREEK 4 ÉTOUFFÉE 6 MAC N CHEESE

11 POUTINE 12 PICKLED EGG SALAD 13 CAESAR 14 PORTLAND 15 BREAKFAST

CHILE RELLENO   SONORAN   BROCCOLI AND CHEESE   SWEET AND SOUR   10 RAPINI

16 CHICKEN FRIED   17 CREAMED CORN   18 PHILLY CHEESE DOG   19 ENCHILADA

For buns, we use Franz Bakery, which is just a few blocks from the plant and the restaurant. The bakery has nailed the hot dog bun: it's not too fleshy and not too crunchy, the perfect vessel to hold up to all the toppings. If you can't get Franz, find a worthy substitute.

TOP 19 FRANKFURTER SPECIALS

SEE IMAGE PREVIOUS PAGE

Nº 1   **REUBEN DOG** To make the Reuben sauce, mix together äioli, ketchup, mustard, pickles, and caraway seeds, and season with salt and pepper. Slather both sides of each bun with sauce. Place a frank in the bun and cover with warm kraut.

Nº 2   **HOUND DOG** Named after Elvis's penchant for PB and banana, this frank went over surprisingly well. To make the peanut butter sauce, heat up sugar, water, peanut butter, a pinch of salt, and sambal. Spread a good slathering of apple butter on the bun, add the frank, top with peanut butter sauce, and garnish with three slices of banana.

Nº 3   **GREEK DOG** As an homage to my Greek heritage, we take house-made tzatziki and mix it with the usual basic Greek salad suspects: cucumbers, tomatoes, kalamata olives, red onions, feta, and dried oregano. The salad is piled onto the dog and garnished with a pepperoncini.

Nº 4   **ÉTOUFFÉE DOG** Because everyone needs a little Cajun or Creole. We cook bay shrimp with onion, celery, green bell pepper, garlic, tomatoes, dried oregano, dried marjoram, and chicken stock. Spoon étouffée on top the dog and garnish with chopped chives.

Nº 5   **MAC N CHEESE** Smoked provolone, white cheddar, and cauliflower make our mac and cheese topping way better than anything from a blue cardboard box. The final dog is also sprinkled with crisped coppa and chives.

Nº 6   **CHILE RELLENO DOG** We make whole chile rellenos and fry them up for use as a topping. The house-made sauce includes guajillo and chipotle chiles for a bit of smokiness, and the garnishes are sour cream and cilantro.

Nº 7   **SONORAN DOG** Hats off to the Southwest. Refried beans (melted in bacon fat) and a creamy avocado sauce are slathered onto the buns before the franks are put in place.

Nº 8   **BROCCOLI AND CHEESE DOG** Blanched broccoli is piled onto the dog, and then topped with as-cheap-as-you-can-find-it cheddar cheese sauce. Should taste like it just came out of a microwave.

Nº 9   **SWEET AND SOUR DOG** Top the frank with sweet-and-sour sauce mixed with sautéed onions and green bell peppers, and garnish with caramelized pineapple.

№ 10 **RAPINI DOG** Top the frank with blanched rapini and five pieces of butternut squash. Drizzle a spoonful of garlic-lemon cream over the top and finish with crumbled ricotta salata.

№ 11 **POUTINE DOG** This frank is a thanks to my co-writer, Meredith, who hails from Montreal. Top each frank with a handful of French fries, spoon on the gravy of choice, and finish with cheese curds.

№ 12 **PICKLED EGG SALAD DOG** Our egg salad is chopped pickled eggs, celery, red onion, and piquillo peppers dressed with mayonnaise, garlic, and dill. Top each dog with a couple spoonfuls of egg salad and garnish with chives and sweet paprika.

№ 13 **CAESAR DOG** We like our Caesar salad nice and anchovy-ey but suggest you make your favorite Caesar salad recipe and place two piles atop the dog. Finish with croutons and two boquerónes.

№ 14 **PORTLAND DOG** The essence of PDX on a hot dog. Thick sliced (OP) bacon with warm roasted hazelnuts and enough chopped braised kale to get in your greens for the day.

№ 15 **BREAKFAST DOG** Scrambled eggs and bacon on a frank. Yes, we eat this for breakfast. We like our eggs scrambled with butter and mushrooms.

№ 16 **CHICKEN FRIED DOG** This is one of OP frankfurter pro Victor Dera's most popular creations. We egg-wash each dog, coat it with seasoned flour, and deep-fry. The dog is dressed with two spoonfuls of Bratwurst Gravy (page 207)

№ 17 **CREAMED CORN DOG** Yes, that's right. We make homemade creamed corn by cooking canned corn in cream, butter, and onions. Dress the dog with two or three spoonfuls of creamed corn and garnish with fried pancetta and chives.

№ 18 **PHILLY CHEESE DOG** Our cheese sauce is made with heavy cream, mushrooms, oregano, and white cheddar. Dress the frank with two spoonfuls of sautéed onions and bell peppers and two spoonfuls of cheese sauce.

№ 19 **ENCHILADA DOG** Victor's enchilada recipe includes Monterey Jack cheese, cilantro, and red onion. Two enchiladas are fried and topped on a frank.

BACON ON A GRILL

MAKES 2½ POUNDS (1.1 KG) BACON; ABOUT 25 STRIPS

3 tablespoons (45 g) fine sea salt

1 tablespoon plus 2 teaspoons (24 g) sugar

¾ teaspoon (3 g) curing salt #1

4 pounds (1.8 kg) pork belly, skin removed

Everyone has an opinion about the best way to make bacon. Big-business producers overcompensate with brine to increase the weight level for sales. This is called "wet bacon." A lot of other flavors are typically added so customers don't notice the excess water. Other producers add pepper, herbs, and all sorts of spices, then smoke the bejesus out of it. Still others add fifty ingredients and cover it in unicorn horn, then finish it with just a touch of whale-bone smoke. (Okay, maybe that last one is an exaggeration.)

To us in the OP household, bacon should have the most basic of flavors. Smoke should be subtle; savory and sweet should be balanced. We coat pork bellies in our cure mixture, being sure to cover every inch, and store them packed in a pan with a tight lid for 10 days of curing. This recipe is the OP bacon recipe adjusted for the home cook. After making this, you will never purchase bacon again.

NOTES: THIS RECIPE TAKES 11 DAYS, WITH 5 HOURS HANDS-ON TIME.

Special Equipment: You will need a grill or smoker, 2 pounds (910 g) of apple wood chips, 1 pound (455 g) of hickory wood chips, and a bag of charcoal. Any type of charcoal without added lighter fluid will work.

1   In a small bowl, whisk together the sea salt, sugar, and curing salt until evenly mixed. In the bottom of a casserole large enough to accommodate the pork belly, sprinkle half of the salt and sugar mixture. Lay the belly on top of it and cover with the rest of the mixture. Using your hands, massage the mixture into the belly, trying to cover the entire belly as evenly as possible, even the squishy indentations. Cover the casserole with its lid or cover tightly with plastic wrap and refrigerate for 5 days.

2   After 5 days, take the pork belly out of the refrigerator. Pour and scrape out all of the liquid and any excess salt and reserve in a bowl. Flip the belly so the bottom side is facing up. Redistribute the liquid and salt across the top of the belly. Cover and refrigerate for another 5 days.

3   Remove the belly from the container and rinse under cold running water, being sure to remove all of the salt. Pat dry using a clean towel.

4   Soak apple wood chips and hickory chips in water to cover for at least 10 minutes. Light the charcoal and, when the coals are ready, pile them up on one side of the grill. Drain the wood chips and place ½ cup (55 g) in a layer on the coals. You should get an even, white smoke. Put the grill grate in place and lay the pork

on the grill as far away from the coals as possible. Place the lid
on the grill. You should grab a beer at this point because you are
in no hurry. The goal is to keep the area of the grill where the
bacon is between 90°F and 150°F (32°C and 65°C) for 2 hours,
and the smoke rising in a steady stream. If the smoke is waning,
add more chips.

5   After about 1½ hours, remove the belly using tongs and get
your nose up in it: you are looking for a sweet smokiness, NOT
a campfire aroma. If you want a bit more smoke, stoke the coals
and add more wood chips. Continue to cook the belly until the
internal temperature is 150°F (65°C), about 30 minutes. When you
hit that sweet spot, remove it from the grill and quickly transfer to
the refrigerator for at least 1 day or for up to 3 weeks before slicing.
To slice, use a sharp knife to cut the belly into ¼-inch (6-mm)
slices. Fry the slices in a skillet over medium heat until crispy.
The uncooked bacon will last for up to 3 weeks in the refrigerator
or 3 months in the freezer.

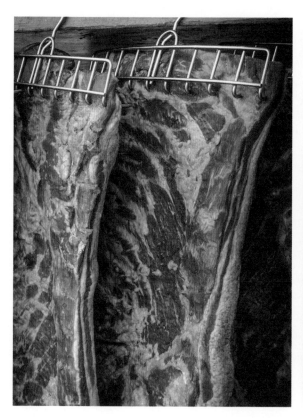

SWEETHEART HAM

This little gem of a ham is called the sweetheart because it's just enough ham for you and your significant other. The cut used to make the ham is called a pork knuckle by butchers. Why, I do not know. We use this completely lean and versatile ham in the OP Benedict (page 194) and in Choucroute Garnie (page 211), and I love to griddle a slice of it during fly-fishing weekends. You will need a brine pump for this recipe. You can buy one online or at any butcher supply store. It is a really great tool—and pretty much the only way to inject brine into ham. And who doesn't want a huge stainless steel syringe hanging on the kitchen wall?

NOTE: THIS RECIPE TAKES II DAYS, WITH 6 HOURS HANDS-ON TIME.

Special Equipment: You will need a brine pump, grill or smoker, 2 pounds (910 g) of apple wood chips, 1 pound (455 g) of hickory wood chips, and a bag of charcoal. Any type of charcoal without added lighter fluid will work. This recipe also requires a size 16 ham net.

1 To make the brine, combine all of the brine ingredients in a large pot over high heat and bring to a simmer, stirring frequently so the sugar does not scorch. Simmer for 5 minutes to ensure that all of the sugar dissolves and the spices and garlic have time to steep. (The brine should smell heavenly—at OP we make it in 50-gallon batches, and the smell as it simmers still makes mouths water.) Remove from the heat, allow to cool, then place in the refrigerator. Once it is no longer hot to touch, whisk in the curing salt. Allow to cool to 44°F (7°C) before using.

2 Get a precise weight on your pork, and then calculate 10 percent of the weight. This is how much brine you need to inject into the meat. Measure out the brine for injecting, making sure to leave out any solids. Poke the needle of the brine pump into the pork, fill the pump with brine, and inject the brine. As you inject, the pork will expand, and a bit of brine may come out; this is normal. Inject the rest of the measured amount of brine into another area of the pork. Place the pork in the remaining brine, cover, and refrigerate for 5 days. After 5 days, rotate the pork and give the brine a stir. Cover and refrigerate for 5 more days.

3 Remove the ham from the brine. Place the ham inside the ham net and tie the ends. Tie the ham to one of the racks in your refrigerator so that it hangs freely, and place a tray under it to catch drips. Keep the ham there for a minimum of 3 hours and a maximum of 6 hours. Air drying before smoking allows the surface of the ham to get nice and tacky so the smoke will stick to it.

CONTINUED

MAKES 1 (3-POUND/1.4-KG) HAM

BRINE

1½ quarts (1.5 liters) water

¼ cup (60 g) fine sea salt

⅓ cup (68 g) granulated sugar

⅓ cup (68 g) brown sugar

Pinch of crushed red pepper flakes

4 black peppercorns

5 bay leaves

¼ teaspoon (1 g) fennel seeds

10 sprigs fresh thyme

1 small onion, peeled and quartered

1 tablespoon (16 g) chopped garlic

1 tablespoon (12 g) curing salt #1

1 (4-pound/1.8 kg) boneless pork sirloin tip or pork knuckle

4   Soak the wood chips in water to cover for 10 minutes. Start your coals, and when they are hot, add them to the grill or smoker. You'll want to start smoking at about 70°F (21°C), so keep the heat as low as you can. Once the heat is nice and even, drain the wood chips and sprinkle about ½ cup (55 g) in an even layer over the coals. You should get a steady stream of white, billowy smoke. Place the ham inside. The temperature should hover around 70°F (21°C) for 1 hour, and there should be a very heavy plume of smoke coming out if the smoker. If you have control of the temperature, increase the heat by 20°F (11°C) every hour until the smoker's temperature is about 210°F (99°C). You should be feeding the smoker with fresh wood chips every 30 to 40 minutes to ensure a beautiful, steady flow of smoke. After 5 hours, check the ham: it should look golden and plump and be firm to the touch, with a internal temperature of 155°F (68°C).

5   Remove the ham from the smoker and let cool for 15 minutes before serving. If not serving right away, store for up to 2 weeks in the refrigerator. Reheat in a 275°F (135°C) oven until the internal temperature is 140°F (60°C), about 1 hour. Remove the ham net or butcher's twine and cut into thin slices.

OP PEPPERETTES

During the fly-fishing season, Tyler, my business/fishing/hunting partner and I do a fair share of roadside tavern trippin' all over Oregon. Whether we're at the One Horse Tavern in Gaston or the Rainbow Room in Maupin (quite possibly the best bar I have ever been to), we always eat a pepperoni stick while slugging down a cold beer. One day Tyler looked at me and said, "Shit, we can make something better than this tangy bomb"—which translates to "We should make these, too."

There are so many great European versions of landjäger (the Swiss-German version of a pepperoni stick), I figured, why not have an OP version or three? This recipe includes: the Kleine Schweine (an all-pork version of a landjäger), the Flaco Paco (a chorizo-style sausage), and the Petit Pierre (a classic sausage from the Jura region of France). The salt, dextrose, and cure are all the same; only the spices change.

NOTES: THESE ARE BEST MADE IN A SMOKER WITH A FAN. THIS RECIPE TAKES 7 HOURS, WITH 3 HOURS HANDS-ON TIME.

Special Equipment: You will need a grinder, stuffer, grill or smoker, 2 pounds (910 g) of apple wood chips, 1 pound (455 g) of hickory wood chips, and a bag of charcoal. Any type of charcoal without added lighter fluid will work.

1   Rinse out your casing by placing one end under the water tap and filling it with about ½ cup (120 ml) of water. Run this water through the casing by pulling up on the end that you filled up, until water comes out the other end of the casing. It will come out a bit cloudy. This is totally normal, as you are removing salt on the inside of the casing. Place the rinsed casing in a bowl of clean warm water to soak.

2   Put all of the parts of your stuffer and meat grinder (including the blades and grinder head), as well as your stand-mixer bowl and paddle attachment, in the freezer to chill. Put the pork shoulder and fatback in the freezer and let chill for about 30 minutes, or until the meat reaches an internal temperature of 32°F (0°C).

3   In a large bowl, mix together the chilled pork and fatback. Set up the grinder with the largest die you have (I use a ⅛-inch/3-mm die). Fill another large bowl about halfway with ice cubes and set it under the grinder. Nestle the chilld stand-mixer bowl in the ice and grind the meat and fat into it. You are looking for good definition between the fat and the lean meat. The mixuture should not look emulsified at all, but should have the texture of finely ground beef, like the beef you would use to make hamburger.

CONTINUED

KLEINE SCHWEINE

1 (4-foot/1.2-m) length (¾-inch/ 18-mm) lamb casing, or the smallest you can find

3 pounds (1.4 kg) boneless pork shoulder, cut in 1-inch (2.5-cm) cubes

Ice cubes, for an ice bath

2½ tablespoons (37 g) fine sea salt

¾ teaspoon (3 g) curing salt #1

1½ teaspoons (7 g) sugar

1 teaspoon (4 g) ground white pepper

¾ teaspoon (3 g) crushed red pepper flakes

¾ teaspoon (3 g) ground caraway

¾ teaspoon (3 g) ground coriander

1 teaspoon (4 g) chopped garlic

Oil, for frying

FLACO PACO

1 (4-foot/1.2-m) length (¾-inch/ 18-mm) lamb casing, or the smallest you can find

3 pounds (1.4 kg) boneless pork, shoulder, cut in 1-inch (2.5-cm) cubes

Ice cubes, for an ice bath

2½ tablespoons (37 g) fine sea salt

¾ teaspoon (3 g) curing salt #1

1½ teaspoons (7 g) sugar

2½ tablespoons (37 g) sweet paprika

¾ teaspoon (3 g) cayenne

1 teaspoon (4 g) ground black pepper

1 teaspoon (4 g) smoked paprika

1 teaspoon (3 g) dried oregano

2 teaspoons (10 g) chopped garlic

Oil, for frying

PETIT PIERRE

1 (4-foot/1.2-m) length (¾-inch/ 18-mm) lamb casing, or the smallest you can find

3 pounds (1.4 kg) boneless pork shoulder, cut into 1-inch (2.5-cm) cubes

Ice cubes, for an ice bath

2½ tablespoons (37 g) fine sea salt

¾ teaspoon (3 g) curing salt #1

1½ teaspoons (7 g) sugar

1 teaspoon (3 g) crushed juniper berries

¾ teaspoon (3 g) ground white pepper

1½ teaspoons (7 ml) red wine

1 teaspoon (5 g) chopped garlic

Oil, for frying

4   Combine all of the seasonings for the variation you're making in the mixing bowl with the ground meat mixture. With the chilled paddle attachment, mix for 3 minutes on medium speed. Here you're looking for what we call "legs" in the lean meat: Take a clump of the mixture and pull it apart. You should see small threadlike pieces trying to hold on to each other.

5   Pinch off a little bit of the meat batter and press it into a patty. Stick the bowl of meat batter in the fridge. In a small skillet over medium heat, fry the test patty in a little oil. Taste it for seasoning. Tweak the seasoning if needed, mixing the batter well (always taking care to keep it cold), and fry up another test patty.

6   Before setting up your stuffer, if possible place the hopper (the part that the meat goes into) in the fridge or the freezer so that it will be nice and cold. When assembling, take a second and make sure that everything is clean and that all parts are on tightly so that nothing will come lose and make a mess. If you are stuffing from your grinder, you will need to remove the blades and dies and place the horn on the end. Get all of the surfaces that the casing will be touching (the horn and the table) really wet with water so that the casing will slide and not tear; if you have a steel or other smooth tabletop, pour about ¼ cup (60 ml) of water on the surface. Using your hands, a spatula, or a wooden spoon, take the meat batter and press it into the hopper of the stuffer. Stuff and link into 6-inch (15 cm) sausage as described in step 9 of Our Basic Sausage (pages 74–75). Let dry for 1 hour on a sheet tray.

7   Soak the wood chips in water to cover for 10 minutes. Start your coals, and when they are hot, add them to the grill or smoker. You'll want to start smoking at about 70°F (21°C), so keep the heat as low as you can. Once the heat is nice and even, drain the wood chips and sprinkle about ½ cup (55 g) in an even layer over the coals. You should get a steady stream of white, billowy smoke. Place the sticks above it and increase the heat every hour by 30°F (18°C), adding more chips to keep the smoke flowing over the sausages until their internal temperature reaches 155°F (68°C), and they look like plump hot dogs with a nice, golden color. This should take about 3½ hours. Taste one and see if you are happy with the amount of smoke. If not, pile on more wood chips. When they're as you like them, turn off the smoker, open up the dampers and keep the smoker at around 200°F (93°C) with the fan on high. Let these skinny little guys dry out and shrivel, about 5 hours. If your smoker doesn't have a fan, use a convection oven at 200°F (93°C) to dry the sausages on a baking sheet. They should shrivel up nicely in about 5 hours. They will keep for 1 month at room temperature, or keep them wrapped in the fridge to prevent drying.

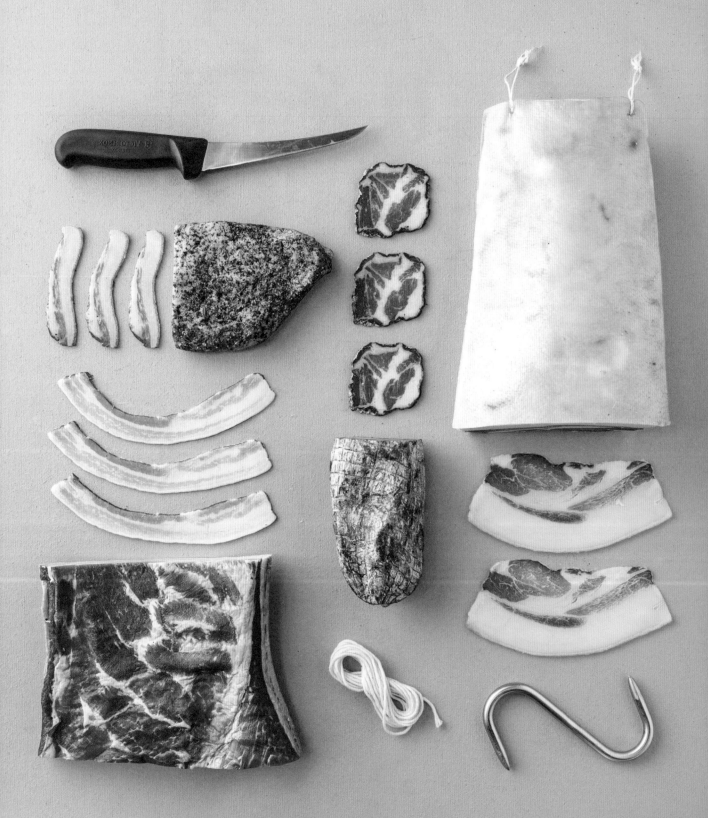

CHAPTER 5

Dry-Cured Meats

Top row, from left: guanciale,
Coppa (page 123), Lomo (page 124).
Bottom row: Pancetta (page 121).

Dry-curing meat is the oldest form of meat preservation. It involves using salt to remove moisture from meat. Salt pulls suspended water out of cells through osmosis; the meat is kept cold during this process to keep microorganisms in check. Once the water is removed, pathogens can no longer grow in the meat.

The technique for all dry-cured meat is simple: add salt and curing salt #2 (nitrate plus nitrite) to fresh meat, then keep the meat cold (under 39°F/4°C). Then rinse off the salt and cure and hang the meat in a slightly humid (relative humidity 83 percent) and cool (58°F/14°C) place with a slight breeze until the meat is dry and has an active water weight (AW) of 0.85 when tested with an active water meter. Active water is the suspended water in the meat. Pathogens need this water to multiply and survive. So by using salt to remove some of this moisture, we are creating an environment in the meat in which pathogens are not likely to survive. You will need a slightly humid area for dry curing your meat, which I understand is a bit confusing. Mild humidity keeps the exterior of the meat moist so the salt can draw the moisture from the center to the exterior. The air circulating around the meat dries the moisture that moves to the surface. If you do not have humidity, the outside will dry up, the moisture in the interior will be trapped, and the meat will eventually be ruined. That's not so hard, right? Well, then.

The percentage charts are ingredient ratios by weight, with the meat serving as the baseline weight. They're especially useful for scaling recipes, allowing you to get consistent recipe results no matter how much meat you have. For more information on how to use them, see page 22.

FOR WHOLE PIECES OF MEAT, 2½ INCHES (4 CM) OR THINNER

In this chapter, try Pancetta (page 121).

*Meat	100%
*Salt	2.5%
*Curing salt #2	0.5%
Spices	1.5%

FOR WHOLE PIECES OF MEAT, 2½ INCHES (4 CM) OR THICKER

In this chapter, try Coppa (page 123) and Lomo (page 124).

*Meat	100%
*Salt	4%
*Curing salt #2	0.5%
Spices	1.5%

* Ingredients marked with an asterisk need to be converted precisely.

I do realize that not all of you are going out and purchase a water activity meter (see page 17). But if you are going to dry cure, I strongly suggest you do. It allows you to know exactly when your product is finished. The other option is to note the exact starting raw weight of your meat. When your product has lost half of its original weight, you know it's ready and safe to consume. Meat that has been properly dry cured theoretically cannot go bad. Welcome to the wonderful world of shelf stability!

Quality Tips

Many components determine the quality of dry-cured meats.

Start with Fresh Ingredients: Beginning with fresh ingredients is important in any form of charcuterie, but in the case of dry curing, freshness is crucial. Imagine discovering after waiting 6 months for your product to finish that it tastes like an old sow's armpit. Remember—this is a race, so why give spoiled meat a head start? Go to your butcher and tell her exactly what you plan on doing. Tell her that you would like the freshest meat she has. She will not only hook you up with the freshest of cuts, but she will also cut it for you.

Weigh Your Meat Precisely: No two cuts of meat will have exactly the same weight. For this reason, it's important to use the percentage charts (left) to adjust the recipes in this chapter to the exact weight of the meat you're using. Assuming that most of you will not be using a water activity meter, you must carefully weigh and record the starting weight of your meat before salt even touches it.

Use a Calendar: Keep careful track on a calendar of every day when you need to handle your meat to ensure that no steps are forgotten. For example, "overhauling" is what we in the meat world call the process of salting and rotating the meat so the salts cure evenly—we even track the days when it's time to overhaul.

Drying: Proper drying conditions are crucial. You need to find a really fine balance between humidity and airflow. If your conditions are too dry and your airflow too fast, you will dry the outside of the product before the middle has a chance to dry out, trapping all the moisture inside of the meat. Eventually the meat will go bad. If you have too-high humidity and not enough airflow, the meat will never dry and eventually will also go bad. So to say that you need to be able to adjust and monitor your drying space is an understatement. Set yourself up with the ability to humidify and dehumidify, using a simple fan with speed adjustments (also see Buy or Make a Dry Box, opposite). I dry at 83 percent relative humidity at a temperature of 58°F (14°C), and an airflow that feels like the wind against your face while at a steady walking pace. That said, there is a lot of hocus pocus involved in the drying process.

I have seen many of my meat-making idols shake their heads in disbelief at the color of a mold, or an unevenly cured product. With a shrug that I know all too well, they conjure up a reason for what went wrong, curse it, and move on. I can only tell you to keep a close eye on your curing environment, and if you see a mold you do not like, use a solution of equal parts water and white vinegar to wipe it off. Great mold is white. However, you will see other colors of mold—blue, green, and also gray. They are by no means bad, but they will give your meat different flavors. White molds have a clean smell to them; the other colors tend to hold a bit of a wet basement smell and taste. Most likely the cause of other colors of mold is too much humidity or not enough airflow. If the mold is ever bright red or black and really fuzzy, toss it out. And if at any moment you smell anything rancid, sour, or just not right, promise me you'll throw away the meat. The smell in a dry curing room should make you hungry, not ill. When making fermented sausage like salami (see chapter 6), an ammonia smell is okay. But if you smell ammonia while making anything else, throw it out and start again.

Buy or Make a Dry Box: This is the most important piece of equipment for dry curing as it's what creates a controllable curing environment. If you're new to this concept, you'll need a large clean, insulated container or closet or room that can be easily sanitized and can, as mentioned above, hold a temperature of 58°F (14°C) at 83 percent humidity with a walking breeze. There are a few Italian manufacturers that produce small curing chambers or dry boxes; they are all really expensive and not as foolproof as one would hope. But you can build one relatively cheaply and easily. Start with a box that has easy-to-clean walls. I have seen all sorts of variations on this, ranging from unused closets with washable walls to an unused home refrigerator, which is my recommendation. Refrigerators are best mostly because they are already insulated. You will need to buy a special thermostat called a temperature controlled outlet. You plug your refrigerator into this thermostat and then plug the thermostat into the wall. It will have a dial on it so you can select a desired temperature, in this case, 58°F (14°C); it will turn on whenever the temperature inside the fridge rises above 58°F (14°C). You will also need a small fan with a speed variation switch to control airflow, a small humidifier that holds about a gallon (4 liters) of water, and a small dehumidifier. Set these last two at 83 percent relative humidity and they will take turns adjusting the environment. For the most part, you will be pulling moisture out of the air once you have a full dry box. But until then you will have to add a bit of moisture, hence the humidifier.

HERE IS A SAMPLE CALENDAR FOR THE RECIPES IN THIS CHAPTER:

DAY 1: Salt and cure

DAY 10: Overhaul

DAY 18: Rinse, hang, and cure (if applicable)

DAY 53: Finish date for pancetta; check water activity

DAY 78: Finish date for lomo and coppa; check water activity

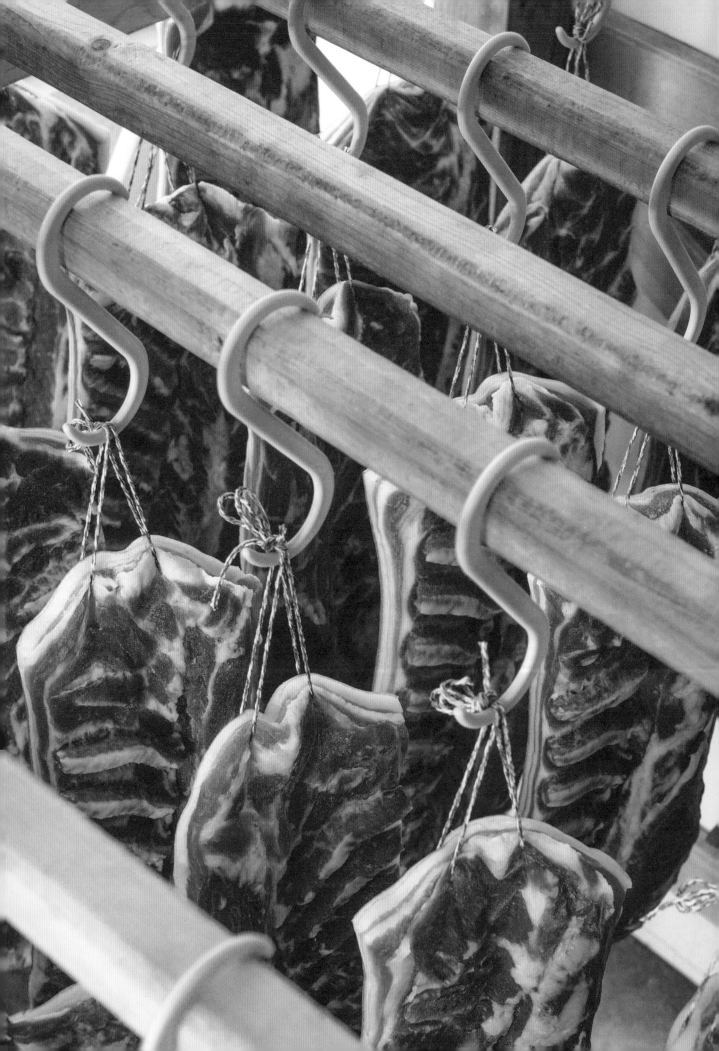

PANCETTA

Pancetta is dry-cured pig belly, the same cut as bacon but not smoked or cooked. All of Europe makes great variations on this product, but my personal favorites are the Italian versions. Pancetta is amazing cut into lardons and tossed in a salad of bitter greens, or sliced thin and baked on pizza. I fully cure mine so you can eat it sliced thin, like you would a ham.

I like to keep my pancetta flat rather than roll it (as it often is) because the curing time is cut in half and the process is really easy this way. Rolling tends to create mold in the center, too. Mold at the center is easy to control if pancetta is the only thing you are making, but most folks I know are curing many different products in their dry boxes, with all sorts of molds and yeast strains. Keeping your pancetta flat gives you the opportunity to rinse off any pesky molds you do not want. Remember, you want white mold if any mold at all, but a bit of variation in color is not the end of everything. Do toss out anything that is red, or black and fuzzy.

I like to cure pancetta with the skin on because there are so many ways to use the cured skin, like simmered into a tomato sauce or cooked with beans. My favorite way to enjoy pancetta is to slice it paper thin and serve it with a bit of lemon squeezed on it, or some melon, or nothing at all. It's also really good on vegetables hot out of the oven—the fat melts into the vegetables, giving them extra pig love.

NOTE: THIS IS AN 18-DAY CURE, PLUS A 35-DAY DRY-CURE TIME, WITH 4 HOURS HANDS-ON TIME.

Special Equipment: You will need a dry box and a water activity machine.

1   Lay the pork belly skin-side down and run your hand over the meat side, feeling for any bones. If you find any, remove them with a sharp knife. Now make sure that the meat is more or less of an even thickness; remove layers or pieces with the knife if it is not. If you don't have a water activity meter, carefully weigh the belly and record its weight: this is the starting weight. The finished pancetta must weigh half as much as the starting weight by end of the dry cure. This moisture loss is absolutely critical, as it helps make the finished product safe to eat.

2   Using a mortar and pestle, grind the pepper, juniper, nutmeg, garlic, bay leaves, and thyme. Add the sea salt, brown sugar, and the curing salt and mix well.

CONTINUED

MAKES 2 POUNDS (910 G)

4 pounds (1.8 kg) skin-on pork belly

1 tablespoon (14 g) crushed black pepper

1½ teaspoons (7 g) crushed juniper berries

¼ teaspoon (1 g) freshly grated nutmeg

2 teaspoons (10 g) chopped garlic

2 bay leaves

5 sprigs thyme

3 tablespoons (45 g) fine sea salt

1¾ tablespoons (20 g) brown sugar

1¾ teaspoons (7 g) curing salt #2

3   Distribute about one-third of the spice mixture in a large baking dish and place the belly skin side down on top. Add the rest of the spice mixture and massage it into all the nooks and crannies, covering the entire belly. Cover the dish with plastic wrap or a lid and refrigerate for 1 week.

4   Remove the baking dish from the refrigerator. Now you're going to do what we in the meat biz call "overhauling". You will see that the belly has given up a bit of moisture. This is good. It should smell clean, not funky or rancid. Take the belly out of the dish and give the liquid a good swirl, mixing in any residual salt or sugar. Place the belly back in the dish, meat side down, and redistribute the mixture as evenly as possible. Replace the cover and refrigerate for 1 more week.

5   Remove the baking dish from the refrigerator. Redistribute the mixture again, as in the last step and return the belly to the dish. The meat should start to feel a bit stiff and some of it should be turning a nice, cured color of pink. Refrigerate, uncovered, for 4 more days. This should make the butter in your refrigerator smell really good.

6   Eighteen days from when you started, the belly will really start to look like a pancetta. Take it out of the refrigerator and give it a good rinse under cold water, removing anything that is stuck to it with your hand. Place the belly on a cutting board and slice a ¼-inch (6-mm) piece from one of the ends; the meat should be an even and beautiful color of pink with bright white fat. Fry this piece in a pan like you would bacon, and taste. At this point your pancetta is ready to cook and eat, though it will be lacking the flavor that will develop if you continue to cure it in your dry-curing chamber.

7   To dry cure, cut two small holes in the skin, just big enough to slip twine through. Run a piece of butcher's twine through each hole, and tie the ends to form a loop. Hang the pancetta by the loops in your curing chamber at 58°F (14°C) and 83 percent relative humidity and let it chill out for 35 days.

8   When the pancetta is done, it will have lost half of its starting weight, and its water activity will have reached 0.85 when measured with a water activity meter. The skin should have turned a very nice color of gold. The cured pancetta will keep forever, in theory. I wrap mine tightly in plastic wrap, store it in the fridge, and try to use it within 3 months.

COPPA

Coppa is dry-cured capicola (page 38)—capicola 2.0. Why have two recipes of the same exact cut, you ask? To show you what a little more salt and time will do to a recipe and how amazing it is that you can produce two completely different products from one cut.

We serve coppa on every chef's choice board at OP because it is the favorite of all of our cooks. Portland ice cream titan Salt and Straw makes a melon ice cream in the summer that they serve with a thin strip of OP coppa.

NOTES: THIS RECIPE REQUIRES A 18-DAY CURE, PLUS A 60 DAY DRY-CURE TIME, WITH 4 HOURS OF HANDS-ON TIME.

Special Equipment: You will need a dry box, a water activity meter, and a size 14 ham net.

1   To make the cure, combine the sea salt, pepper, and curing salt in a bowl and whisk well. Completely cover the coppa with the cure mix and then place in a casserole dish. Cover tightly with plastic wrap and refrigerate for 1 week.

2   After 1 week, overhaul the meat—that is, flip it over. Reapply any cure mix that may have fallen off. Cover again with plastic wrap and refrigerate for another 11 days.

3   To make the rub, mix together the red pepper flakes, cayenne, sweet paprika, and coriander. Remove the coppa from the refrigerator and rinse well under running water. Pat dry and place in a clean casserole dish. Sprinkle the rub all over the meat.

4   Place the coppa in a tight-fitting ham net; this will help it to keep its form and dry evenly. If you don't have a water activity meter, carefully weigh the meat now and record its weight; this is the starting weight. The finished product must weigh half as much as the starting weight by the end of the dry cure. This moisture loss is absolutely critical, as it helps make the finished product safe to eat. Hang in a dry box for 60 days at 58°F (14°C) and 83 percent relative humidity, until the coppa has lost half of its starting weight or its water activity has reached 0.85 when measured with a water activity meter. It is very likely that a bit of mold will appear on the outside of your coppa. If it is nice and white, you may want to keep it. If it is of a strange looking color, you can wipe it off with an equal-part water and white vinegar solution. The coppa should feel really firm to touch, similar to an unopened can of soda with just a bit of give. Remove from the net and slice thinly. The unsliced coppa will keep for up to 1 year in the refrigerator wrapped in plastic wrap.

MAKES 1.5 POUNDS (680 G)

CURE

¼ cup (60 g) fine sea salt

1 teaspoon (5 g) crushed black pepper

½ teaspoon (2 g) curing salt #2

3 pounds (1.4 kg) pork coppa (see Note page 38)

RUB

1 teaspoon (7 g) crushed red pepper flakes

1 teaspoon (7 g) cayenne

2 tablespoons (34 g) sweet paprika

Pinch of ground coriander

LOMO

MAKES 2 POUNDS (910 G)

4-pound (1.8 kg) Danish pork loin (boneless, skin-on)

⅓ cup (72 g) fine sea salt

1¾ teaspoons (7 g) curing salt #2

1 tablespoon (14 g) ground black pepper

In butcher talk, lomo is a piece of boneless, center-cut Danish pork loin dry-cured with the skin on. Any quality butcher who knows his or her way around a hog will easily make this cut happen for you. Danish loins are usually brined, then roasted really hot so that the skin turns into a crackling. The Danish love the crackling on a roast so they keep it all on.

The brilliance of a lomo is that you get intact lardo, with the loin cured in the manner of prosciutto, but in about half the time and with much less risk of rot because the cut is boneless. It's truly the best of all possible worlds.

This is one of my all-time favorite products, and the only one I sent to the Good Food Awards in 2012. I decided if it didn't win, I would stop making meat. Thank God it won, because I love making meat!

NOTE: THIS IS AN 18-DAY CURE, PLUS A 60-DAY DRY-CURE TIME, WITH 4 HOURS OF HANDS-ON TIME.

Special Equipment: You will need a dry box and a water activity machine.

1 Lay the loin skin side down on a cutting board. Run your hand along the loin, feeling for any bone chips or shards. If you find any, remove them using a sharp knife. If the butcher has gouged the loin in harvesting it, try your best to smooth it out so you have a nice, even surface with no cuts. If you don't have a water activity meter, carefully weigh the loin and record its weight: this is the starting weight. The finished lomo must weigh half as much as the starting weight by the end of the dry cure. This moisture loss is absolutely critical, as it helps make the finished product safe to eat.

2 Put the sea salt, curing salt, and pepper in a bowl and whisk to combine well. Sprinkle one-third of this mixture in the bottom of a baking dish that is large enough to hold the loin. Lay the loin in the dish skin side down. Distribute the rest of the mixture evenly over the surface. Cover again with plastic wrap and refrigerate for 9 days.

3   After 9 days, overhaul the meat. To do so, flip it so that the skin is now facing up. Redistribute the salt mixture over the surface, trying to cover as much of the meat as possible. Re-cover with plastic wrap and refrigerate for another 9 days.

4   After 9 days, rinse the salt mixture off of the loin with cold running water. It should feel a bit firmer and you should smell a hint of pepper. At one of the ends, cut two small holes in the skin. Run a small piece of twine through each hole and tie the ends to form a loop. Hang the loin by the loops in your dry box at 58°F (14°C) and 83 percent relative humidity for 60 days. Every once in a while, check on it and think, "This is going to taste good." When the lomo is ready, it will have lost half of its starting weight and its water weight will have reached 0.85 when measured with a water activity meter. The skin should be a beautiful golden brown color.

5   Serve the lomo cut crosswise into paper-thin slices. To slice it, you must first cut away the skin with a sharp knife, but remove the skin only on the section that you will be slicing. This will prevent the fat from oxidizing and will ensure that the meat stays in tip-top shape. If you have difficulty slicing the lomo so thinly, ask your butcher—he or she might be happy to, if paid in lomo. Unsliced lomo will keep in the refrigerator, wrapped in plastic wrap, for up to 1 year.

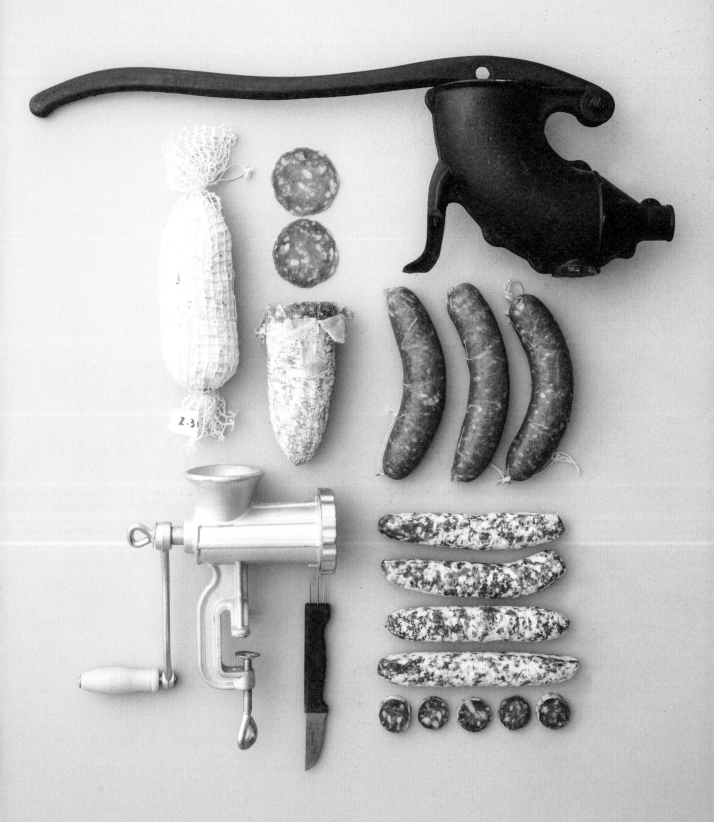

CHAPTER 6

Fermented, Dry-Cured Salami

Making fermented, dry-cured salami is like meat alchemy. So many things can go wrong in the process that when you do pull it off, it feels like a win.

The secrets to a successful fermented product are: meticulously cleaning the meat of all sinew and fat; selecting hard, premium fatback; scrupulously weighing your ingredients; grinding the meat yourself at the proper temperature; stuffing your casings tightly but not too tightly; fermenting the sausage at a constant temperature of 73°F (23°C); and then drying it in a dry box (which you've probably made yourself). Simple, right?

In addition to these secrets, there are two critical steps unique to making dry-cured salami. The first is the fermentation step, for which you use a lactic acid starter culture, which transforms dextrose, a sugar, into lactic acid. Using a calibrated pH meter (see page 132), you test each batch of salami to ensure it finishes at a pH of 4.8 or lower (this means you have a high enough level of lactic acid in your salami to make it safe to eat). This all takes place in a fermentation chamber (see page 132 for instructions on how to make one of these), in which a temperature of 73°F (23°C) and a relative humidity of 95 percent is maintained. This fermentation step happens over the 48 hours after you've stuffed your sausages.

From top: Salami Etna (page 143), Nduja (page 153), Saucisson d'Arles (page 140).

The percentage charts are ingredient ratios by weight, with the meat serving as the baseline weight. They're especially useful for scaling recipes, allowing you to get consistent recipe results no matter how much meat you have. All meat portions add up to 100 percent. For more information on how to use them, see page 22.

CLASSIC SALAMI

Ones to try are Loukanika (page 135), Saucisson d'Arles (page 140), and Salami Etna (page 143).

*Lean ham	82%
*Fatback	18%
*Salt	2.6%
*Curing salt #2	0.2%
*Dextrose	0.5%
Spices	1.5%

For distilled water and starter culture, use manufacturer's suggested amounts.

CHORIZO

One to try is Chorizo Andalucía (page 149).

*Pork shoulder meat	95%
*Fatback	5%
*Salt	2.6%
*Curing salt #2	0.2%
*Dextrose	0.5%
Spices	1.5%

For distilled water and starter culture, use manufacturer's suggested amounts.

* Ingredients marked with an asterisk need to be converted precisely.

The second step is drying. You allow salt to pull moisture to the exterior of the sausages and use a slight airflow to evaporate the moisture. This is done at a temperature of 58°F (14°C) and a relative humidity of 83 percent, which encourages the growth of the white mold you will learn to love. This step takes at least 18 days, after which you use a water activity meter to measure the amount of moisture that is still in your product. This all might seem a bit daunting at first, and it is. But closely follow the instructions and you will be just fine.

Quality Tips

Salami making is a very difficult thing to teach. A lot of techniques and practices together add up to the best possible product. But there is one absolute rule: get that pH down to 4.8 within 48 hours. As with any craft, good product is the result of getting a feel for it, which comes with practice. Please use that pH meter and be safe. Otherwise, practice the techniques and use the tips below, pay close attention to your product as you're making it, taste it when it's done, and learn.

Choose Your Meat Carefully: For making salami, I use lean and trimmed pork leg meat, with no visible fat or sinew at all, and grind it with pure fatback. (The advantage of taking all of the sinew out of the leg is so that when the lean meat melts away you won't have any chewy bits of sinew in your sausage. This gives you better mouthfeel and texture. You trim out all the fat you can so that you are in control of your ratio of lean to fat, except for chorizo, which is meant to have a more rustic texture.)

Grind Your Meat Carefully: When grinding meat for salami, you really do not want to develop too much myosin (see page 70) in the meat. It is a balancing act: you need myosin to bind but you also want the meat to breathe so the moisture can come out. (If you're a baker, gluten in bread is an analog: you develop it for structure, but not so much that the loaf is tough.) Your best chance at getting the right amount of myosin is to have grinder blades that are as sharp as a sushi chef's knives so they don't crush and mash the meat.

Use a Fine-Mesh Sieve: We pass all the crucial salami-curing ingredients—sea salt, curing salt, and dextrose—through a fine mesh sieve before adding them to the meat. We do this to eliminate the possibility of clumping. If there is a big clump of dextrose in your meat batter, for example, you will get overactive fermentation, and the sourness will disintegrate the meat completely, leaving you with a hollow salami. Fermentation will make any clumping apparent, with a "cure burn" or "salt burn," which turns the meat brown or hollow. Once these ingredients are passed through a sieve, we use a whisk to mix in the spices. This creates a shorter mix time.

Use a Good Starter Culture: Starter culture (see "What is Starter Culture," right) is your chance to add a personal touch to your salami. Most commercial cultures are produced in Europe, and each is designed to create a different flavor in the finished product. For example, tangy salami is de rigueur with domestic salami companies, but I prefer a much more subtle and natural taste to my salami. Through experimentation, I have formulated my own culture, and I use it to ferment the meat over a relatively long period (which is to say days, not hours). It would be really hard for you to reproduce the exact flavor that I get from my culture. I suggest you use one called Bactoferm LHP, which you can purchase from SausageMaker.com. This online source has many great cultures for you to choose from. Some are developed for an Old World flavor, while others are more New World.

The job of a culture, first and foremost, is to make your sausage's pH drop, ensuring you have a safe product. At OP, we use a degree chart created by meat safety experts; it lists, by time and temperature, the likeliness of bacteria to spread before the pH drops low enough to suppress it. Based on these, I suggest you ferment at 73°F (23°C) and that you reach a pH of 4.8 or lower in 48 hours. The clock starts ticking the second your meat gets to a temperature of 70°F (21°C) or higher—the danger zone for pathogen proliferation. If by hour 48 your pH is still above 4.8, you need to discard your meat.

Starter culture comes in freeze-dried packs. To formulate it, 1 hour before you plan to mix it into your meat, place the manufacturer's suggested amount of starter directly into room-temperature (70°F/21°C) distilled water. This cool (not cold) water will allow the culture to wake up a bit and get ready to produce some acid. Use distilled water only, since it contains none of the contaminants found in every municipal water supply, which may inhibit the culture. Also be sure to use the exact amount of water and culture recommended by the manufacturer—with most cultures, you use half a pack of culture, with water weighing 0.5 percent of the protein weight.

Mix Cold and Quickly: When grinding and mixing meat to make sausage, you want to do it quickly and keep it cold—the same goes for salami. I suggest you keep your meat in the fridge whenever you are not handling it and to grind into a bowl nestled in an ice bath whenever possible. When I need to fully bind a product and am using a standard mixer, I usually mix it for 8 to 10 minutes. But for fermented, dry-cured salami, I only mix for 3 minutes. You want to just incorporate the ingredients so they barely bind.

What is Starter Culture?

STARTER CULTURE *consists of lactic acid bacteria (LAB), mostly* Lactobacillus curvatus *and* Staphylococcus xylosus, *which are found naturally in meat. With the starter, you inoculate your meat with a bunch more of the good LAB than you would get naturally—enough so that the pH of your meat drops low enough to inhibit pathogen growth.*

THE METHOD *of freeze-drying LAB and using it in precisely measured amounts is only forty-odd years old, which is quite new when you consider that cavemen were preserving meat. Before starter cultures were available, meat makers would do what we call "back slopping," which is the process of taking a bit of a salami batch that had a great pH drop (and therefore a good active LAB population) and folding it into the next batch—kind of like how you make sourdough bread using a bit of the last batch of dough. However, the stakes are different: if your culture doesn't work in bread baking, your bread won't rise. But if the starter culture doesn't work properly in making fermented, dry-cured salami, you can make someone pretty sick. So embrace modern science and use a good commercially prepared culture. (Like everything else charcuterie-related, I suggest buying culture at SausageMaker.com.)*

Use a pH Meter: A trustworthy *charcutiére* never produces a batch of salami without checking the pH. If you do not own, plan to use, or know how to calibrate and operate a pH meter, you have no business making salami. Using a meter is the only way to be sure that the lactic acid bacteria are converting the dextrose in your sausages into lactic acid and to check if the pH has dropped to 4.8. This change is not something you can smell or see.

Build a Proper Fermentation Chamber: After you add the culture to your salami batch, you have 48 hours to get your pH to 4.8. Do this by placing the sausages in a fermentation chamber. In the controlled environment of the fermentation chamber, you are heating and activating the cultures you added to your meat so they transform all of the dextrose to lactic acid before any bad pathogens have a chance to multiply too much—which is happening simultaneously in the very same controlled environment. If the pH drops fast enough, you'll keep the pathogens at bay.

A fermentation chamber is easy to build yourself. You need a few things: a small space heater that gives off radiant heat (not one with a fan on it—you want little to no airflow so the salami casing stays nice and moist); a humidifier that runs on fresh, clean water; and a clean and sanitized large box, closet, or room that seals as tightly as possible. (You may also need a really understanding roommate who doesn't mind the smell of souring meat.) You want to create a steady temperature of 73°F (23°C) with 95 percent relative humidity; to keep these stable while you are fermenting, you will need a humidistat on your humidifier and a thermostat on your heater. The temperature and humidity should be kept as steady as possible, but the product will not be ruined if the temperature deviates by 5°F (3°C) or if the relative humidity fluctuates between 85 and 100 percent.

Cure in a Dry Box: To make fermented, dry-cured salami, you need to give the salami a chance to sweat—or rather, give the salt in the meat mixture time to pull moisture from the batch so it evaporates. For this to happen, you need to create the right conditions in a controlled environment—that is, a dry, sanitized container. These conditions are 58°F (14°C) and 83 percent humidity. I prefer to use a dry box that creates a cycle of airflow and stillness rather than a steady airflow, ideally 30 minutes of airflow (about the speed of walking, or 1½ miles an hour) followed by 15 minutes of very little to no airflow.

The end goal of the dry-curing period is evenly cured salami. But there are salami landmines along the way. If you see a dark line around the outside of your salami when you cut into it, or if you give it a gentle squeeze and it feels hollow, you most likely have what is called "casehardening." This happens when the outside of the salami gets too dry (and hard) before the inside has a chance to dry enough. Most likely, the problem—assuming you kept your humidity at 83 percent the entire time the salami was in the box—was too much airflow.

Generally speaking, a 1½-inch (4 cm) casing should take about 3 weeks to cure. As a rule of thumb, with every ½ inch (1.3 cm) added to your casing width, you will need to increase drying time by 2 weeks. So if a 1½-inch (4 cm) casing takes 3 weeks to dry, a 2-inch (5 cm) sausage will take about 5 weeks to dry. The time increases if the humidity is too high or there is not enough airflow. Dry curing is really a process that takes patience and tinkering to get right. You are looking for the final product to be about half the weight (or less) of the raw lean meat that went into the sausage. This can be measured by weighing the salami and comparing it to the weight of the meat you started with. Better yet, use a water activity meter to measure the water weight—it should be 0.85.

Understand the Basics of Mold: Use a commercial mold, Bactoferm 600 Mold (available, of course, at SausageMaker.com). This is a white mold that is strong enough to overpower most other molds you may encounter (see below). We use this as a starter mold at OP, and it's great for home salami making. Use it on every batch.

I've spoken with salami masters overseeing hundred-year-old dry rooms who are still trying to figure out why, all of a sudden, a mold change occurred. It's a learning process for even the best *charcutiéres*. Clean, white mold, *Penicillium nalgiovense*, is the norm and is good; it's what's in your freeze-dried packet of Bactoferm 600. It is also what you are looking for when you gaze upon your salami and, in an ideal world, it is the only mold you would have. But this is very rarely the case.

White mold is what you want, but not all nonwhite molds are evil; they are just trying to tell you something. If your white mold has a gray tint, there is most likely too much moisture, or the temperature is too low. A yellow tint could be saying there is too much heat in the dry box. In both cases, adjust accordingly.

If your salami begins to develop a fuzzy black or reddish black mold, discard it immediately and sanitize the dry box. Such a mold probably grew from a rogue spore in your environment; a really good wash, rinse, and sanitization of your dry box will most likely get rid of the problem for future batches. (Honestly, these bad molds very rarely appear, and you will probably never have to deal with them.)

What Makes Salami Salami

The relative acidity or alkalinity in a substance is measured by pH on a 14-point scale. Pure water has a pH of 7, which is completely neutral. The lower the number, the more acidic something is. Coffee checks in at around 5.3 to 5 (fairly acidic), and lemon juice is around 2 (very acidic). The reason we use acid in fermenting meat is that it keeps pathogens in check.

ON A PRACTICAL LEVEL, THE WAY IT WORKS IS THIS: *The lactic acid bacteria (LAB) in the starter that is mixed into your salami will get really active as the meat warms up. They look for dextrose to consume, and when they do, they release lactic acid. The buildup of acid drops the pH. However, what also happens as the meat starts to warm up is the growth of pathogens like* Clostridium botulinum. *You are holding your meat at a temperature that's in what is commonly referred to as the danger zone. It's a race inside your sausage: you need heat to get the starter working fast enough to make enough acid, but the same heat is also making the pathogens multiply. The only way to keep the pathogens from multiplying is to be sure that your pH drops to 4.8 before they have a chance to multiply to the degree that they can't be checked by all that nice acid you've been creating.*

Mold: Yes, it's true. The white stuff on the outside of your salami is mold, and it does some great things. First, it keeps the outside moist so the salami will dry properly, and second, it gives your salami a unique flavor found in no other cured meat.

Meat and Salt: Salami is ground meat, usually 30 percent fat and 70 percent lean, mixed with salt, which not only helps with flavor but also helps the meat dry.

Lactic Acid Starter Culture: Lactic acid bacterial strains, which you buy from a sausage-making supplier, consume dextrose (see below), releasing lactic acid and lowering the pH to 4.8 in your salami. This is accomplished in the fermentation step, and if a low enough pH doesn't occur within 48 hours, your salami is DOA (see "Your Salami on Acid," left).

Dextrose: Up to this point, charcuterie recipes in this book that call for sugar have called for either regular granulated sugar or brown sugar. Not fermented, dry-cured salami. Instead, we use dextrose to help the starter culture more easily produce lactic acid. Why does dextrose make this easier? Because dextrose is the most fine-grained sugar available, so it has less mass, and the smaller the mass, the less energy it takes for the starter to transform the sugar to lactic acid—you get the maximum conversion rate from your starter, driving down the product's pH to the level necessary essential for safety and flavor. Dextrose also has less sweetness, which works better with fermented products. Granulated sugars, with their larger grain mass, may not be fully transformed into lactic acid before the starter has run out of energy or is stalled by too high a pH. This could result in a small amount of residual sugar that will give a bit of sweetness to your sausage—a flavor effect that's amplified if you have a really sour sausage (think sweet-and-sour pork). In some sausages, it is a sign of quality to have a bit of sweetness. To me, it's just confusing and not great tasting, so I work with dextrose. You can buy it at SausageMaker.com

Curing Salt #2 (Nitrate plus Nitrite): Curing salt keeps pathogens (namely *Clostridium botulinum*) from spreading like mad, preserves color, and gives your salami that "cured flavor." The combination of fermentation and long curing time makes it critical to use curing salt #2, which contains both nitrite as well as nitrate for an added layer of protection.

LOUKANIKA

When I was growing up, my family had an acre of land that my dad desperately tried to turn into a true, working Greek-style farm. We lived off the land as much as possible, and of course, being thrifty as all Greeks are, we never let a thing go to waste.

My father, knowing next to nothing about the science of meat, routinely produced loukanika out of the extra trim from the animals we butchered. *Loukanika* is the Greek word for sausage; I, however, associate it with this type of salami. Using a hand grinder and a cast-iron stuffer, he mixed up batches of the salami, then hung them in the garage to dry—no matter what the season. Sub-zero temperatures with arctic winds? Yep. Hotter than 100°F (38°C) in the middle of summer? Why not? I always assumed he included copious amounts of garlic and cumin so that if any of the sausages went rancid we couldn't tell.

Fast-forward twenty years to 2009, when (as a joke), I made a 25-pound batch of loukanika for my sister to thank her for help working with the USDA. I told her that this was absolutely a one-time thing; it wasn't a recipe I wished to spend any more time with. Without me knowing, Michele entered the loukanika in the Good Foods Awards, and sure enough, it won. And so I will be making this salami until the day I die.

There are many, many loukanika recipes out there, and the only commonality I can see is the use of orange zest. I use cumin and garlic in absurd proportions because that's what I remember my dad doing. So this recipe offers a slightly more refined flavor, and careful fermentation and dry curing means a safer salami, too.

NOTES: YOU WILL NEED A STARTER CULTURE SUCH AS BACTOFERM LHP, DISTILLED WATER (TO HYDRATE THE STARTER CULTURE), AND BACTOFERM 600 MOLD FOR THIS RECIPE. THIS RECIPE TAKES 22 DAYS, WITH 5 HOURS OF HANDS-ON TIME.

Special Equipment: You will need a grinder, stand mixer, stuffer, hanging rack, fermentation chamber, pH meter, dry box, and, in an ideal world, a water activity meter.

1. Rinse out your casing by placing one end under the water tap and filling it with about ½ cup (120 ml) water. Run this water through the casing by pulling up on the end that you filled up, until water comes out the other end of the casing. It will come out a bit cloudy. This is totally normal, as you are removing salt on the inside of the casing. Place the rinsed casing in a bowl of clean warm water to soak.

CONTINUED

MAKES 9 SAUSAGES, 5 OUNCES (140 G) EACH

1 (8-foot/2.5-m) length (1¾-inch/45-mm) natural hog casing

3 pounds (1.4 kg) boneless pork leg, cut into 1-inch (1.3-cm) cubes

10 ounces (280 g) pork fatback, cut into ½-inch (1.3-cm) cubes

Starter culture (see Notes)

Distilled water (see Notes)

1 tablespoon (13 g) chopped garlic

1 tablespoon (10 g) ground cumin

2 tablespoons plus 2 teaspoons (40 g) fine sea salt

1¾ teaspoons (8 g) dextrose

¾ teaspoon (3 g) curing salt #2

¾ teaspoon (3 g) minced orange zest

Ice cubes, for ice bath

Bactoferm 600 Mold

2   Put all of the parts of your stuffer and meat grinder (including the blades and grinder head), as well as your stand-mixer bowl and paddle attachment, in the freezer to chill. Put the pork and fatback in the freezer and let chill for about 30 minutes, until the meat reaches an internal temperature of 32°F (0°C). In a large bowl, toss together the chilled pork and fatback and return it to the freezer.

3   Pour the manufacturer's suggested amount of starter culture into the corresponding amount of distilled water. Set aside. Using a mortar and pestle, grind together the garlic and cumin, then mix in the sea salt, dextrose, and curing salt. Put the mixture through a fine-mesh sieve to make sure there are no clumps; clumps cause "cure burn" (see pages 128–29). Add the orange zest and set aside.

4   Set up the grinder with the ⅓-inch (8-mm) die. Fill a bowl halfway with ice cubes and set it under the grinder. Nestle the stand-mixer bowl in the ice. Grind the meat mixture into the chilled stand-mixer bowl, and then check the internal temperature; it should be 39°F (4°C) or lower. If it isn't, return the ground meat to the freezer until it reaches this temperature.

5   Add the spice mixture to the chilled ground meat. Using the chilled paddle attachment, mix on low speed for 1 minute. Add the culture and its water, then mix for another 3 minutes. The meat batter should show good definition between the fat and the lean meat and you should see no clumping of spices. You are also looking for what we call "legs" in the lean meat: Take a clump of the mixture and pull it apart. You should see thread like pieces trying to hold on to each other (see image, page 73). Bring out your trusty thermometer and check the internal temperature again. If it's above 39°F (4°C), return the bowl to the freezer for 10 to 15 minutes, or until the meat batter reaches this temperature.

6   Assemble your stuffer, making sure that everything is clean and that all parts are on tightly so that nothing will come loose and make a mess. Get all of the surfaces that the casing will be touching (the horn and the table) really wet with water so that the casing will slide and not tear. Remove the meat batter from the mixer bowl and portion it into three balls, each about the size of a softball. Hand-pack these tightly to remove any air—you have to be diligent about this. If you have a pocket of air, that area will oxidize, turning the meat brown and making it taste like a wet, moldy basement. Now stuff the meat portions one on top of another into the hopper and fill the casing. When casing the meat, you want the sausage to have the consistency of an overripe banana in its peel—when you squeeze your fingers to pinch the casing at each end of your desired length, there should be a light resistance,

but not enough to burst the casing. Link the sausages into 6-inch (15 cm) links by twisting each sausage in the opposite direction as the previous one (see pages 74–75). Tie every two sausages with a loop to hang the meat from. If you don't have a water activity meter, carefully weigh the meat now and record its weight; this is the starting weight. The finished product must weigh half as much as the starting weight by the end of the dry cure. This moisture loss is absolutely critical, as it helps make the finished product safe to eat.

7   Hang the sausages in the fermentation chamber at 73°F (23°C) with 95 percent relative humidity. Using the width of two fingers as a measure, space the salami so they do not touch each other on the hanging rack. Mix the mold following the manufacturer's directions, put it in a clean spray bottle, and mist the hanging salami over their entire surface—two or three light sprays on each salami should do it.

8   After 24 hours, start checking the pH of the salami every 12 hours or so using your pH meter. You only need to check one link. You can test this link repeatedly until you hit the 4.8 mark, but discard it when you do hit the mark because mold can form in the holes. If the pH is close to 4.8, you can check more often than every 12 hours. After 48 hours, the salami should reach a pH of 4.8 or lower; if it does not reach this pH within 48 hours of going into the fermentation chamber, you must discard the salami and start over. Once the pH is 4.8, remove the salami and transfer it to your dry box set to a temperature of 58°F (14°C) and 83 percent relative humidity. The salami should take 3 weeks to dry.

9   After 3 weeks, check if the salami is ready. If you own a water activity meter meter, the active water weight should be 0.85. Otherwise, weigh the salami; it should have lost at least half of its starting weight. To serve, thinly slice the loukanika. (To channel your inner Greek, make a Greek salad and slice loukanika on top, sit outside on your deck, open a bottle of retsina, and enjoy.) Store the unsliced salami in a breathable container in the refrigerator for up to 2 months.

Spanish board, French board, Italian board.

SAUCISSON D'ARLES

MAKES 9 SAUSAGES,
5 OUNCES (140 G) EACH

1 (8-foot/2.5-m) length
(1¾-inch/45-mm) natural
hog casing

3 pounds (1.4 kg) boneless lean pork
leg, cut into 1-inch (2.5-cm) cubes

10 ounces (280 g) pork fatback, cut
into 1-inch (2.5-cm) cubes

Starter culture (see Notes)

Distilled water (see Notes)

2 tablespoons plus 2 teaspoons (40 g)
fine sea salt

1¾ teaspoons (8 g) dextrose

¾ teaspoon (3 g) curing salt #2

Ice cubes, for ice bath

Bactoferm 600 Mold

VARIATIONS

SAUCISSON D'ALSACE

Pinch of ground cinnamon

Pinch of freshly grated nutmeg

Pinch of ground cloves

½ teaspoon (2.5 g) chopped garlic

1 teaspoon (5 g) ground white pepper

¼ teaspoon (1 ml) rum

SAUCISSON SEC

1¾ teaspoons (8 g) ground
black pepper

1 tablespoon (18 g) chopped garlic

If you want a lesson on how hard it is to make the simplest things, look no further than this recipe. It's a salami flavored only with salt and mold. Without any hesitation, I can say this is my favorite product because of its simplicity. But if you make a mistake or rush any of the steps, you will taste it in the finished sausage. There is no spice to mask errors, no smoke or mirrors. If you buy cheap pork, the salami will taste cheap. If you rush the fermentation with more heat, it will taste too tangy. However, if you nail it with the best raw materials and good technique, you can taste so many nuances, namely whatever the pig ate—say, grass and cherries in the spring, or corn in the winter. Of course, something this simple isn't everyone's idea of perfection, so I've also included two more highly seasoned variations that we make at OP.

In my humble opinion, the French make two things better than anyone else in the world: wine and *saucisson*. So make this *saucisson*, or one of the variations, and while you are waiting for it to dry, find yourself a delicious bottle of wine. Once the salami is finished, find a perfect spot to have a picnic and eat your sausage, reflecting on how awesome you and the French are for making great *saucisson*.

NOTES: YOU WILL NEED A STARTER CULTURE SUCH AS BACTOFERM LHP, DISTILLED WATER (TO HYDRATE THE STARTER CULTURE), AND BACTOFERM 600 MOLD FOR THIS RECIPE. THIS RECIPE TAKES 22 DAYS, WITH 5 HOURS HANDS-ON TIME.

Special Equipment: You will need a stuffer, grinder, hanging rack, fermentation chamber, spray bottle, pH meter, dry box, and, in an ideal world, a water activity meter.

1 Rinse out your casing by placing one end under the water tap and filling it with about ½ cup (120 ml) of water. Run this water through the casing by pulling up on the end that you filled up, until water comes out the other end of the casing. It will come out a bit cloudy. This is totally normal, as you are removing salt on the inside of the casing. Place the rinsed casing in a bowl of clean warm water to soak.

2 Put all of the parts of your stuffer and meat grinder (including the blades and grinder head), as well as your stand-mixer bowl and paddle attachment, in the freezer to chill. Put the pork and fatback in the freezer and let chill for about 30 minutes, until the meat reaches an internal temperature of 32°F (0°C). In a large bowl, toss together the chilled pork and fatback and return it to the freezer.

3   Pour the manufacturer's suggested amount of starter culture into the corresponding amount of distilled water. Set aside. If you are making one of the spice mix variations, grind the spices together using a mortar and pestle. Now mix the ground spices with the sea salt, dextrose, and curing salt. Put the mixture through a fine-mesh sieve to make sure there are no clumps; clumps cause "cure burn" (see pages 128–29). Add the rum if you are making the Saucisson d'Alsace and set aside.

4   Set up the grinder with the ⅓-inch (8-mm) die. Fill a bowl halfway with ice cubes and set it under the grinder. Nestle the stand-mixer bowl in the ice. Grind the meat mixture into the chilled stand-mixer bowl, and then check the internal temperature; it should be 39°F (4°C) or below. If it isn't, return the ground meat to the freezer until it reaches this temperature.

5   Add the cure mixture to the chilled ground meat. Using the chilled paddle attachment, mix on low speed for 1 minute. Add the culture and its water, then mix for another 3 minutes. The meat should show good definition between the fat and the lean meat and you should see no clumping of spices if you are making one of the spice variations. You are also looking for what we call "legs" in the lean meat: Take a clump of the mixture and pull it apart. You should see threadlike pieces trying to hold onto each other (see image, page 73). Bring out your trusty thermometer and check the internal temperature again. If it's above 39°F (4°C), return the bowl back to the freezer for 10 to 15 minutes, or until the meat batter reaches this temperature.

6   Assemble your stuffer, making sure that everything is clean and that all parts are on tightly so that nothing will come lose and make a mess. Get all of the surfaces that the casing will be touching (the horn and the table) really wet with water so that the casing will slide and not tear. Remove the meat batter from the mixer bowl and portion it into three balls, each about the size of a softball. Hand-pack these tightly to remove any air—you have to be diligent about this. If you have a pocket of air, that area will oxidize, turning the meat brown and making it taste like a wet, moldy basement. Now stuff the meat portions one on top of another into the hopper and fill the casing. When casing the meat, you want the sausage to have the consistency of an overripe banana in its peel—when you squeeze your fingers to pinch the casing at each end of your desired length, there should be a light resistance, but not enough to burst the casing. Link the sausages into 6-inch (15 cm) links by twisting each sausage in the opposite direction as

CONTINUED

the previous one (see pages 74–75). Tie every two sausages with a loop to hang the meat from. If you don't have a water activity meter, carefully weigh the meat now and record its weight; this is the starting weight. The finished product must weigh half as much as the starting weight by the end of the dry cure. This moisture loss is absolutely critical, as it helps make the finished product safe to eat.

7   Hang the tied sausages in an incubator at 73°F (23°C) with 95 percent relative humidity. Using the width of two fingers as a measure, space the salami so they do not touch each other on the hanging rack. Mix the mold following the manufacturer's directions, put it in a clean spray bottle, and mist the hanging salami over their entire surface—two or three light sprays on each salami should do it.

8   After 24 hours, start checking the pH of the salami every 12 hours or so using your pH meter. You only need to check one link. You can test this link repeatedly until you hit the 4.8 mark, but discard it when you do hit the mark because mold can form in the holes. After 48 hours, the salami should reach a pH of 4.8 or lower; if it does not reach this pH within 2 days from going into the incubator, you must discard the salami and start over. Once the pH is 4.8, remove the salami and transfer it to your dry box set to a temperature of 58°F (14°C) and 83 percent relative humidity. The salami should take 3 weeks to dry.

9   After 3 weeks, check if the salami is ready. If you own a water activity meter, the active water weight should be 0.85. Otherwise, weigh the salami; it should have lost at least half of its starting weight. To serve, slice thinly. Store the salami in a breathable container in the refrigerator for up to 2 months.

SALAMI ETNA

I discovered Etna from a producer in Sicily. The only ingredients added to the pork and fat were sea salt, lemon zest, and pepper. It took me 3 years to get this right.

NOTES: YOU WILL NEED A STARTER CULTURE SUCH AS BACTOFERM LHP, DISTILLED WATER (TO HYDRATE THE STARTER CULTURE), AND BACTOFERM 600 MOLD FOR THIS RECIPE. THIS RECIPE TAKES 22 DAYS, WITH 5 HOURS OF HANDS-ON TIME.

Special Equipment: You will need a stuffer, grinder, hanging rack, fermentation chamber, spray bottle, pH meter, dry box, and, in an ideal world, a water activity meter.

1 Rinse out your casing by placing one end under the water tap and filling it with about ½ cup (120 ml) water. Run this water through the casing by pulling up on the end that you filled up, until water comes out the other end of the casing. It will come out a bit cloudy. This is totally normal, as you are removing salt on the inside of the casing. Place the rinsed casing in a bowl of clean warm water to soak.

2 Put all of the parts of your stuffer and meat grinder (including the blades and grinder head), as well as your stand-mixer bowl and paddle attachment, in the freezer to chill. Put the pork and fatback in the freezer and let chill for about 30 minutes, until the meat reaches an internal temperature of 32°F (0°C). In a large bowl, toss together the chilled pork and fatback and return it to the freezer.

3 Pour the manufacturer's suggested amount of starter culture into the corresponding amount of distilled water. Set aside. Using a mortar and pestle, mix together the pepper, sea salt, dextrose, and curing salt. Put the mixture through a fine-mesh sieve to make sure there are no clumps; clumps cause "cure burn" (see pages 128–29).

4 Set up the grinder with the ⅓-inch (8-mm) die. Fill another bowl halfway with ice cubes and set it under the grinder. Nestle the stand-mixer bowl in the ice. Grind the meat mixture into the chilled stand-mixer bowl, and then check the internal temperature; it should be 39°F (4°C) or lower. If it isn't, return the ground meat to the freezer until it reaches this temperature.

5 Add the cure mixture and the pistachios and lemon zest to the ground meat. Using the chilled paddle attachment, mix on low

CONTINUED ON PAGE 147

MAKES 9 SAUSAGES, 5 OUNCES (140 G) EACH

1 (8-foot/2.5-m) length (1¾-inch/45-mm) natural hog casing (or the largest diameter your butcher can get)

3 pounds (1.4 kg) boneless lean pork leg, cut into 1-inch (2.5-cm) cubes

10 ounces (280 g) pork fatback, cut into 1-inch (2.5-cm) cubes

Starter culture (see Notes)

Distilled water (see Notes)

½ teaspoon (2 g) ground black pepper

2 tablespoons plus 2 teaspoons (40 g) fine sea salt

1¾ teaspoons (8 g) dextrose

¾ teaspoon (3 g) curing salt #2

¼ cup (60 g) whole shelled pistachios

1½ teaspoons (7 g) minced lemon zest

Ice cubes, for ice bath

Bactoferm 600 Mold

speed for 1 minute. Add the culture and its water, then mix for another 3 minutes. The meat should show good definition between the fat and the lean meat and you should see no clumping of seasonings. You are also looking for what we call "legs" in the lean meat: Take a clump of the mixture and pull it apart. You should see threadlike pieces trying to hold onto each other (see image, page 73). Bring out your trusty thermometer and check the internal temperature again. If it's above 39°F (4°C), return the bowl to the freezer for 10 to 15 minutes, or until the meat batter reaches this temperature.

6   Assemble your stuffer, making sure that everything is clean and that all parts are on tightly so that nothing will come lose and make a mess. Get all of the surfaces that the casing will be touching (the horn and the table) really wet with water so that the casing will slide and not tear. Remove the meat batter from the mixer bowl and portion it into three balls, each about the size of a softball. Hand-pack these tightly to remove any air—you have to be diligent about this. If you have a pocket of air, that area will oxidize, turning the meat brown and making it taste like a wet, moldy basement. Now stuff the meat portions one on top of another into the hopper and fill the casing. When casing the meat, you want the sausage to have the consistency of an overripe banana in its peel—when you squeeze your fingers to pinch the casing at each end of your desired length, there should be a light resistance, but not enough to burst the casing. Link the sausages into 6-inch (15 cm) links by twisting each sausage in the opposite direction as the previous one (see pages 74–75). Tie every two sausages with a loop to hang the meat from. If you don't have a water activity meter, carefully weigh the meat now and record its weight; this is the starting weight. The finished product must weigh half as much as the starting weight by the end of the dry cure. This moisture loss is absolutely critical, as it helps make the finished product safe to eat.

7   Hang the sausages in a fermentation chamber at 73°F (23°C) with 95 percent relative humidity. Using the width of two fingers as a measure, space the salami so they do not touch each other on the hanging rack. Mix the mold following the manufacturer's directions, pour it into a clean spray bottle, and mist the hanging salami over their entire surface—two or three light sprays on each salami should do it.

8   After 24 hours, start checking the pH of the salami every 12 hours or so using the pH meter. You only need to check one link. You can

CONTINUED

test this link repeatedly until you hit the 4.8 mark, but discard it when you do hit the mark because mold can form in the holes. After 48 hours, the salami should reach a pH of 4.8 or lower; if it does not reach this pH within 48 hours of going into the incubator, you must discard the salami and start over. Once the pH is 4.8, remove the salami and weigh it; take careful note of the weight. Finally, transfer the salami to your dry box set to a temperature of 58°F (14°C) and 83 percent relative humidity. The salami should take 3 weeks to dry.

9   After 3 weeks, check if the salami is ready. If you own a water activity meter, the active water weight should be 0.85. Otherwise, weigh the salami; it should have lost at least half of its starting weight. To serve, slice thinly. Store the unsliced salami in a breathable container in the refrigerator for up to 2 months.

CHORIZO ANDALUCÍA

My favorite region for food and drink in all of Spain is Andalucía. I find it so brilliant how these people often use a hint of clove, or even sometimes cinnamon, in their meat and chorizo recipes. The flavors pair so perfectly with a delicious sherry like amontillado or oloroso.

We sell three chorizos at OP now, but when we opened, I had twenty different types on the menu. That is when Michelle (the brains of the operation) stepped in to reveal that no one could tell the differences among the twenty flavors but me. So I chose the three versions that are most different from one another and did away with the rest. Here is one of them.

NOTES: YOU WILL NEED A STARTER CULTURE SUCH AS BACTOFERM LHP, DISTILLED WATER (TO HYDRATE THE STARTER CULTURE), AND BACTOFERM 600 MOLD FOR THIS RECIPE. THIS RECIPE TAKES 22 DAYS, WITH 5 HOURS HANDS-ON TIME.

Special Equipment: You will need a grinder, stuffer, hanging rack, fermentation chamber, spray bottle, pH meter, dry box, and, in an ideal world, a water activity meter.

1   Rinse out your casing by placing one end under the water tap and filling it with about ½ cup (120 ml) of water. Run this water through the casing by pulling up on the end that you filled up, until water comes out the other end of the casing. It will come out a bit cloudy. This is totally normal, as you are removing salt on the inside of the casing. Place the rinsed casing in a bowl of clean warm water to soak.

2   Put all of the parts of your stuffer and meat grinder (including the blades and grinder head), as well as your stand-mixer bowl and paddle attachment, in the freezer to chill. Put the pork and fatback in the freezer and let chill for about 30 minutes, or until the meat reaches an internal temperature of 32°F (0°C). In a large bowl, toss together the chilled pork and fatback, and return to the freezer.

3   Pour the manufacturer's suggested amount of starter culture into the corresponding amount of distilled water. Set aside. Using a mortar and pestle, grind together the spices and garlic, then mix in the pepper, sea salt, dextrose, and curing salt. Put the mixture through a fine-mesh sieve to make sure there are no clumps; clumps cause "cure burn" (see pages 128–29).

CONTINUED

MAKES 9 SAUSAGES, 5 OUNCES (140 G) EACH

1 (8-foot/2.5-m) length (1¾-inch/45-mm) natural hog casing

3 pounds (1.4 kg) boneless pork shoulder, cut into 1-inch (2.5-cm) cubes

2½ ounces (70 g) fatback, cut into 1-inch (2.5-cm) cubes

Starter culture (see Notes)

Distilled water (see Notes)

1¾ teaspoons (7 g) smoked paprika

1½ tablespoons (20 g) sweet paprika

1¾ teaspoons (7 g) ground black pepper

¾ teaspoon (3 g) ground cloves

1½ teaspoons (6 g) cayenne

1 tablespoon (18 g) chopped garlic

2 tablespoons plus 1 teaspoon (37 g) fine sea salt

1¾ teaspoons (8 g) dextrose

¾ teaspoon (3 g) curing salt #2

Ice cubes, for ice bath

Bactoferm 600 Mold

4   Set up the grinder with the ⅓-inch (8-mm) die. Fill another bowl halfway with ice cubes. And set it under the grinder. Nestle the stand-mixer in to the ice. Grind the meat mixture into the chilled stand-mixer bowl, and then check the internal temperature; it should be 39°F (4°C). If it isn't, return the ground meat to the freezer until it reaches this temperature.

5   Add the cure mixture to the chilled ground meat. Using the chilled paddle attachment, mix on low speed for 1 minute. Add the culture and its water, then mix for another 3 minutes. The meat should show good definition between the fat and the lean meat and you should see no clumping of seasonings. You are also looking for what we call "legs" in the meat: Take a clump of the mixture and pull it apart. You should see thread like pieces trying to hold on to each other (see image, page 73). Bring out your trusty thermometer and check the internal temperature again. If it's over 39°F (4°C), place the bowl back in the freezer for 10 to 15 minutes, or until the meat batter reaches this temperature.

6   Assemble your stuffer, making sure that everything is clean and that all parts are on tightly so that nothing will come lose and make a mess. Get all of the surfaces that the casing will be touching (the horn and the table) really wet with water so that the casing will slide and not tear. Remove the meat batter from the mixer bowl and portion it into three balls, each about the size of a softball. Hand-pack these tightly to remove any air—you have to be diligent about this. If you have a pocket of air, that area will oxidize, turning the meat brown and making it taste like a wet, moldy basement. Now stuff the meat portions one on top of another into the hopper and fill the casing. When casing the meat, you want the sausage the consistency of an overripe banana in its peel—when you squeeze your fingers to pinch the casing at each end of your desired length, there should be a light resistance, but not enough to burst the casing. Link the sausages into 6-inch (15 cm) links by twisting each sausage in the opposite direction as the previous one. Tie every two sausages with a loop to hang the meat from. If you don't have a water activity meter, carefully weigh the meat now and record its weight; this is the starting weight. The finished product must weigh half as much as the starting weight by the end of the dry cure. This moisture loss is absolutely critical, as it helps make the finished product safe to eat.

CONTINUED

7 Hang the sausages in a fermentation chamber at 73°F (23°C) with 95 percent relative humidity. Using the width of two fingers as a measure, space the salami so they do not touch each other on the hanging rack. Mix the mold following the manufacturer's directions, pour it into a clean spray bottle, and mist the hanging salami over their entire surface—two or three light sprays on each salami should do it.

8 After 24 hours, start checking the pH of the salami every 12 hours or so using the pH meter. You only need to check one link. You can test this link repeatedly until you hit the 4.8 mark, but discard it when you do hit the mark because mold can form in the holes. After 48 hours, the salami should reach a pH of 4.8 or lower; if it does not reach this pH within 48 hours of going into the incubator, you must discard the salami and start over. Once the pH is 4.8, transfer the salami to your dry box set to a temperature of 58°F (14°C) and 83 percent relative humidity. The salami should take 3 weeks to dry.

9 After 3 weeks, check if the salami is ready. If you own a water activity meter, the active water weight should be 0.85. Otherwise, weigh the salami; it should have lost at least half of its starting weight. To serve, sliced thinly. Store the unsliced salami in a breathable container in the refrigerator for up to 2 months.

NDUJA

Nduja is meat making at its nerdiest. It's 60 percent fat, which gives it a soft, spreadable texture. Making it involves emulsifying, fermenting, and cold smoking. When it's done correctly, you will have a wonderfully versatile product. You can eat it raw smeared on bread or crumble it atop pizza, but it shines most when used like butter to finish a sauce. For example, when adding oil or butter to a dish of clams or mussels, substitute nduja, which melts like butter and gives a crazy-amazing fermented meat flavor.

Warning: This is a raw product and is not dried; it is fermented below a pH of 4.2, which is what makes it safe to consume. You let the pH get really low so no pathogens survive. If this doesn't make sense to you, it's probably not a good idea for you to attempt making it. In any case, this recipe absolutely requires a pH meter (see page 17). You may also notice that this recipe has way more dextrose than the other fermented recipes. This is because including greater amounts of dextrose will trigger bacteria that ravage the dextrose, releasing lactic acid and bringing down the pH. This is a tricky recipe to master, so we have not provided a percentage chart.

NOTES: YOU WILL NEED A STARTER CULTURE SUCH AS BACTOFERM LHP, DISTILLED WATER (TO HYDRATE THE STARTER CULTURE), AND BACTOFERM 600 MOLD FOR THIS RECIPE. THIS IS A 3-DAY RECIPE, WITH 4 HOURS OF HANDS-ON TIME.

Special Equipment: You will need a grinder, stuffer, incubator, pH meter, 2 pounds (910 g) apple wood chips, 1 pound (455 g) hickory wood chips, and a bag of charcoal. Any type of charcoal without added lighter fluid will work.

1 Rinse out your casing by placing one end under the water tap and filling it with about ½ cup (120 ml) water. Run this water through the casing by pulling up on the end that you filled up, until water comes out the other end of the casing. It will come out a bit cloudy. This is totally normal, as you are removing salt on the inside of the casing. Place the rinsed casing in a bowl of clean warm water to soak.

2 Put all of the parts of your stuffer and meat grinder (including the blades and grinder head), as well as your stand-mixer bowl and paddle attachment, in the freezer to chill. Put the pork and fatback in the freezer and let chill for about 30 minutes, until the meat reaches an internal temperature of 32°F (0°C). In a large bowl,

CONTINUED

MAKES 6 (3-INCH/7.5 CM) SAUSAGES; SERVES 18 TO 20

1 (8-foot/2.5-m) length (1¾-inch/45-mm) natural hog casing

1½ pounds (680 g) boneless pork shoulder, cut into 1-inch (1.3-cm) cubes

1½ pounds (680 g) fatback, cut into 1-inch (1.3-cm) cubes

Starter culture (see Notes)

Distilled water (see Notes)

¼ cup (60 g) chopped, drained, oil-packed Calabrian peppers, plus ¼ cup (50 g) oil from the peppers

2 cups (225 g) crushed ice, plus additional ice cubes for an ice bath

3 tablespoons (45 g) fine sea salt

¾ teaspoon (3 g) curing salt # 1

1 tablespoon plus 1 teaspoon (20 g) dextrose

2 teaspoons (9 g) smoked paprika

1½ tablespoons (20 g) sweet paprika

2 teaspoons (10 g) ground black pepper

2 teaspoons (9 g) cayenne

1 tablespoon (18 g) chopped garlic

toss together the chilled pork and fatback with the Calabrian peppers and the pepper oil. Put the bowl in the freezer.

3   Pour the manufacturer's suggested amount of starter culture into the corresponding amount of distilled water. Set aside.

4   Set up the grinder with the ¼-inch (6-mm) die. Fill another large bowl halfway with ice cubes and set it under the grinder. Nestle the chilled stand-mixer bowl in the ice. Mix the crushed ice into the meat mixture, then check the internal temperature; it should not exceed 39°F (4°C). Pass the meat mixture twice through the grinder, into the stand-mixer bowl; check the temperature again to make sure it does not exceed be 39°F (4°C). If it does, return the meat to the freezer until the temperature comes down. Change to the smallest die you have—a ⅛-inch (3-mm) die would be perfect—and run the meat mixture through two more times. (If you do not have a smaller die, run the meat through the ¼-inch/6-mm die four more times, for a total of six passes.) After each pass through the grinder, if the temperature of the meat mixture exceeds 39°F (4°C), return the bowl to the freezer. Your goal is a uniform color and texture: light pink and the consistency of pudding.

5   Add the sea salt, curing salt, dextrose, smoked paprika, sweet paprika, black pepper, cayenne, and garlic to the ground meat mixture and mix with the chilled paddle attachment on low speed until all of the ingredients are incorporated, about 4 minutes.

6   Assemble your stuffer, making sure that everything is clean and that all parts are on tightly so that nothing will come lose and make a mess. Get all of the surfaces that the casing will be touching (the horn and the table) really wet with water so that the casing will slide and not tear. Load the hopper, packing the meat down firmly to get as much air out as possible. Stuff the casing and tie off the end. Link the sausages into 3-inch (7.5 cm) links, by twisting each sausage in the opposite direction as the previous one (see pages 74–75). You should have six sausages.

7   You want to incubate this in your fermentation chamber at 73°F (23°C) with a relative humidity of 95 percent with very little to no air flow. This is the exact same way that you will ferment all of your other salamis. However, this one has a lot more dextrose in it to form lactic acid and will have a much lower pH, which is very important to this product as the pH is the only way to keep the pathogens in check. In other words, you are fermenting it to be so acidic that pathogens will not be likely to multiply. I ferment mine

for only 48 hours at 73°F (23°C) and 90 percent humidity. The bottom line being that you need to get a pH of less than 4.2 in under 48 hours to be sure that the nduja will be safe to consume.

8   One your sausage has reached a pH of 4.2, start preparing to smoke it. Soak wood and chips in water to cover for at least 10 minutes. Once you have your charcoal burning, remove the grill and place the charcoal on one side of the bottom of your grill. Put about ⅓ of the soaked wood chips on the hot coals, and then place your grill back over the coals. You should start to see and smell smoke.

9   Place your meat on the grill at this point, as far away from the coals as possible. Place the lid on your grill, with the air holes open and, if possible, directly over the meat, so that the airflow will pull the smoke over the meat. Let your meat begin to smoke. Once you see that the smoke coming out is starting to dissipate, take the lid off the grill, stoke your coals, and add 2 or 3 cold coals and more wood chips. Once you are happy with the stream of smoke, slowly raise the temperature of your grill by adding coals. Slowly smoke for 3 hours, keeping the temperature under 90°F (32°C), with a steady stream of cool smoke. If the smoker temperature begins to climb, crack the door or vent and allow some fresh cool air in (and some hot air out). The internal temperature of your sausage should never exceed 90°F (32°F), so a really cool smoke is what you are looking for. The color of your sausage should be nice and golden, and it should be firm to the touch.

10 Once it is all golden and delicious looking, remove it from the grill and place it in your fridge to cool for at least an hour or until the temperature is 39°F (4°C) or less. Peel back the casing from one tip using a sharp pairing knife. Cut a small round of the sausage about ½ inch (1.3-cm) thick. It should be nice and soft with a texture of a spreadable pâté with a very beautiful reddish-pink color. Smear on a crusty piece of bread with some olive oil and crunchy salt. Take a small second to think how great it is that you are eating raw fermented meat that taste so damn good. Once you have eaten all that you can possibly consume, wrap any leftover sausages in plastic wrap and store in your fridge. Nduja will keep for only 4 weeks. It is not a shelf-stable product and has a high amount of moisture that can still sour quickly.

INTERMISSION

BACK TO WILDHAUS

ALP TRIPPIN' IN CHICKEN-SKIN PAJAMAS

It was 1997, five years after my dad died. I was nineteen and, after dropping a Burton snowboarding sponsorship, I had no idea what to do. But I had always loved cooking, and the restaurant business was in my blood. I decided I wanted to go to the CIA, but as we couldn't afford it, my mom suggested I go back to Greece and cook at a friend's restaurant. In retrospect, that would have been fantastic: century-old ovens, goat butchery, upping my fish game, and quiet village living. But I wanted chef whites, a busy dining room, and fancy-pants customers. I wanted action.

So I called our family friend Dieter Reineke, a restaurateur in Chicago, for help. He connected me with Annegrit Schlumpf, a former employee of his who had recently returned to her hometown of Wildhaus, in the Swiss Alps. Dieter told me that Annegret's new place of work, the Alpenrose Hotel, would take on one apprentice per year. I don't know why (maybe because my parents hid garlic in my clothes for good luck?), but Annegrit agreed to take me on.

Within a few days I had sold everything I owned for the price of a ticket from Salt Lake City to Zurich. I knew next to nothing about where I was going, only that Wildhaus was in an area called the Toggenburg in northeastern Switzerland near the borders with Austria and Lichtenstein, that it had a population of 1,500 or so, and that I had a job waiting for me there.

After arriving in Zurich, I took the train to Nesslau, and from there it was a thirty-minute bus ride to Wildhaus. When I arrived, I found the most picturesque, quaint alpine town imaginable, complete with towering cliffs, church bells echoing in the valley, layer upon layer of cow-filled meadows, and a very small ski resort dotted with gondolas, T-bars, and chalets. I called up to the hotel and Johannes, the dishwasher, came cruising down in a beat-up black Renault hatchback. The kitchen he ushered me into was filled with natural light and was sparkling clean, with the kind of logical organization you would expect from the Swiss.

There was a full butchery section, complete with a rail system that transported the hanging elk, cow, or ibex from outside to the cooler and then to the cutting room. Off to one side was a tank with lake trout, so *truite au bleu* could be made to order. There was a separate bakery where fresh bread was made daily—and I mean bread bread, made with real wheat, with real crust—as well as croissants, brioche, and strudel. And, of course, there was an entire wall stacked with Swiss chocolate.

Even with all this daily activity, the whole kitchen was immaculate; if not for the bustling dining room, you would think it was rarely used.

The Alpenrose Hotel sits about a quarter of the way up the Gamsalp Mountain, just above the base village. The large windows in the kitchen face upward toward the Oberdorf piste, so when I first looked out, I could see a steady stream of skiers tearing down toward me. Although this detail initially seemed like a dream come true, it would, of course, became a source of torture during the eighty-some hours a week I worked over the next four years.

It was here that I first met Urban Neussbaumer, the hard-living chef de cuisine of the Alpenrose. Ah, Urban, a man who had worked at some of the biggest hotels in the Alps, who rested his sirloins in clarified butter, and for whom the phrase "too early for a drink" didn't exist. Urban took me to the back door of the restaurant and pointed out my room, just up from the kitchen. A one-minute straight shot down on skis and a five-minute walk up after service. Not bad.

I also met Fäger Brunner, my Swiss guide–coworker–cooking partner and accomplice in arms. Fäger is the kind of guy who can climb 2,300 meters, make a traditional *schlorzifladen* (pear paste tart), kill a bear with his own two hands, and ski off-piste for days with nothing but a sleeping bag, chocolate, and an avalanche balloon. Fäger became one of my closest friends, and still is today.

This page, top, Wildhaus, and bottom, Fäger Brunner. Opposite page, Fäger Brunner raising the flag. Previous page, Alp trippin'.

A year and a half later, my childhood pal Eric Moore couldn't resist joining me, and the three of us became inseparable. (Eric now owns two great bars in Portland, The Richmond and The Freehouse, where you can find both amazing alpen macaroni and a full OP meat menu.) On our days off, Fäger, Eric, and I had nothing to do but explore, hike, dream up dishes, talk about girls we didn't know, and ski and snowboard (which, ironically, made me love the sport once again). Lunches were a skiable feast—we'd trek as high or as far as we could, then share extraordinary dishes matched only by extraordinary views.

For ten years—ever since leaving Switzerland, really—I had been looking for a reason, an excuse to go back to Wildhaus. So much of what I do, and who I am, is inspired by my time in this tiny mountain village. Everyone there—from the young to the very old—works so damn hard, six days a week, with only two weeks off a year. This dedication fosters true craftsmanship: whether it's Jörg Brügger making *bündnerfleisch*, or Jakob Knaus making *alpkäse*, each day they do the exact same thing, but the result is always different and never perfect. The craft and the product are alive. And to me, alive and changing is better than perfect.

This page, the intrepid team from left, Eric Wolfinger, Jess Hereth, Elias Cairo, Meredith Erickson, Fäger Brunner, and Alison Christiana. Opposite page, top, Bueger Stump, and bottom, Elias Cairo.

This traditional way of working is what I strive for with the meat plant at Olympia Provisions. So as we at OP were beginning to reach critical mass in terms of expansion, I needed a reminder of my past in order to find our way forward. Because Wildhaus had influenced me in such a profound way, I decided to go back.

Over the course of ten days in June, Meredith and I visited Swiss sausage makers, local heroes, and old friends—with Fäger as my guide. We saw people living simply in the most extraordinary of places. The next pages trace our journey with photos, and anecdotes. (You can also use what follows as an itinerary. We want you to.)

Die Tat ist Alles, Nicht der Ruhm

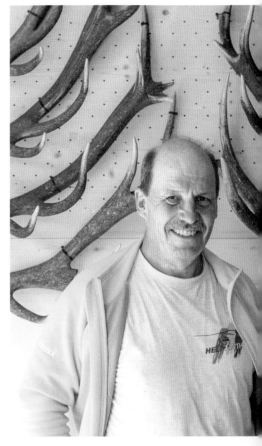

The task is everything, not the glory.

This is the motto of Stump's Alpenrose; it's carved in wood on the dining room wall, right above the family table where the staff usually sits. This is where it all started for me, and so where better to begin this trip than dinner here?

A little context: Stump's is a country inn and restaurant built as a small guesthouse for tired and thirsty climbers. It was taken over by the Stump family in 1912, when grandfather Stump bought it using money won in a ski jumping competition. His two sons, Roland and Bueger, eventually inherited the inn and are running it today. Under them it has become one of the most popular hotels in the Toggenburg area. That's partly due to its wellness program (brine stream bath? check; mountain hut sauna? check; fresh springs pond for swimming? check) and partly due to its alpine charm (it's normal to have a cow stick its head in your room).

Roland and Bueger were my bosses back in the nineties, and they still felt like my bosses when I visited twelve years later (funny how we remain the dominion of our first mentors). Roland runs the day-to-day administration of the hotel, along with the floor of the restaurant and the wine program. An elegant man, he is the perfect host. Bueger, the older brother, is another story. I would say that he is my mentor and hero, but I know he will read this and think I am a baby, so I won't say that. Bueger is a butcher, cook, forager, *jägermeister* (master hunter), maintenance man, and, in retirement, a successful helicopter pilot. You gotta love a man this diversified.

I remember arriving at work at 6:00 a.m. to see Bueger stepping off his CAT tractor after plowing the surrounding area. He'd walk into the cold room, having been up for hours already, and begin butchering fresh steinbucks, breaking them down perfectly within minutes. He was a machine. Usually around that time, his wife, Marlyse, a World Cup downhill skier, would bring down his three small daughters to

have breakfast together at the family table. He made the kitchen rounds with Urban and tasted everything: the consommés had to be perfect; the spätzle long enough to hold sauce; the elk meat tender, but not overcooked; and the sauce thickened with blood had to shine like a new car.

Jägermeister is a title of prestige, especially in Wildhaus, which is a completely self-sustaining township. In order to officially be named *jägermeister*, one has to have a sponsor—a sort of godfather—from whom to learn the traditions. You need to understand the movement of your prey throughout the spring and fall. You need to know the ins and outs of rifle responsibility and practice it over a number of years. In short, you can't just walk into a Walmart in Switzerland, buy a gun and a few beers, and try your luck in the woods. There, you would be fined and banned, and earn the mockery of the village if you shot a healthy animal or a prize buck. Mounted on one of Bueger's walls at home are twelve sets of antlers, showcasing his proudest claim in life. Over twelve years, he had followed this elk, collecting the antlers it shed each year. He waited for it to slow and become sick. In its eighteenth or nineteenth year, when the elk was too weak to stand, he killed it.

Though technically retired, Bueger still works six days a week as a helicopter pilot. He mainly transports foodstuffs and rescues mountain livestock from certain death. He says he does it to "stay young, strong, healthy." I originally came to Alpenrose because of the strength of its kitchen, nothing more. I thought I wanted to become a cook first and foremost—a restaurant owner like my dad. Looking back, it was Bueger who planted the seed of sausage making in me.

* * *

The dinner at Alpenrose was a homecoming of sorts; the food was heartwarming, and really at a higher level than my cooking all those years ago—I would have had my ass handed to me by chef Stefan Radzuweit and crew. The charcuterie board was piled with *bündnerfleisch* (dried cured beef tenderloin), *mostbrockli* (smoked and mountain-dried beef eye), *bauernspeck* (pork belly peppered, smoked, fried, and cured), *fleischkäse* (oven-roasted baloney), *landrauchschincken* (pork leg peppered, smoked, and dried), and so on. Roland opened a couple of bottles from Swiss winemaker Jann Marugg. Rich veal cutlets were passed around, along with *truite en bleu*, vegetables, and the lightest, most delicious brats I've ever had. We told tales and toasted with *alpenbitter* as diners around us enjoyed steak tartare made tableside. All was right with the world. We fell asleep drunk, happy, and excited to be in the mountains.

The Trek Begins

The next morning, we left the Toggenburg Valley and headed east for the hour-long journey by car to the Appenzell Alps. Guiding us was Säntis, the king of these mountains at 8,200 feet (2,500 meters). We parked in the town of Wasserauen and took the *luftseilbahn* (gondola) to the Family Sutter's Berggasthaus Ebenalp restaurant for lunch.

The vista at the Ebenalp is endless. To the north is Lake Constance (the Bodensee), with Germany just beyond. To the east are the snow-capped mountains of Austria. If you squint, you can see the mountains of Lech, one of the best-kept skiing secrets of the Alps. And squint we did, as it was already 95°F (35°C) at noon. The sun was blazing and our thirst was something strong. We took a seat, reviewed the menus, and reminded one another that this was only the first of many lunches, so everyone should just calm down. A round of *zitronenpanachés*, the Swiss answer to the German *radler* and the British shandy (half lemonade, half pilsner) was ordered.

The Alpstein range has the highest density of restaurants in the Swiss Alps, twenty-seven in all. We know this because every time we sat down to a meal—starting in the Ebenalp—there were the same placemats: a thoughtfully illustrated watercolor map of the Alpstein detailing the whereabouts of each hut, or basic inn. It's only when you factor in the scale—every hut is at an extremely high altitude and must figure out the best way to provision itself—that this number becomes truly impressive.

Our first meal turned out to be one of our best meals: a simple toggi schnitzel (Swiss Cordon bleu) with alpen macaroni, applesauce, and a killer *fitness teller salat* (an array of local salads). The descent from the Ebenalp to our next destination was a southwesterly meandering route around the back of the mountain, zigzagging on a narrow trail. We walked down the trail toward the Aescher, a famed 170-year-old hut built into the curve of the mountain, where we were headed for dinner and where we would camp for the night. Fäger told us about working there, about routinely cooking lunch for four hundred-plus people and about sleeping up there through the five-month season, ten days on, two days off, often working eighteen hours per day.

The current owners of the Aescher are Bernard Knechtle; his wife, Nicole; and Bernard's father, Benny. Bernard also works in the off-season as a butcher for the sausage maker Franz Fässler (more about Franz later). The Aescher is officially known as the Berggasthaus Aescher-Wildkirchli; Wildkirchli is the name of a system of caves in the Appenzell that housed hermits beginning in the 1600s. In the 1850s, the last of the hermits apparently fell to his (or her) death, leaving his or her furnishings behind in the cave. The restaurant has stood nearby for more than 170 years and through many incarnations.

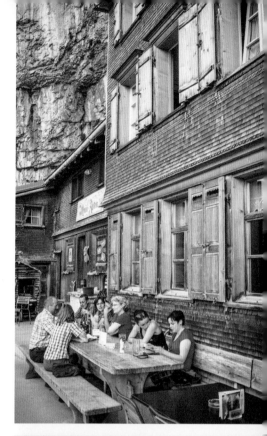

Opposite page, top, the Aescher, and bottom, Benny Knechtle. This page, top, the deck of the Aescher, and bottom, pork steak with herb butter and the Aescher's famous rösti with alpkäse *cheese.*

Tourists typically come for the cave and its adjacent small church. We came for the rösti.

Fäger described how a restaurant perched on the edge of a cliff, with no road, no mailing address, no accessible purveyors, and no access to public water, actually works. "The food arrives via cable car three times per week. The bottom of the cable car opens and a large pallet is slowly lowered into the cave adjacent to the Aescher. The cave is basically the stockroom. The temperature in the cave is around 5°C (41°F); thankfully, this is ideal for potatoes, as we mostly serve rösti. In the same cave, there is the water reservoir, a swimming pool–sized tub containing 120,000 liters (31,680 gallons) of spring water that drips down from the rocks above and accumulates. The water must last from May through November, the entirety of the Aescher's season."

And so rösti—raw potatoes grated and then fried—is the house specialty by necessity. Pasta and rice would use too much water; only potatoes, which provide their own water, work here. Aescher's rösti is made in a gigantic pressure cooker off to the side of the hut. The only indication that magic is happening is the opening of a valve pipe and intermittent release of steam through a tiny wooden window. We sat down for dinner: rösti with speck and eggs, rösti with *alpkäse* cheese, rösti with sausage, and rösti with a simple green mountain salad.

Bernard and I sat at the *stammtisch* (the big wooden family table you see in every hut) drinking apple brandy and talking about charcuterie until sunrise. Bernard, being the macho mountain man he is, constantly disappeared and then reappeared with one or another of his homemade wares. There was ibex salami cured with pepper, smoked elk *shubli* (a mix of ibex, pork, and elk, smoked then cured) and my favorite, canned pork belly. He cures it skin-on and slow-cooks it in a can until the skin is tender. He then cools it, seals it, and transports it to the restaurant so that throughout the summer, whenever anyone orders a meat board, all he has to do is open a can and slice out a healthy chunk (alongside a drop of mustard and a slice of bread, of course). The pork belly tastes wild and intensely flavorful. It tastes of something you could only find in a place like the Aescher. This is *terroir*. Bernard tracks animals over their lifetimes, butchers them beautifully, utilizes all the parts, and cures them perfectly. It is rare to find this approach anywhere in the world and almost impossible to find it at such high quality. I simply love seeing how Bernard works. He is a third-generation butcher who gets after it day in and day out with so much pride. A lifelong work ethic is engrained in the people who live in the mountains: Do it for life or until your children take over, and do it with as little ego as possible. It is totally the opposite of the get-rich-fast stuff; it's all about building a job and a life that you love. I hope one day to set up a similar approach at OP in Oregon.

Opposite page, top, Franz Fässler, and bottom, siedwurst.

Franz Fässler at Metzgerei Fässler

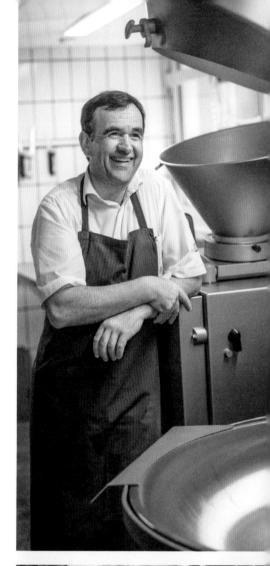

The most famous butcher/sausage maker in the region is Franz Fässler, whose specialty is *siedwurst*. Our reason for visiting was to see his shop and watch him at work. Tough to find outside of the Alps, *siedwurst* is like a Swiss cousin to *weisswurst*. They are both emulsified sausages, similar in size but with one big difference: *siedwurst* is mostly beef and *weisswurst* is all pork. This is why *siedwurst* has a pinkish color, compared to all-white *weisswurst*.

The basic recipe for *siedwurst* is 80 percent beef trim, 10 percent pork shoulder, and 10 percent pork fatback, plus fresh nutmeg, white pepper, caraway, and cardamom. Small wooden skewers tied onto the casings bookend the sausages; this is the mark of *siedwurst*, and a calling card of Appenzell. We looked on as Franz's son Benjamin tied the sausages onto the skewers with a ninja-quick motion. Taking pity on us, he slowed to one-quarter time to give us a tutorial in tying. Soon everyone was tying and, except for the hum of the machinery, it felt like we were back in the meat department at OP for a moment.

After being tied, the sausages are poached for twenty minutes. Franz drained the vat and, while the sausages were still hot, peeled them like bananas. He brought out a loaf of *bürli* (country bread) from the front of his shop (a showcase for meats, locals cheeses, and every Lindt chocolate bar imaginable) and diced the sausages for us to try. They tasted like a sausage that has stood the test of time. We washed it down with *flauder ilsfee* (apenzeller elderflower iced tea).

Next he showed us *burespeck*, a blackened bacon referred to as "farmer's bacon," which is made according to a relatively simple recipe: pork belly is cured for a week in salt. Every two days, the belly is turned (overhauled) and then rubbed in juniper and rosemary and brushed with a bizarre-looking black lacquer of burnt sugar and water. The bacon is then slowly smoked up and down (that is, at 104°F/40°C, then 176°F/80°C, then 104°F/40°C) over the course of two days, giving the bacon an out-of-this-world depth of flavor. Most Americans think of speck as smoked country ham from Südtirol. But in Switzerland, that is known as *landrauchschinken*. The speck we were learning about at Fässler's is closer to what Americans know as bacon. But this bacon, the *burespeck*, is served cold.

We spent a morning watching the Fässler operation—a fourth-generation butcher who still works by hand. Sure, there was machinery on a small scale, but the handwork is his signature. Franz and his wife and son work six days per week, continually tweaking and perfecting their products. While Franz was teaching us how to make speck, he was also monitoring batches, answering the phone, giving customers change, and overseeing the nonstop cleaning required of any meat

plant. You could see the mastery in his muscle memory. He understood what was happening at every level of his business. Elegant isn't a word you associate with the meat business, but that's exactly what he was.

We left inspired (and full). We parked the car at the base of Wasserauen and started what became a hot and very sweaty one-and-a-half hour hike toward the Seealpsee, a mystical lake we had spotted from the Aescher.

On our way, we came across a small hut with a pen of five or six happy hogs. Like in a fairytale, the door swung out and a young and handsome bearded Swiss greeted us. Slim and wearing the typical light blue wool edelweiss shirt covered by a leather apron, he told us he couldn't have us in right then as he was making *alpkäse* and fresh air would interrupt his cellar's humidity. For a moment, it felt like we were in Williamsburg, Brooklyn. He told us his name was Michael Graff and this was his family's hut, known as the Little Alp of Seealpsee. His pigs and goats fed off the whey from his cheese, and he fed off his pigs and goats. He was sweet and proud and he let us drink from his spring.

We continued to the Seealpweiden, a large alp owned by the Appenzeller Brewery and leased to Adolph Fässler (no relation to Franz). Adolph and his wife sell their cheese from their small hut. It's normal for passersby to stop in for a *panaché* and chat before purchasing fresh butter, goat cheese, or pure cow's milk *alpkäse*.

He showed us to his cellar and told us he had been born in this hut and spent all of his sixty-three summers here. Down below there was a stream that ran through his cellar. The humidity of the stream plus the subterranean temperature worked as his fridge, keeping the raw milk cold before he makes it into cheese and butter. Along the walls there were birthday cake–size wheels of cow's milk cheese. He gave us each a spoonful of cheese and said that, on a typical day, he can make a maximum of eighteen wheels. It tasted like ice cream. We bought butter and a quarter of a wheel, and, as we were racing against the sun, we wedged these gems into our backpacks and said goodbye.

The Berggasthaus Forelle, whose name means "trout mountain inn," is a magical inn and restaurant at the foot of the Seealpsee. It's in a tight valley surrounded by trees and high alps, the kind of place where you would expect to see wizards and elves. But nope, it's just groups of Swiss-Germans swimming naked and drinking Alstätten wines. We sat down to a few pretty little bottles of Heini Haubensak (AOC St. Gallen) and ordered a few *truites en bleu* and a couple of plates of woodland garlic spätzle with *alpkäse* cheese, crispy onions, and applesauce.

This page, top, Adolph Fässler standing in the kitchen where he has made cheese for sixty years, and bottom, Michael Graff looking devilishly handsome.

Family Knaus

Six hours later, at 4:30 a.m., we were back in the Toggenburg Valley, drinking instant coffee outside of a van. The air was crisp and it was absolutely silent. Even the surrounding cows were still asleep. The idea was to hike up to Alp Troosen (6,889 feet/2,100 meters), observe, and partake in a little vertical transhumance at the dairy of the Family Knaus, and maybe even catch the sunrise.

After a rigorous forty-five minute ascent we arrived at the hut and were met by a herd of sleepy dairy cows queuing for milking. Melchior Knaus, the son of Jakob (the cheese maker), greeted us quickly. He wore a belt with a stool attached to it, making easier his constant over-and-under movement among his beloved cows. We watched him work tirelessly throughout the morning, gently milking, removing the odd burr from his animals, replacing milk cans, and generally keeping order in the barn. He only broke once, to watch the sun come up over the Scharfsberg ("sheep mountain"). "The best twenty seconds of my day is when the mountain splits the sun in two," he said.

Just below, in a small and humid hut, we watched Jakob work his alchemy in a large copper pot, transforming the milk into Alpkäse. Though each alpine cheese is a similar product, it's the individual cheese maker who gives each its nuance. Jakob, for example, puts a knife's tip of his own alpine grass into the vat. The grass particles spread throughout the mixture and a gas forms around each particle, creating little holes in the cheese. That is Jakob's mark.

From the cows munching to the final wheel being shelved, we watched the entire process from sunrise (5:00 a.m.) to 1:00 p.m. In the afternoon, we munched on large hunks of the alpine cheese; in it we could taste the diversity of the pasture and purity of the milk.

The Knaus family has been doing this for three generations: taking the cows up to graze from May to September, dealing with every weather condition imaginable, seeing very few people, and often working eighteen-hour days. And when you're there you can see why; it's completely intoxicating.

This page, top, alpkäse, *and bottom, Melchior Knaus.*

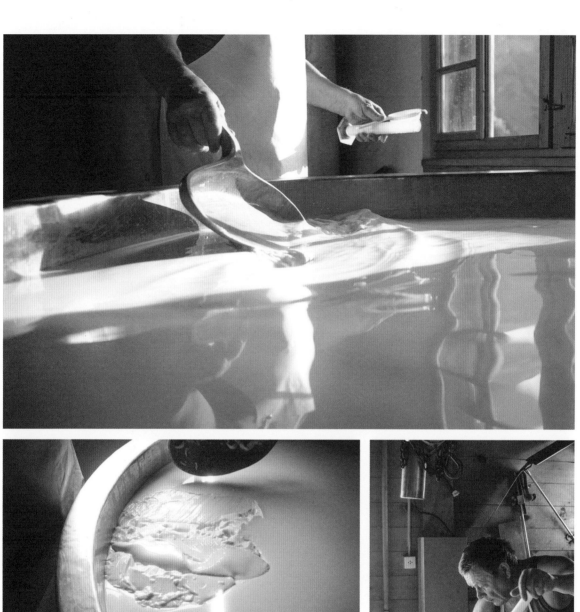

Family Knaus, making cheese.

This page, top, Jörg Brügger in his Alpen dry room, bottom, pancetta drying. Opposite page, top, Bündnerfleisch in the press, and bottom, Bündnerfleisch out of the press. Previous page, Jakob Knaus trimming alpkäse.

Bündnerfleisch

The next day we drove one and a half hours directly south, just west of Davos and so close to the Italian border that we could feel it. Things there are just slightly slower, and people are just slightly tanner. The goal this day: to meet the last independent *bündnerfleisch* maker, Jörg Brügger at Brügger Parpan. Parpan is a teeny village in the township of Graubünden and, like Champagne or Appenzeller cheese, Bündnerfleisch can only be the real deal if it's made in Graubünden. This is because of its particular climate, or rather its position in the world, which is essential to every aspect of the process (this of course doesn't stop good people from making decent *bündner* elsewhere). For a comparison, I would say that taste-wise *bündner* is similar to bresaola in Italy or *viande des grisons* in France.

Jörg explained to us that his great-grandfather had been a farmer in Parpan and that during winter months, he had extra beef shoulder and thigh meat, but no way to preserve it. To avoid wasting the meat, his great-grandfather developed a technique of curing it with white wine and salts and then seasoning and hanging it in his cooler. But he also needed three other components that he didn't have: natural humidity, temperature, and airflow. He needed to cure the meat first in a cooler temperature and then finish it in a warmer temperature. He found land down the road from his original farm, a perfect spot of where the valley bends and the north wind (the *Bise*) and south wind (the *Föhn*) meet. There was also a fresh alpine stream: the key to humidity. And so he began to build. He built a log house where the upper floor had two sections: one inner space surrounded by gridded logs (for the second round of curing) and an outer periphery for the meat to hang above the stream in the outdoors (for the first round of curing). He began to sell his wares, selling out as soon as each batch was complete.

Eventually Jörg's grandfather took over the operation and refined the product one step further. He realized that if he wanted to dry meat more evenly, it made sense to press it. And so he built a wooden and steel press (see photo, right), the same one Jörg uses today. The following paragraphs explain how to make *bündnerfleisch* à la Brügger.

Butcher one leg of beef into five individual pieces: bottom round, top round, eye round, knuckle, and knuckle round.

Create a cure of white pepper, nitrate, and fine sea salt. Sprinkle the cure in the bottom of a large plastic bin with a spigot at the bottom. Rub each of the meat pieces with the cure and shake it off gently. Start with the biggest piece of meat—the bottom round—and place it at the bottom of the container. Layer in the rest of the meat according to size so that the smallest piece is at the top.

Each day, drain the container twice, recycling the cure by pouring it over the top again. (The salt turns to liquid when it pulls moisture out of the meat.) Having a really large container with a spigot in the bottom is key. Jörg also wedges in a salt meter and checks the salinity daily. The smallest pieces at the top finish first (after two weeks) and go to hang first. The rest follow in due time, with the biggest piece (the one at the bottom) curing for five weeks. When we asked for a visual cue to know when the meat is ready, Jörg said, "I could lie to you and say there is a way to know, but it's futile to talk of it; it's a learned trade. You have to touch each piece to know. You have to work at it."

An aside: This curing method blows my mind. Of all my travels in the global meat universe, this is the most finely tuned, well-honed product I have ever seen. I couldn't believe the simplicity of the process. Why didn't I figure it out? It gave me goose bumps—or, as the Swiss would say, *hühnerhaut pyjamas* ("chicken-skin pajamas").

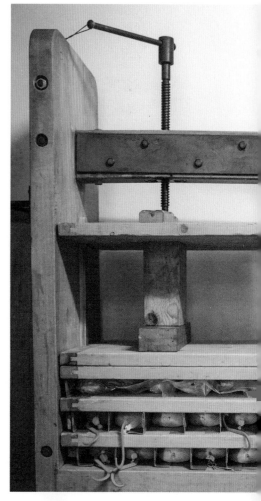

Next, the meats are netted and moved to the balcony. Outside during the winter, the gems are kept cold, and the alpine air whips them into arid shape. It's out here that the first molds begin to appear as the crystals begin to dry. When this happens, the meat is moved inside, where it's about 50°F (10°C) degrees warmer (there's no heat, the meat is just sheltered slightly by the log walls). During the height of production, this room holds up to ten thousand pieces of *bündner-fleisch*. Each piece has to be rotated daily and pressed nine times during its curing cycle.

This is when we realized that Jörg is a complete slave to his meat. It's just him and one assistant. He has to be one hundred percent tuned in to the wind, temperature, and humidity. He needs to know what the weather has done, what it's doing, and what it will do next. If he gets it wrong or is unlucky with the weather, then, like a wine producer, he will lose his stock and his income for the year. He only makes one "vintage" of meat a year.

Jörg makes thirty thousand pieces to sell per year. "What I do is the opposite of what many young people are doing today; it's more work for less money, to ensure perfection," he told us as we picnicked on sliced *bündner*, bread, and hunter's wine. "With technology, people can make it twice as fast. There is one plant down the road that creates my entire inventory in one week. You have to be quite strong to do this work, and my daughters, at this point, cannot. So if you know someone who is looking to get into the *bündner* business . . . "

The Hike up to the Rotsteinpass

This pass sits at 6,961 feet (2,122 meters) and straddles the border of Appenzellerland and Toggenburg. It's completely wild and rocky and extremely steep, and has snow cover pretty much year-round.

We took the tram up to Mt. Säntis in full cloud cover. We couldn't see thirteen feet (four meters) in front of us, which I think might have been a blessing for the first timers: we could not see the traverse across the snow fields, or the small wire to hold onto the side of the mountain, or the depth of the plunge below. Our goal was the Berggasthaus Rotsteinpass, to visit the Wyss Räss family (Cäcilia and Albert Wyss Räss III, and Albert Wyss Räss IV), with whom I spent time as an apprentice. And also to eat one of my favorite things in the whole world: authentic *hirsh peffer*, essentially an elk or ibex stew thickened with pig's blood. Why is this *hirsh peffer* the best I've had? Because both Alberts are tremendous hunters and cooks; they kill the animals in the fall, prepare the stew off site in the winter, and then can it in order to transport it to the hut to serve to hungry hikers throughout the summer.

This page, top, Berggasthaus Rotsteinpass, and bottom, en route to Rotsteinpass. Opposite page, a tricky trail section en route to dinner.

Just as we came within sight of the restaurant, the sun began to shine through the clouds and we could hear horns cracking and smashing. Starting out, we thought we might see one steinbock (alpine ibex), but we saw about thirty, all on the front steps of the restaurant, and all in a big ole rutting match over one female. Albert III said he has never

This page, top, Hans Neffs on his porch, and bottom, Hans's hut. Opposite page, fitness teller salat. *Previous page, steinbock (ibex) on the move above Wildhaus.*

in his fifty-some years seen anything like it. It was surreal to then step inside and enjoy the most incredible *hirsh peffer*, better even than I remember it, served on fluffy polenta. It still blows my mind that the Swiss love the mountains so much that they can actually support restaurants in such crazy locations.

On our last afternoon, we went up to the hut of local legend Hans Neffs. Hans's hut is a fifteen-minute hike up from the Alpenrose and, when I was apprenticing, Hans would often yell at me to come have a beer and smoke a cigarette. With a tough exterior, a heart of gold, and the eyes of someone who has seen a whole lot of good and bad, Hans is the ultimate Toggenburg personality.

We cooked all afternoon on the *schwenker*, a simple outdoor campfire grill, making the classics of the region that we had tasted over the last week. Fäger made *sauerbraten* and *siedfleisch*; our photographer, Eric, made *alpenbrod*; and the rest of us made *fitness teller salat*, organized our wine stash (i.e., drank), and prepared the tiny hut for company. Around 5 p.m., Hans and Roland, and Bueger and Marlyse and their daughter, Tina, came up. They were our guests, and we drank to them for hosting us during this week, for the impact they had on me more than twenty years ago, and for their relentless inspiration to make products with integrity and love.

This page and opposite, scenes from the meal at the hut, and next spread, the final toast.

PART

2

THE
RESTAURANTS
AND THEIR RECIPES

Stories of restaurant beginnings are too often told with the seriousness of Genesis or the drama of VH1's *Behind the Music*. Even if it went that way, I wouldn't tell it like that. The story of what OP is, and how it came to be, is quite straightforward: the idea was always to have a restaurant with a USDA-approved meat plant beside it. But as my role was to build the plant and run it as head salumist, I only had half of the equation figured out. Though I didn't know it at the time, the second half of the plan was catalyzed when I met Nate Tilden. (On the same day, as fate would have it, I was nearly electrocuted while cooking dinner outdoors for my sister Michelle. But that's another story.)

At the time, Nate was not yet the co-owner of the perpetually busy Clyde Common and Spirit of 77. He was a line cook at Castagna, the restaurant in town that constantly had a two-hour line and was absolutely bananas from the time it opened until it closed. Nate was working the oven/fryer station and he hired me to be the grill/sauté man. Two cooks, plus 150 to 200 diners, plus all the dishes made to order equals some of the best times I've ever had cooking. Nate and I became fast friends.

Within months, I was working as the sous chef alongside Nate, until he was serendipitously approached by the Ace Hotel to run Clyde Common within the hotel. I carried on at Castagna, but after four years there, I was majoring in meat-making with a minor in restaurants. I was working big hours, but in my mind I was plotting my own provisions company.

Having watched our parents slave away in their own restaurants and having worked as a cashier herself since the age of six, Michelle didn't want any part of restaurant life. She was, however, the CFO at a large corporation and was willing to invest in me, thinking I would sell my wares here and there, mostly at farmers' markets, and aiming to break even.

In 2008, Michelle and I met Tyler Gaston, a country-singing line cook who was sweating his ass off nightly in the Clyde kitchen. Hailing from Oklahoma, Tyler is a man of many talents: he's sailed the seas in the Navy, mined uranium in Wyoming, worked oil fields in the Midwest, fly-fished most of Montana and Oregon, and cooked in some of the best kitchens in Portland, Chicago, and Seattle. Magnanimous and incredibly hardworking, Tyler connected instantly with Nate, Michelle, and me on the idea of a meat plant and a sidekick restaurant that could be a showcase for the products, but not limited to just that.

Opposite page, Alex Yoder,
OP's executive chef.

The only piece missing was the advisor, the Rick Rubin-esque sage who could seal the seams of our wooden boat as we set out to sea. We found that sage in Marty Schwartz, a friend of Nate's who was a regular at both Clyde Common and Castagna. Any night of the week, Marty would be at the bar of either restaurant, drinking whiskey, ordering whatever was vegetarian, and (usually) talking to a beautiful woman. But who is Marty Schwartz? Here are the things we know: He's from Massachusetts. He lived in Los Angeles at some point. He attended the Berklee College of Music. He has played at Red Rocks and is rumored to have a guitar named after him. He has a private farm in the mountains and an island off the coast of Panama. He has two awesome kids. All who know him love him.

The team had coalesced. Now we needed space. One came up for rent in southeast Portland's landmark Olympic Mills building, and Nate, Marty, and Michelle thought it would be the perfect spot for our endeavor. We could provide lunch and dinner to the folks who worked inside as well as those who worked at the neighboring Produce Row. Isolated almost directly under the Morrison Bridge (within five minutes of leaving OP you can be on the freeway to either San Francisco or Seattle), this area can't really be called a neighborhood. It's more of a thoroughfare for wholesale distributors, homeless folks, truck drivers, and the occasional restaurant. It's the Cannery Row of Portland. Regardless, by now you know that I am Greek and, therefore, fervently superstitious. So the fact that the building had the word "Olympic" in its name—I mean, it was already a done deal. That is, until the U.S. Olympic Committee told us it was game over for us using the word "Olympic" in our name. So now we're Olympia Provisions.

We agreed to the lease and began a three-month refurb. We all worked twenty-hour days, welding, painting, meat making, and building nonstop. Nate held the vision, designed the restaurant, and began the process of hiring employees; he's an absolute talent magnet. Nate's dad, Steve Tilden, a former general contractor and current artist, lent us his studio overlooking the Columbia River and put aside all of his other work to weld our meat cases and racks and build the stools and countertops. Marty stepped in and did whatever was needed (which he still does to this day); he was a pH tester for the sample meats, delivery driver, real estate agent, and our wise counselor—someone to buy us a drink and slowly talk us off the ledge when things looked bleak. Jeremy Pelley and Fritz Mesenbrink at OMFG Company designed our oft-imitated but never duplicated (okay, it's been duplicated many times) meat sign, branding, and labeling, for which they were paid in sausages.

I would like to say we had fun in the beginning and it all took off, but that would be a lie. In reality, it was terrible. I realized that being USDA-approved means that you do have a boss . . . the government.

I worked long days. My time spent cleaning the plant equaled the time spent actually making meat. Tyler worked double shifts in the restaurant for years. Every week, we would be at Pioneer Square or Jamison Square waiting for people to buy products from our pretty little farmers' market booths.

Just as I was considering an out—serving coffee at a diner or drinks at a sports bar was looking so damn good at this point—we won four Good Food Awards for our loukanika, saucisson d'Arles, pork liver mousse, and pickles! We swept all of the big houses, though it had zero emotional effect on me. But from this moment, the phone started ringing. From Bi-Rite Market in San Francisco, Sam Mogannam (to whom I cannot give enough credit) called requesting a wholesale app, as did Dean & DeLuca. (We didn't even know what a wholesale app was.)

At this point, Michelle chose to leave her cushy job and slug it out full-time as our CFO and co-owner. She was handling sales out of the prep kitchen, the only place that had any space for a desk. But in actuality, there wasn't that much to handle; we were completely maxed out. As soon as the meat was made, it was packaged and out the door. In my wildest dreams, I imagined that we would have two, maybe three accounts, but by 2011 we had close to three hundred.

Within one year of our awards sweep, the OP Southeast restaurant was heaving, and the meat plant was splitting at the seams. In early 2011, we leased a large, gorgeous space on Thurman Street in northwest Portland just under the Fremont Bridge, a corner building with many windows and heavy pedestrian traffic—it was a Greek man's dream. The area has bridges, train tracks, plenty of homeless folks, and a grown-up crowd. The space was more or less exactly what I was looking for—it had natural light, floor drains, and all the electricity I could ever use. It was a turnkey meat shop/restaurant. We moved in and all was perfect . . . for two years, until the meat shop outgrew the space and we moved again, strangely enough, back to southeast Portland in the old Tazo tea plant, two blocks from where we had been originally.

The restaurants, with their constant moving parts (new menus, wine, customers, and other things we don't have to deal with in the meat plant), keep us grounded, and we often say the locations are like siblings: they share the same lineage but each has its own identity. OP Southeast is still our HQ (you know, first-born and all), where Alex Yoder makes the kind of food I always want to eat. OP Northwest has a respectful sophistication to it. The wine lists at both locations, chosen by Jess Hereth, are Eurocentric, refreshing, and made by like-minded producers—ergo, simply what you'd want to drink with our charcuterie.

As the sun moves from east to west over the course of the day, the OP atmosphere also changes, lazy brunch giving way to business lunch, followed by wine time, and then dinner service. The chapters are organized accordingly, and represent a typical day at OP.

THE OP BENEDICT

SERVES 4

HOLLANDAISE REDUCTION

2 large shallots

6 sprigs fresh thyme

2 tablespoons black peppercorns

1 bottle (750 ml) white wine
(as you will reduce this to under
2 tablespoons, go cheap)

1 cup (240 ml) champagne vinegar

HOLLANDAISE SAUCE

1 pound (455 g) unsalted butter

4 egg yolks

2 tablespoons Hollandaise Reduction
(above)

Juice of 1 lemon

2 tablespoons kosher salt

8 eggs

4 English Muffins (page 198), halved

1 pound (455 g) thinly sliced
Sweetheart Ham (page 111)
or applewood smoked ham

1 teaspoon smoked paprika

1 bunch chives, thinly sliced

Maldon salt

TO SERVE (OPTIONAL)

Laser Potatoes (page 196)

Many folks rate a breakfast or brunch restaurant on the quality of its eggs Benedict, and I truly feel that those people will find their holy grail right here at Olympia Provisions. In a DIY town like Portland, our Benedict is for sure the most DIY, which may make it the most DIY in the country. From the English muffin that is mixed, rolled, cut, seared, and baked in the oven to the sweetheart ham that is butchered, brined, injected, netted, and smoked, you would be hard pressed to find another eggs Benedict that has been given more love. We serve this with a side of our famous Laser Potatoes (page 196).

To streamline cooking, it's best to make the hollandaise reduction a day ahead of time. Before you start on the actual hollandaise, make sure all of the provisions are close at hand: the sliced English muffins, the ham, the eggs, the garnishes. It all comes together a bit quickly in the end so you'll want to have everything near. Set out the garnishes (smoked paprika, chives, Maldon salt) in little bowls so they are easily accessible.

1. To make the hollandaise reduction, slice the shallots into thin rounds and add them, along with the thyme, peppercorns, wine, and vinegar, to a large pot and bring to a boil over medium-high heat. Boil the mixture until the liquid has reduced to a total volume of 2 tablespoons, about 40 minutes. Strain the liquid through a doubled layer of cheesecloth, lifting the cloth out of the strainer and squeezing it until all the liquid is extracted. Discard the solids and refrigerate the liquid.

2. Preheat a large griddle to medium-high and begin heating a large pot with about 4 inches (10 cm) of water; you'll want the water simmering when the hollandaise is done. Prepare and assemble your ingredients for the hollandaise and for the final preparation. It all goes quickly once you start, and to serve the best eggs Benedict, you need to have all the pieces hot and ready at the same time.

3. To make the hollandaise sauce, put the butter in a small saucepan over low heat. Gently melt the butter, without stirring, until it becomes liquid and separates into fat (floating on top) and milk solids/water (settled at the bottom). While the butter is melting, put the egg yolks in a large flame-resistant bowl along with the hollandaise reduction. Whisk the yolks and reduction until combined. Place the bowl over low heat on your stove and whisk until the yolk mixture is warmed, then start whisking vigorously

to aerate the mixture. Keep the bowl over the burner and whisk, whisk, whisk until the mixture starts to hold stiff ribbons. Skim the foam off of the butter. Carefully dip a ladle into the melted butter so that only fat (the clearer top layer) flows into it. Add this clarified butter to the yolk mixture in a slow, steady stream, continually whisking, until the mixture becomes very thick and hard to whisk. At this point, dip your ladle down into the bottom of the butter pan to get some of the milk solids and water there; add this to the yolk mixture, whisking continually, to thin it out. Continue to alternate between clarified butter and milk solids until all the clarified butter has been mixed in and the hollandaise coats the back of a spoon (you may not use all of the milk solids). It's important to work as quickly as possible when making the hollandaise so it does not get too cool. Finish the sauce by whisking in the lemon juice and kosher salt. Keep in a warm spot near your stove until ready to serve.

4   Once the hollandaise is made and your griddle is hot, it is time to poach the eggs, toast the muffins, and heat the ham. Check that the water you started heating earlier is at a rolling simmer. Crack each egg into a cup or glass to aid in slipping them into the water. Stir the water to create a whirlpool, and quickly slip all of the eggs into the water. Lower the heat so the water is at a gentle simmer, and poach the eggs for 3 to 4 minutes, until the whites are set but the yolks are still runny. Meanwhile, toast the muffins and heat the ham on the griddle.

5   As the eggs are finishing, place two muffin halves on each of four plates and top each half with a portion of hot ham. With a slotted spoon, lift the eggs from the water and place one atop the ham on each muffin half. Ladle ¼ cup (60 ml) of hollandaise sauce over each. Garnish with smoked paprika, chives, and Maldon salt. Serve with a wedge of Laser Potatoes, if you like.

Variations: For Eggs Florentine, substitute ½ cup (110g) of blanched, well-drained spinach for the ham on each serving.

For Steak Benedict, substitute 2 thin slices of prime rib, heated on the griddle, for the ham in each serving. Top the beef and egg with 1 cup (30 g) of arugula.

LASER POTATOES

SERVES 12

12 tablespoons (175 g) unsalted butter, plus 3 tablespoons (42 g) for coating

4 cups (435 g) finely julienned onion

5 pounds (2.25 kg) Yukon gold potatoes, peeled

Fine sea salt and ground black pepper

Nothing epitomizes the Olympia Provisions endeavor to bridge tradition and future as this exquisitely simple but unique dish. When we were starting the brunch program at OP, we racked our brains to create an easy-to-execute potato dish. Akin to pommes dauphinois, Chef Colin's elegant solution gave us the perfect brunch potato—"the potatoes of tomorrow, today." The name is attributed to an ornery cook who told a customer we achieved the uniform thickness of the sliced potatoes with the help of a class 5 laser. If you don't have a laser at home, however, a Japanese mandoline will suffice.

1   Preheat the oven to 400°F (204°C). Combine the butter and onions to a large pot over medium heat and sweat the onions until they are tender and translucent, without browning, about 4 minutes. While the onions are sweating, slice the potatoes ⅓₂ to ¹⁄₁₆ inch (1 to 2 mm) thick on a mandoline into a large bowl. Add the onions and mix until the potatoes are coated with butter and the onions are evenly distributed. Add salt until you can just taste the saltiness over the sweetness of the onion and season lightly with pepper.

2   Cut a piece of parchment paper to fit a 10-inch (25-cm) cast-iron skillet, and press into the bottom of the pan. Layer the potato mixture into the pan until it is heaping full (see photos, right). Pour over any excess butter from onion mixture. Once the pan is full, cut another parchment paper cartouche and place it on top of the potato pile. Cover the pan with aluminum foil.

3   Place the pan on a baking sheet lined with parchment paper and bake for 1¾ to 2 hours, until you can pierce the potatoes with a skewer without resistance. To achieve a crispy surface, remove the foil and the top parchment and broil for the last 10 minutes.

4   Remove the pan from the oven and let cool for at least 45 minutes. Gently press the potatoes with a spatula until flat on top. Refrigerate to meld the flavors, at least 5 hours or up to overnight.

5   When ready to serve, preheat the oven to 400°F (204°C). Coat a baking sheet with 3 tablespoons melted butter. With a knife or spatula, carefully cut around the edge of the pan to loosen the potatoes. Invert the pan onto a cutting board or large plate and carefully remove the parchment paper. Trim any dark or ragged edges off the top of the potatoes, and cut into twelve wedges. Place as many wedges as you want to serve on a baking sheet and bake until golden brown and hot, 12 to 15 minutes. Wrapped with plastic and stored in the refrigerator, the unsliced potatoes will keep for 1 week.

ENGLISH MUFFINS

MAKES ABOUT 12 MUFFINS

¾ cup (180 ml) lukewarm water

1½ teaspoons active dry yeast

1 tablespoon plus 2 teaspoons (25 g) sugar

3 tablespoons (45 g) unsalted butter, plus extra butter for frying (optional)

¾ cup (180 ml) whole milk

4 cups (440 g) unbleached all-purpose flour, plus extra flour as needed and for rolling

1 tablespoon plus ¾ teaspoon fine sea salt

1 tablespoon cornmeal, for dusting

Canola oil for greasing the skillet

These muffins are made fresh daily by our pastry chef, Melissa McKinney, who says the key to balancing their flavor is adding the right amount of fine sea salt. She takes care to let the ingredients do the talking: "I want peach desserts to taste like a fresh peach. Raspberries to taste like raspberries. I like chocolate to taste deep and intense, and not overpowered with other flavors. For these muffins, it's just pure, high-quality ingredients. I make them straight up and basic." You will need a 3-inch (7.5-cm) round cutter for this recipe. Enjoy them toasted or fried with salted butter, jam, marmalade or lemon curd.

1 Combine the water, yeast, and sugar in a mixing bowl (if mixing by hand) or in the bowl of a stand mixer. Stir with a wooden spoon to break up the yeast and dissolve the sugar.

2 In a small pan over medium heat, melt the butter with half of the milk. Once the butter is melted, add the remaining milk to the melted butter mixture to cool it down. Add the butter and milk mixture to the yeast mixture, then add the flour and salt on top of the wet ingredients. If mixing by hand, beat the ingredients with a wooden spoon until they combine and form a dough. Turn the dough out onto a floured work surface and knead until you have a cohesive ball of dough that's neither too sticky nor too stiff; this will take about 4 minutes.

3 If using a stand mixer, attach the dough hook and mix on low speed until the ingredients combine and begin to resemble a dough. Increase the speed to medium and mix until the dough forms a ball, about 2 minutes. If the dough ball doesn't pull away from the bottom of the mixing bowl, knead in flour in small amounts until it does.

4 Put the dough in an oiled container, cover, and let rest for 30 minutes. It will double in volume, so make sure your container is large enough.

5 Line a large rimmed baking sheet with parchment paper and dust it with the cornmeal. Once the dough has doubled, turn it out onto a floured surface, and then fold the dough over itself, as if closing a book. Using a rolling pin, roll out the dough to a ¾-inch (2-cm) thickness. Using a 3-inch (7.5-cm) round cutter, cut out as many muffins as you can, placing them 1 to 2 inches (2.5 to 5 cm) apart on the prepared baking sheet. Moisten your hands with warm water, gather up the dough scraps, and pat them together.

CONTINUED

Roll out the scraps to a ¾-inch (2-cm) thickness, cut out as many rounds as you can, and place them on the baking sheet with the others. Lightly moisten another baking sheet with water and place it upside down over the muffins to keep them from drying out while the dough rises. Allow the muffins to rise at room temperature until doubled in size, about 30 minutes. Preheat the oven to 350°F (176°C).

6   When the muffins have doubled in size, preheat a cast-iron skillet or ovensafe griddle over medium heat. Drizzle 1 tablespoon of canola oil in the pan and place the muffins in the skillet, leaving at least 1 inch (2.5 cm) of space between them; you'll need to work in batches.

7   Cook for about 3 minutes until light golden on bottom, and then flip with a spatula. Cook for 3 minutes on the other side, then place the pan into the oven and bake for 5 minutes, until dark golden. Remove the muffins and let cool.

8   To serve, slice the muffins horizontally and toast until a light golden color or lightly butter and fry cut side down in a pan over medium heat.

FLAPJACK ATTACK

At the end of every brunch service, the OP kitchen cooks up this grand staff meal of perishables: pancakes, poached eggs, bacon, and hollandaise—an attack on the senses, the hangover, and the heart.

1 In a bowl, whisk together the flour, sugar, baking powder, and kosher salt. In another bowl, whisk together the egg, milk, and oil. Add the wet ingredients to the dry, and give a couple of stirs.

2 Place a skillet or griddle over medium heat and melt some butter on it. Ladle 2 or 3 tablespoons of batter into the pan for each pancake and cook until golden on each side, about 3 minutes total, melting more butter in the pan as needed to make eight pancakes.

3 To serve, put two pancakes, four slices of bacon, two poached eggs, and ½ cup (120 ml) of hollandaise on each plate.

SERVES 4

1 cup (110 g) unbleached all-purpose flour

1 tablespoon sugar

1 tablespoon baking powder

½ teaspoon kosher salt

1 egg

1 cup (240 ml) whole milk

2 tablespoons canola oil

Unsalted butter, for cooking the pancakes

16 slices bacon (page 108), cooked

8 eggs, poached

2 cups (480 ml) Hollandaise (pages 194–95)

KIELBASA HASH

SERVES 4

5 tablespoons (70 g) unsalted butter

2 cups (340 g) julienned white onion

3 tablespoons canola oil

2 pounds (910 g) Yukon gold potatoes, diced into ¼-inch (6-mm) cubes

10 ounces (280 g) fatty bacon, sliced into lardons

11 ounces (320 g) kielbasa, sliced into ¼-inch (6-mm) coins

8½ ounces (240 g) oyster mushrooms, thinly sliced

Leaves from 1 head frisée

4 eggs

This is a hefty dish for breakfast, or a perfect lunch or dinner after you've come in from the cold.

1 Preheat the oven to 425°F (218°C).

2 In a small pot over very low heat, melt the butter and add the onions. Cook for 35 to 40 minutes, stirring occasionally, until the onions are completely translucent but not at all browned. Remove from the heat and set aside.

3 While the onions cook, in a large frying pan over medium heat, warm the canola oil. Add the diced potatoes and sear them until dark golden brown, 3 to 5 minutes. Spread the potatoes on a baking sheet and bake for 15 minutes, until tender. Set the potatoes aside.

4 Fill a pot three-quarters full of water and bring to a simmer over medium heat; you'll use this to poach the eggs. In the same pan you used to sear the potatoes, cook the lardons and kielbasa over medium heat for about 2 minutes, until they release a bit of fat. Add the mushrooms and cook for another 3 minutes, until the lardons are nice and rendered and the mushrooms are golden brown. Drain in a colander and set aside.

5 Check that the water you started heating earlier is at a rolling simmer. Crack each egg into a cup or glass to aid in slipping them into the water. Stir the water to create a whirlpool and quickly slip all of the eggs into the water. Lower the heat so the water is at a gentle simmer and poach the eggs for 3 to 4 minutes, until the whites are set but the yolk is still runny.

6 While the eggs are poaching, in a large bowl, toss the onions, the potatoes, and the kielbasa mixture with the frisée. Divide the hash among four bowls. When the eggs are ready, use a slotted spoon to lift them from the water; place one atop each serving.

BAKED EGGS PEPERONATA

Chiles, eggs, and goat cheese baked and served in one cocotte big enough to share, with a scattering of kale chips and some toasted baguette? Done.

1. Preheat the oven to 325°F (163°C).

2. Toss the kale with the ¼ cup (60 ml) of olive oil until glossy and season lightly with sea salt. Spread the kale in an even layer on a baking sheet and toast in the oven until crisp, 8 to 10 minutes. Remove from the oven and set aside.

3. Place a 6- to 8-inch (15- to 20-cm) casserole dish in the oven and increase the oven temperature to 375°F (191°C). Let the dish heat until it's nice and hot, about 5 minutes. Remove it from the oven, add the 1 teaspoon of olive oil, and crack the eggs into the dish. Bake the eggs until the whites are set but the yolks are still runny, about 10 minutes. Remove from the oven and scatter the piquillo peppers, Anaheim chiles, and ancho chile over the eggs. Sprinkle with the chèvre. Return to the oven and bake for 3 minutes longer, until the chiles and cheese are warm.

4. Serve in the baking dish, garnished with the kale chips and with the toasted bread alongside.

SERVES 4

1 bunch kale, stemmed, and coarsely chopped

¼ cup (60 ml) plus 1 teaspoon extra virgin olive oil

Fine sea salt

6 eggs, at room temperature

4 jarred piquillo peppers, diced

4 Anaheim chiles, seeded, roasted, and diced

1 ancho chile, seeded, roasted, and diced

6 ounces (170 g) crumbled chèvre

1 sourdough demi-baguette, sliced and toasted

SWEET CREAM BISCUITS

These biscuits are perfect for soaking up gravy and are thus a necessary addition to any lumberjack breakfast. This recipe is the brainchild of our first pastry chef, Amelia Lane. To make these biscuits, you will need a 3-inch (7.5-cm) round cutter. Do not listen to antiquated advice about using a drinking glass instead of a cutter—this compresses the sides of the dough and prevents the biscuits from rising like a cylinder.

1 Preheat the oven to 375°F (191°C). Line a baking sheet with parchment paper or spray it with nonstick spray. In the bowl of a stand mixer fitted with the paddle attachment, combine the flour, kosher salt, sugar, baking powder, and chilled diced butter. Mix on the lowest speed until the butter is broken down into pieces the size of peas. Stop the mixer and feel the mixture with your fingers. If there are some pieces larger than others, press them flat between your thumb and forefinger. Turn on the mixer again to low speed and, while it is running, slowly add the buttermilk and cream. The dough will look wet and soft and midway through and you'll think, "This can't take the rest of the cream!" Just let it mix for a few turns of the paddle, and you will see that the cream is being absorbed by the flour. Once all the liquid is incorporated, let the dough sit in the bowl for a few minutes to allow the flour to absorb even more of the liquid.

2 Sprinkle some flour on your work surface. Turn the dough out of the bowl onto the work surface and sprinkle with a little flour. Gently press the dough with your hands into a rectangle. Use a rolling pin to roll out the dough until it is ¾ inch (2 cm) thick. Dip a 3-inch (7.5-cm) round cutter into some flour, cut out a biscuit, and place on the prepared baking sheet. Repeat this process, dipping the cutter into flour after each cut.

3 To make the salty butter, in a small saucepan over low heat, melt the butter with the kosher salt. Using a pastry brush, brush salty butter over the tops of the biscuits. Bake for 20 to 22 minutes, until the biscuits are golden brown and feel firm and springy to the touch. Store any leftover biscuits in an airtight container at room temperature; they will keep for 3 to 4 days.

MAKES ABOUT 12 BISCUITS

4 cups (440 g) unbleached all-purpose flour, plus extra flour for rolling and cutting

3½ teaspoons kosher salt

1 teaspoon sugar

1 tablespoon plus 2 teaspoons baking powder

½ cup (120 g) unsalted butter, diced and chilled

⅓ cup (90 ml) buttermilk

3 cups (720 ml) heavy cream

SALTY BUTTER

2 tablespoons unsalted butter

½ teaspoon kosher salt

BRATWURST GRAVY

What can we say? We love gravy. Gravy connects us to the great Western expansion that brought a lot of settlers to Oregon. Classic white cream gravy was a way to make almost anything on the trail palatable—or quite delicious, actually. At OP we are lucky enough to serve gravy on tender, yielding biscuits instead of hardtack, but it makes even those better, too. Of course, the use of OP bratwurst and some slightly advanced techniques make this gravy better than your grandma's.

1   In a small pot over low heat, melt the bacon fat. As it begins to liquefy, slowly whisk in the flour until thoroughly incorporated. Immediately remove from heat. Using a spatula, transfer the roux to a container and place in the fridge. Keep it there until it's good and solid, 20 to 25 minutes.

2   While the roux is cooling, heat a heavy medium-size pot over medium heat. Add the brat forcemeat to the pot. Using a wooden spoon, stir the forcemeat until the fat starts rendering and the forcemeat begins to brown, about 10 minutes. Remove from heat and drain, discarding the fat.

3   Remove the roux from the fridge and pop it out of its container. Cut it into Ping-Pong ball size pieces. Add the milk to a large pot and bring to a simmer over medium-high heat. Whisk the roux into the milk piece by piece, adding the next as soon as the previous one dissolves, whisking the whole time. The roux will bring down the milk's temperature, so the simmer will stop. When all the roux pieces have been added, bring the roux back to a simmer. Turn down the heat to low. Whisk occasionally, until you have a rich and savory flavor and the taste of flour is gone; this will take 10 minutes. Add the forcemeat, paprika, cayenne, pepper, and kosher salt, stirring to incorporate. Serve the gravy right away, or let cool and refrigerate in an airtight container for up to 10 days.

4   To reheat, pour ¼ cup (60 ml) milk into a medium pot. Using a wooden spoon, stir the cold gravy into the milk in four or five additions. Set the pot over low heat and allow the gravy to warm through while stirring occasionally, 5 to 6 minutes.

MAKES ABOUT 1 QUART (1 LITER)

¼ cup (60 ml) rendered bacon fat

¼ cup (50 g) unbleached all-purpose flour

1 pound (455 g) bratwurst forcemeat (see page 80)

1 quart (1 liter) whole milk, plus extra milk if reheating

½ teaspoon sweet paprika

½ teaspoon cayenne

1½ teaspoons coarsely ground black pepper

Kosher salt

: *On the way out of Portland, swing by Portland's* Lauretta Jeans *for cookies and pie. Drive down Division Street, home of* Stumptown, Pok Pok, *and* Ava Gene's *until 82nd Street. Hang a right and then take a left on Powell until you hit the I-26. Take the south ramp and, within 15 minutes, you're at the bottom of Mount Hood. This is called the Government Pass. At one point, you'll see the Timberline Lodge, which is the exterior of the Overlook Hotel from the movie* The Shining. *Continue following signs to Warm Springs, a Native American reservation. Cross a bridge that spans the Deschutes River. Hang a left at the blue abandoned gas station and drive down the dirt road for 5 minutes. You'll end at the parking lot for the Mecca Flats.*

Step out and fish for 4 hours and make everyone else wait in the car and drink on the riverbank. At this point, you're only about 1½ hours away from Portland.

To continue toward Camp Sherman, get back on I-26 south toward Madras, where it turns into the I-97. At the town of Redmond, stop at the Tumble On In for a refreshing beer and hop back in your car (safely!) and get back onto highway I-97, and follow signs for Camp Sherman. It's in the Ponderosa Forest, and looks like it should be crawling with ewoks.

On the way back, go over Santiam pass and through the Willamette Valley Corridor, hitting up the cute town of Sisters and the Sisters Coffee Company.

The Bonanza Trail

The month of October is my favorite time of year. It's when 4:00 p.m. can't come fast enough—especially on a Friday—and I can jump in my truck with Leather (my Brittany Spaniel) and Jess (my girlfriend and OP's wine buyer and restaurant manager) and head for the country. We are well positioned in Portland, just an hour's drive to some of the most scenic waters in the country: the McKenzie, Deschutes, and Metolious rivers. Mt. Hood National Forest alone has one hundred fifty different lakes, of which a good percentage are healthy and fishable.

Apart from making meat, my two passions are fly-fishing and pheasant hunting. If this whole meat-making thing doesn't work out, I would gladly bid farewell to city life and apply to work for the Forest Service or the Department of Agriculture.

Knowing this, customers and friends often ask me where to go that's within a two-hour drive from Portland. My answer to them (and to you) is Lake Creek Lodge in Camp Sherman, a Northwestern haven perfectly located along the Metolious in the heart of the Deschutes National Forest. I can't suggest any nearby restaurants, as cooking (and drinking) outdoors is a big part of the experience.

CHOUCROUTE GARNIE

The Thirty Years' War, which came to an end in 1648, gave Europe the concept of a strong sovereign state and gave France choucroute garnie. With the annexation of Alsace and Lorraine, France gained important strategic and gastronomic high ground. But enough dusty history. What of the dish? Sauerkraut, cooked with bacon, stock, and dry white wine, then garnished with pork—lots of pork. I'll give you the knowledge to make all of the components on the following pages, and here you can bring them together in one grand dish. (Or you can slide over to OlympiaProvisions.com to get a choucroute garnie kit, and still impress the hell out of your dinner guests.) Don't forget a crisp salad and copious amounts of crisp Riesling (Albert Boxler or Dönnhoff will do nicely) as perfect accompaniments.

SERVES 8

2 bay leaves

10 black peppercorns

16 small fingerling potatoes

8 slices bacon, cut crosswise into thin lardons

2½ pounds (1.1 kg) Kielbasa, cut crosswise

4 Bratwurst, cut crosswise (page 80)

4 Frankfurters, cut crosswise (page 101)

2½ pounds (1.1 kg) Sauerkraut (page 212)

1 tablespoon caraway seeds, toasted

2 cups (480 ml) chicken stock

1 cup (240 ml) dry Riesling

8 (⅛-inch/4-mm) slices Sweetheart Ham (page 111) or other good-quality smoked ham

Whole-grain mustard, for serving

1   In a medium pot, bring plenty of salted water to a boil along with the bay leaves and peppercorns. Taste the water—you want it to be saltier than the cooked potatoes. Add the potatoes and boil until tender when pierced with a fork, about 20 minutes. Drain and let cool, and then slice each potato in half lengthwise. Set the potatoes aside.

2   In a large Dutch oven over medium-low heat, sauté the bacon until crisp and its fat has rendered, about 20 minutes. Using a slotted spoon, transfer the bacon to a small bowl and set aside. Increase the heat to medium and add the kielbasa, bratwurst, and frankfurters to the pot. Cook, stirring occasionally, until the sausages are lightly browned, about 5 minutes. Add the sauerkraut, caraway seeds, chicken stock, Riesling, and the cooked bacon and stir to combine. Cook, covered, until the sauerkraut is crisp-tender (as cooked cabbage should be), about 15 minutes. Add the potatoes and stir in, then add the ham slices on top and continue to cook until the potatoes and ham are just heated through, 5 to 6 minutes. Divide the dish evenly among eight plates, and top each with a dollop of mustard.

SAUERKRAUT

MAKES 2½ POUNDS (1.1 KG)

4½ tablespoons (40 g) kosher salt

2 large green cabbages, a little over 2½ pounds (1.1 kg) total weight

8 ounces (227 g) fresh horseradish, peeled, rinsed, and sliced into ⅛-inch (3-mm) strips

3 bunches fresh dill, trimmed of the bottom ½ inch (13 mm) of stem

3 tablespoons caraway seeds, toasted

We keep jars of this kraut at OP Southeast and have an employee, "Pickle Joe," who does nothing but pickle part of the year. Serve this as part of Choucroute Garnie (page 211) or atop franks or brats.

1 Make the kraut brine by stirring 2 tablespoons (24 g) of the kosher salt into 4 cups (1 liter) of room-temperature water. Rinse the heads of cabbage under running water and peel away their largest outer leaves and any leaves with damaged spots. Cut the cabbages into quarters, then trim away the core from each cabbage quarter.

2 With either a mandoline or a sharp chef's knife, finely shred the cabbage until you have 2½ pounds (1.1 kg). Place the shredded cabbage in a sterilized large bowl. Add the remaining 2½ tablespoons (22 g) kosher salt and the caraway seeds and mix thoroughly.

3 Place half of the cabbage in a sterilized narrow square plastic container large enough to hold all of the cabbage and still have at least several inches of room at the top. Push the cabbage down firmly into the bottom of the container. You want to create a firmly packed and even layer here, with no air pockets. Next, add half of the dill and half of the horseradish, both distributed evenly over the cabbage. Add the remaining cabbage, pressing to make a firmly packed even layer. Add the remaining dill and horseradish and distribute as before.

4 Fill a clean resealable plastic bag (one with a surface area similar to that of the opening of your container) with water, seal it, and place on top of the packed cabbage, arranging the bag so it covers the cabbage completely. Top the bag with one or more sterilized plates heavy enough to hold the bag in place and small enough to fit inside the container. Now slowly pour the kraut brine into the container, letting it drip around the plastic bag. Pour until the cabbage, dill, and horseradish are submerged by at least 2 inches (5 cm). Seal the container, the bag and plates inside, with a snapping lid or cover tightly with plastic wrap. Store the container in a spot with a temperature between 60°F (15°C) and 65°F (18°C) for 3 weeks.

5 At the 3-week mark, open the container. The cabbage will have softened and darkened in color and the mixture will smell funky but not bad. In the case of this kraut, the smell is stronger than the taste—this recipe produces a very clean-tasting kraut. If there is a wee bit of mold on top, it's okay: simply skim it off with a slotted spoon; you can still eat what is below. Drain the sauerkraut in a large strainer; discard the dill and horseradish. Kept refrigerated in a lidded container, the kraut will last for up to 2½ months.

CHICORIES SALAD

If I could package and sell Alex Yoder's wizardry with salads and vegetables, we would all die healthy, and I would die wealthy. I often look around the OP dining room in awe that a charcuterie shop could be so busy, and just when I'm about to pat myself on the back, I realize each table has four vegetable dishes, a bottle of wine, and maybe, maybe, a charcuterie board.

1   To make the croutons, preheat the oven to 325°F (163°C). Slice the baguette crosswise into ⅛-inch (3-mm) slices. Lay these out on a baking sheet and drizzle with the olive oil, making sure to get a little on each slice. Season with salt. Bake for 7 minutes, or until golden and completely crisp. Set aside to cool.

2   To make the salad, using a mortar and pestle, pound the garlic with a pinch of kosher salt to a smooth puree. Transfer the garlic to a heavy bowl and whisk in the egg yolk and mustard. Combine the vegetable oil and olive oil in a cup with a spout and begin whisking the oil, drop by drop at first, into the egg yolk–garlic mixture. As the mixture thickens, add the oil in a thin, steady stream, whisking continuously, until all of the oil is incorporated. If the mixture is too thick, whisk in a teaspoon or two of water to thin it out. Whisk in the lemon juice and one-third of the grated Grana Padano. Season to taste with kosher salt and pepper and set the dressing aside.

3   Cut the radicchio quarters crosswise into ½-inch (13-mm) slivers. In a large bowl, combine the radicchio with the frisée, Catalonian chicory, and half of the remaining grated cheese. Add the dressing and mix until the greens have a tendency to stick together. Add the croutons and mix again, adding more dressing if necessary to lightly coat the croutons.

4   Divide the salad among six plates and top evenly with the remaining grated Grana Padano. Divide the anchovies equally among the salads and finish each salad with more black pepper.

SERVES 6

BAGUETTE CROUTONS

1 day-old baguette

½ cup (120 ml) extra virgin olive oil

Kosher salt

CHICORIES SALAD

3 cloves garlic, degermed

Kosher salt

1 egg yolk

1 tablespoon Dijon mustard

¾ (180 ml) cup vegetable oil

¼ cup (60 ml) extra virgin olive oil

2 tablespoons lemon juice

8½ ounces (240 g) Grana Padano cheese, grated on a microplane (about 3 cups)

Ground black pepper

1 head radicchio, quartered and cored

2 heads frisée, trimmed

1 bunch Catalonian chicory or puntarelle or dandelion greens, cut into 1-inch (2.5-cm) lengths

18 white anchovies packed in oil and vinegar

WINTER DENSITY ROMAINE WITH ANCHOVY VINAIGRETTE

SERVES 4

15 anchovy fillets

3 cloves garlic, degermed

1 teaspoon Dijon mustard

1 egg yolk

¾ cup (180 ml) extra virgin olive oil

¼ cup (60 ml) vegetable oil

Lemon juice

Kosher salt

2 heads Winter Density romaine,
    or regular young romaine

16 oil-cured olives, pitted, halved, and
    submerged in extra virgin olive oil

¼ cup (20 g) julienned red onion

2 tablespoons coarsely chopped
    fresh tarragon

2 eggs, soft-boiled

Ground black pepper

A cross between regular romaine and Bibb lettuce, Winter Density romaine is the perfect salad green to serve with a charcuterie board. Sheldon Marcuitz, owner of a local farm called Your Kitchen Garden, grows a lot of it for us. Both he and his wife, Carol Laity, hold PhD's in scientific fields, but turned from growing things in petri dishes to growing vegetables in the rich soil of the Willamette Valley.

1   Using a mortar and pestle, pound the anchovy fillets and garlic cloves until very smooth. If the mixture looks oily, add a few drops of water and pound more to make it creamy. Transfer this mixture to a heavy bowl and add the mustard and egg yolk; whisk to combine. Combine the olive oil and vegetable oil in a cup with a spout, and, starting drop by drop, whisk the oil into the anchovy-garlic-egg mixture. Once the dressing has thickened somewhat, you should be able to add the oil a little more quickly, so long as you whisk continuously. Season to taste with lemon juice and kosher salt. Often this dressing will not require more salt, as the anchovies are already very salty. Set aside.

2   Remove any damaged or leathery outer leaves from the heads of lettuce. Trim the base of each head and halve lengthwise. Submerge in a bowl of water and gently separate the leaves with your fingers to remove any sand or dirt, keeping the halved heads attached at the base. Once clean, set aside to dry on kitchen towels.

3   To assemble the salads, place a halved lettuce head cut side up on each of four plates. Drizzle anchovy vinaigrette onto the center of each lettuce half, allowing it to drip over the sides and create a small pool on the plate. In a similar manner, scatter a portion of oil-cured olives on and around the lettuce, allowing the oil they have been submerged in to drip all over. Scatter onion and tarragon across the lettuce. Carefully peel and halve the soft-boiled eggs and place one half in the pool of dressing next to each lettuce half. Season the entire salad with black pepper.

Variation: This also works well with the OP house dressing. To make, combine ½ cup (120 ml) mustard, ¼ cup (60 ml) honey, ½ cup (120 ml) champagne vinegar, and 4 teaspoons minced shallot. Whisk continuously while adding 1 cup (240 ml) vegetable oil and ¾ cup (180 ml) Arbequina olive oil. Season with fine sea salt and ground black pepper.

CARDOON SALAD WITH CORONA BEANS AND PIAVE CHEESE

SERVES 2

1 medium bunch cardoons
(about 2 pounds/910 g)

1 lemon, halved

1 cup (170 g) dried corona beans,
soaked overnight in water to cover

2 onions, peeled

2 bay leaves

1 carrot, peeled

Kosher salt

¼ cup (60 ml) red wine vinegar

1 tablespoon minced garlic

4 teaspoons dried oregano

½ teaspoon crushed red pepper flakes

¾ cup (180 ml) extra virgin olive oil

2 ounces (60 g) Piave cheese, grated,
or substitute Grana Padano

12 kalamata olives, pitted and halved

12 leaves flat-leaf parsley, coarsely
chopped

Ground black pepper

Both cardoons and corona beans require time and care to cook properly. Undercooked, the cardoons will be tough and stringy, the beans unappetizingly crunchy and grainy. Overcooking, however, is also not an option, as everything will turn to mush. Slow-roasting both beans and cardoons, as opposed to boiling, will help you cook them perfectly.

1   Preheat the oven to 350°F (176°C). Fill a bowl with water, squeeze in the juice from the lemon halves, and then drop in the halves. Cut the base off the cardoons to separate the stalks (just like you would do with celery). Trim each stalk of its leaves and remove any damaged or discolored parts. As you finish trimming each stalk, place it in the lemon water. This will keep it from discoloring and will also clean it. Once all the stalks are trimmed and clean, cut them into 10-inch lengths. Put the pieces back in the lemon water and set aside.

2   Drain the corona beans and, in a large baking dish, combine them with 1 onion, 1 bay leaf, and the carrot and cover with water by several inches. Cover the dish with foil and bake for 3 hours.

3   When the beans have been in the oven for 1 hour, drain the cardoons and discard the lemon halves. Put the cardoons, the remaining onion, and the remaining bay leaf in a medium baking dish and add water to cover. Salt the water as if you were cooking pasta. Cover the dish with aluminum foil and bake alongside the beans until the cardoons are tender when pierced with a fork, about 4 hours. Using a slotted spoon, transfer the cardoons to a bowl and set aside to cool.

4   When the beans have been in the oven for 3 hours, remove the dish from the oven and stir with a slotted spoon. Add more water if necessary to keep the beans generously covered. Replace the foil. Return the dish to the oven and bake until the beans are tender and creamy on the inside, about another 2 hours. They should be done around the same time as the cardoons. Let the beans cool in their cooking liquid, and then drain.

5   In a medium bowl, combine the vinegar, garlic, oregano, and red pepper flakes and season with kosher salt. Drizzle in the olive oil while whisking continuously.

6   Cut the cardoon stalks crosswise into 1-inch (2.5-cm) pieces. In a large bowl, combine the cardoons, the drained corona beans, the cheese, olives, and parsley and toss with as much of the vinaigrette as desired. Divide the salad between two plates and season to taste with black pepper.

VEGGIE BANH MI

Here at OP, we do everything we can to get into the vegetarians' good graces. This is a sandwich for which we'd face a backlash if it weren't on the menu for just one day. It's also popular among the staff because, well, there is more to life than pork!

1   Preheat the oven to 400°F (204°C).

2   To make the pickled vegetables and jalapeños, put the carrots and turnips in a medium heatproof bowl and put the jalapeños in a small heatproof bowl. In a small saucepan, combine the wine, vinegar, sugar, kosher salt, ginger, and coriander seeds. Bring to a boil over high heat. Pour three-quarters of the hot pickling liquid over the carrots and turnips and pour the remainder over the jalapeños. Let both cool to room temperature, about 15 minutes. Drain the vegetables and the jalapeños and set aside separately.

3   Place the portobello mushroom tops on a baking sheet and sprinkle liberally with salt and pepper. Bake for 35 to 40 minutes, until the mushrooms have lost their water and are crispy and blackened on the edges. Remove from the baking sheet and cut each mushroom in half.

4   Toast the bread. In a small bowl, whisk together the mayonnaise and sriracha. When the rolls are toasted, slather each with a liberal amount of sriracha mayonnaise. Put three mushroom halves on one side of each roll, then lay about 8 cucumber slices on top of the mushrooms. Spoon a portion of the pickled veggies and jalapeños on top. Finish with cilantro and a sprinkle of Maldon salt.

MAKES 4 SANDWICHES

PICKLED VEGETABLES AND JALAPEÑOS

½ cup (100 g) thinly sliced carrots

½ cup (100 g) thinly sliced turnips

3 jalapeños, seeded and sliced

1 cup (240 ml) white wine

1 cup (240 ml) white wine vinegar

¼ cup (55 g) sugar

2 tablespoons kosher salt

1 nub of ginger about the size of your thumb, sliced thinly

2 teaspoons coriander seeds

6 portobello mushrooms, stemmed and cleaned

Fine sea salt and ground black pepper

4 hoagie rolls, cut lengthwise

¾ cup (150 g) mayonnaise

1½ tablespoons sriracha

½ cucumber, sliced thinly

1 bunch cilantro, stems on, torn into 2-inch (5-cm) pieces

Maldon salt, to finish

THE OP CURED MEATS SANDWICH

This is an absolute and direct rip-off of the classic East Coast Italian grinder. We feel that every element of the traditional sandwich is crucial and irreplaceable. We just bettered it by bettering the meat, and now it's perfect.

1   Preheat the oven to 350°F (176°C).

2   To make the dressing, combine the red pepper flakes and oregano in spice grinder and pulse until finely ground. Add to a bowl with the garlic, kosher salt, oils, and vinegar and mix together. Transfer to a squeeze bottle.

3   To make the aïoli, using a mortar and pestle, pound the garlic with a pinch of salt until completely smooth. Scrape the garlic into a heavy ceramic bowl, add the egg yolks, and whisk to combine. Combine the canola oil and olive oil in a cup with a spout and, starting a drop at a time, begin whisking the oil into the egg yolk mixture. When the aïoli thickens somewhat, begin pouring in the oil in a thin, steady stream, whisking continuously, until all of the oil has been emulsified. You're looking for a nice, thick aïoli here, about the same consistency as mayonnaise. If it becomes too thick, add a few drops of water. Adjust the seasoning with sea salt and add lemon juice to taste.

4   To assemble the sandwiches, cut along the length of each roll, leaving one edge intact. Place the rolls in the oven and heat until warm, 6 to 7 minutes. Spread a generous amount of aïoli on the inside of each roll and layer capicola and salami cotto on top. Top the meat with lettuce, onion, and pepperoncini. Shake the dressing to re-emulsify, then drench the veggies with dressing and sprinkle with flaky salt and pepper. Cut the sandwich in halves, open a bag of Tom's potato chips, and enjoy.

MAKES 4 SANDWICHES

ITALIAN DRESSING

½ teaspoon (2.5 g) crushed red pepper flakes

Pinch of dried oregano

1 teaspoon (5 g) finely minced garlic

½ teaspoon kosher salt

1 tablespoon extra virgin olive oil

¼ cup (60 ml) canola oil

2 tablespoons red wine vinegar

AÏOLI

2 large cloves garlic, degermed

Fine sea salt

2 egg yolks

1½ cups (360 ml) canola oil

½ cup (120 ml) extra virgin olive oil

Lemon juice

4 soft sandwich rolls

8 ounces (227 g) Capicola (page 38)

8 ounces (227 g) Salami Cotto (page 92)

½ head iceberg lettuce, shaved

4 very thin slices red onion

1 cup (150 g) sliced pepperoncini

Flaky sea salt, such as Maldon

Coarsely ground black pepper

The OP sandwich lineup.

OP CHORIZO SANDWICH

MAKES 4 SANDWICHES

4 ciabatta rolls, halved

4 Fresh Chorizo sausages
(1 pound/455 g) (page 149)
or your favorite alternative,
sliced lengthwise

½ cup (120 ml) aïoli (see page 219)

8 thin slices manchego cheese

8 piquillo peppers, julienned

2 cups (60 g) arugula

Olive oil

Lemon juice

Maldon salt, to finish

Not that I ever ate this sandwich in Spain, but I would put some solid money down that it would win the heart of many a hungry Spaniard—even more so if we could smoke cigarettes inside the restaurant . . . while eating.

1 Warm the rolls.

2 Heat a griddle or skillet over high heat, and then sear the chorizo cut side down until hot throughout, about 4 minutes.

3 Slather the top and bottom of each roll with 1 tablespoon of aïoli and lay two slices of cheese on each bottom half. Place two sausage halves on top of the cheese and layer with a portion of piquillo peppers and arugula. Drizzle with olive oil and lemon juice and sprinkle with Maldon salt. Cover with the top half of the roll.

THE RANDY

MAKES 4 SANDWICHES

4 ciabatta rolls

¾ cup (180 ml) extra virgin olive oil,
plus additional for toasting

¼ cup (60 ml) champagne vinegar

Kosher salt

8 cups (130 g) frisée

4 teaspoons minced shallot

2 cups (226 g) crumbled blue cheese,
preferably buttermilk blue

1 cup (140 g) coarsely chopped toasted
hazelnuts

2 Fuji or Honeycrisp apples, halved,
cored, and cut into thin half moons

Ground black pepper

1 cup (240 ml) aïoli (see page 219)

1 pound (455 g) Sweetheart Ham
(page 111), thinly sliced

This was originally a hearty fall vegetarian sandwich featuring local apples and hazelnuts. When we started doing lease negotiations with Randy, our landlord at the new meat shop, it came up that it was a favorite sandwich of his. When negotiations were slowing down, we asked if he'd give us a deal if we put the sandwich back on the menu and name it after him. He said yes! So now it is The Randy, and we make it the way he likes to order it: with the addition of sweetheart ham.

1 Halve each ciabatta roll and brush the cut sides with olive oil. Heat a large nonstick skillet over medium heat and toast the cut sides of the rolls until golden, about 3 minutes; you may need to toast in batches. Let the rolls cool.

2 Combine the oil and vinegar in a jar with a tight-fitting lid and shake to emulsify. Season to taste with salt.

3 In a large bowl, combine the frisée, shallot, blue cheese, hazelnuts, and apples and the vinaigrette. Season to taste with ground black pepper.

4 To assemble the sandwiches, spread 2 tablespoons of aïoli on the cut side of each ciabatta half. Divide the ham evenly among the four bottom halves, then top each with one-quarter of the salad. Cover with the top half of the rolls. Cut each sandwich in half.

ASPARAGUS AND GARLIC CREAM ON TOAST

SERVES 4

32 spears asparagus, woody ends
    trimmed off

½ cup (120 ml) extra virgin olive oil

Kosher salt and ground black pepper

1½ cups (360 ml) heavy cream

4 cloves garlic, smashed

2 teaspoon lemon zest

4 slices como or other rustic bread
    slices, each about 1 inch (2.5 cm)
    thick

4 eggs

The Oregon asparagus season begins at the end of April, runs for about 8 weeks, and then promptly ends. We get ours from Hermiston, Oregon, from a farmer who calls himself the Aspara-guy. During the season, we serve this open-faced veggie sandwich at lunch.

1   Preheat the oven to 400°F (204°C).

2   In a large bowl, toss the asparagus spears with ¼ cup (60 ml) of the olive oil and season with kosher salt and pepper. Spread out on a baking sheet and roast until just barely cooked, about 5 minutes. Let cool. Once the asparagus spears are cool, chop them into 1-inch (2.5-cm) lengths.

3   In a deep pot over medium heat, simmer the cream with the garlic cloves until the cream has reduced by half, 18 to 20 minutes. Remove from the heat, remove and discard the garlic cloves, and add the lemon zest. Season to taste with salt and pepper.

4   In a large nonstick sauté pan over medium heat, warm 3 tablespoons of the remaining olive oil. Toast the bread until golden brown on both sides, about 3 minutes. Transfer the toast to four warmed plates.

5   Add the chopped asparagus to the cream mixture and return the pot to low heat. Warm the mixture until just heated through, about 3 minutes. Spoon the asparagus and garlic cream over the four pieces of toasted bread, dividing it evenly.

6   In a large nonstick sauté pan over medium heat, working in batches if necessary, fry the four eggs sunny side up, which should take about 4 minutes. Top each asparagus toast with a fried egg and serve immediately, each plate accompanied by a steak knife.

PORK PISTACHIO PÂTÉ SANDWICH

This sandwich celebrates the simple yet decadent combination of bread, butter, and pâté.

1   In a large nonstick skillet over medium heat, heat a little olive oil. Working in batches, toast the cut side of each roll until golden, about 3 minutes. Let cool completely.

2   Meanwhile, in a bowl, combine the frisée, shallot, and chives and season to taste with olive oil, lemon juice, salt, and black pepper.

3   Spread 1 tablespoon of butter on the toasted side of each kaiser roll half and sprinkle with Maldon salt. Spread 1 tablespoon of mustard on each bottom half. Divide the pâté evenly among the bottoms, and then do the same with the frisée mixture. Cover with the top half of the rolls and cut each sandwich in half.

MAKES 4 SANDWICHES

Extra virgin olive oil

4 kaiser rolls, halved

2 cups (35 g) frisée

1 tablespoon minced shallot

3 tablespoons minced chives

Lemon juice

Maldon salt

Ground black pepper

½ cup (115 g) unsalted butter, at room temperature

¼ cup (60 ml) Dijon mustard

1 pound (450 g) Pork Pistachio Pâté (page 45), cut into ¼-inch (6-mm) slices

HAND PIES

2 cups (220 g) all-purpose flour,
plus extra flour for rolling

½ cup (120 g) cold unsalted butter,
diced

½ teaspoon fine sea salt

½ cup (120 ml) cold water

3 tablespoons whole-grain mustard,
plus more for serving

1 tablespoon plus 1 teaspoon
heavy cream

1 egg

12 ounces (340 g) Pork Rillettes
(page 27)

Gherkins, for serving

With these hand pie, we created what are essentially elegant Hot
Pockets—haute stoner food to accompany the gourmet pot grown here
in the Pacific Northwest. *Food & Wine* enjoyed them (the hand pies,
not the pot) so much that they named them a 2010 dish of the year.
These perfect little packages come to the table straight from the oven
and are served with whole grain mustard and gherkins.

NOTE: IF YOU WANT TO SERVE MINI HAND PIES AS SMALLER BITES,
JUST CUT EACH RECTANGLE IN HALF AND DIVIDE THE RILLETTES INTO
TWELVE BALLS RATHER THAN SIX.

1   Combine the flour, butter, and sea salt in the bowl of a food
processor and pulse until the butter is the size of peas. Add the
water slowly while pulsing until the dough comes together. Turn
the dough out onto a work surface. Shape it into a rectangle,
packing it tightly, and wrap with plastic wrap. Refrigerate for
1 hour.

2   Line a baking sheet with parchment paper. Sprinkle a little flour
on your work surface. Using a rolling pin, roll the chilled dough
into a 12-inch by 12-inch (30-cm by 40-cm) square. Cut into six
rectangles, each 4 inches by 6 inches (10 cm by 15 cm). In a small
bowl, combine the mustard and the 1 tablespoon of cream, mix
well, and divide among the six rectangles, placing it in a dollop
near the shorter end of the rectangle about ½ inch from the
edge. Make an egg wash by whisking the egg and the remaining
1 teaspoon of cream in a small bowl and brush around the edges
of the dough. This is the glue to hold together our pockets. Scoop
the rillettes into six balls and place on top of the mustard. Fold the
other end of the dough over the rillettes. Tuck the top left corner
of the dough near the bottom right corner, and the top right corner
into the bottom left corner. Crimp together the edges of the dough,
sealing them.Brush the hand pie with egg wash and place on the
prepared baking sheet. Shape the rest of the pies and refrigerate for
15 minutes or for up to 1 hour. Once chilled, the hand pies can be
frozen for up to 1 month.

3   When ready to bake the hand pies, preheat the oven to 400°F
(204°C). Bake pies on the baking sheet for 20 minutes, or until
golden. Serve warm with mustard and gherkins.

GARLIC ALMOND SOUP

SERVES 8

2½ pounds (1.1 kg) blanched almonds

Fine sea salt

4 quarts (4 liters) water

9 brioche rolls, crusts removed and cut into 1-inch (2.5-cm) cubes

8 large cloves garlic, degermed

2 cups (480 ml) vegetable oil

2½ cups (600 ml) extra virgin olive oil

½ cup (120 ml) sherry vinegar

½ pound (227 g) green garlic, sliced thinly on the bias, or substitute green onions

Ground black pepper

This soup is a creation of Alex Yoder (our chef at OP Southeast) creation, so I'll let him take it: "*Ajo blanco* is a classic soup from Andalucía in Spain that is traditionally garnished with peeled green grapes. This recipe reimagines *ajo blanco* to eliminate the grainy texture of the original: because the classic soup already contains bread, it just seemed natural to strain out the leftover almond solids and use the bread as a thickener."

1   Line a large strainer with cheesecloth and set the strainer over a 4-quart (4-liter) bowl or container. Put one-quarter of the blanched almonds in a blender with a pinch of sea salt and pour in just enough of the measured water to cover the almonds. Puree; as the mixture thickens, slowly add more water until you have added 1 quart (1 liter). Pour this mixture into the prepared strainer. Repeat this process three more times until all of the almonds and water have been pureed together. Cover with a cloth and let sit for 8 hours, so that all of the liquid strains out from the solids.

2   After 8 hours, discard the almond solids from the strainer. You should have about 2 quarts (2 liters) of liquid remaining. To this liquid, add the brioche, garlic cloves, vegetable oil, 2 cups (480 ml) of the olive oil, and another good pinch of sea salt. Stir to combine, cover, and let sit for at least 2 hours in the refrigerator.

3   Put eight serving bowls in the refrigerator to chill. Working in batches, puree the mixture in a blender and pass the pureé through a fine-mesh strainer set over a container; discard any solids that you cannot press through.

4   Stir in the sherry vinegar and taste for salt and acid. Serve chilled in the chilled bowls garnished with the green garlic, the remaining ½ cup (120 ml) of olive oil, and black pepper. (Without garnishes, this soup will keep in an airtight container in the refrigerator for up to 5 days.)

BABY OCTOPUS WITH CHICKPEAS AND AIOLI

This dish, which is very rich and unctuous for a seafood dish, gives you six big, perfect bites. We've dubbed it "the octo-snack," and it makes a wonderful appetizer served before a light main.

1 Preheat the oven to 400°F (204°C).

2 Toast the nora chiles on a baking sheet for 4 minutes, then let cool. We just want a bit of heat here. Once cool, break the stems off the chiles and remove their seeds. Simmer the chiles in the water until they are soft, about 1 hour. With a slotted spoon, transfer the chiles to a blender and process with just enough cooking liquid to allow the chiles to fully break down. Discard the remaining cooking liquid. Push the contents of the blender through a fine-mesh strainer into a small bowl and set aside.

3 In a small saucepan, combine the octopuses, 1 cup (240 ml) of the olive oil, the vegetable oil, the bay leaf, and a pinch of kosher salt and bring to a simmer over medium heat. Cover, lower heat to medium-low, and cook, stirring occasionally, until the octopuses are tender, about 1 hour. Remove the octopuses from their cooking liquid and discard the liquid.

4 Empty the can of tomatoes into a strainer set over a bowl and crush the tomatoes with a wooden spoon until they are drained of all their liquid. Set aside ¼ cup (50 g) of the tomato solids; reserve the remaining tomato solids and juice for another use.

5 Preheat the oven again to 400°F (204°C). In a blender, combine the tomato solids, the chile puree, piquillo peppers, paprika, smoked paprika, cayenne, honey, and a pinch of kosher salt and puree until smooth, about 1 minute. With the motor running, pour in the sherry vinegar in a thin, steady stream, and then slowly pour in the remaining 5 tablespoons of olive oil. Season to taste with salt and pepper. (At the restaurant, this preparation is called roasted chile sauce, and we use it in a handful of dishes.)

6 In a large sauté pan over low heat, combine the octopuses with the chickpeas, ½ cup (120 ml) of the chickpea cooking liquid, and ½ cup (120 ml) of the roasted chile sauce. Season to taste with kosher salt and black pepper and additional roasted chile sauce, if desired.

7 Transfer the contents of the sauté pan to a large baking dish or to six individual casserole dishes and bake for 10 minutes until heated through. Top with the aïoli and green onions, and serve.

SERVES 6 AS AN APPETIZER

4 ounces (115 g) dried nora chiles or chile negro

3 cups (720 ml) water

12 baby octopuses, cleaned

1 cup plus 5 tablespoons (315 ml) extra virgin olive oil

1 cup (240 ml) vegetable oil

1 bay leaf

Kosher salt

1 (14-ounce/410 g) can diced tomatoes

½ cup (120 g) jarred piquillo peppers

1 tablespoon paprika

Pinch of smoked paprika

Pinch of cayenne

3 tablespoons honey

5 tablespoons (75 ml) sherry vinegar

2 cups (350 g) cooked chickpeas, cooking liquid reserved

Ground black pepper

¼ cup (60 ml) aïoli (see page 219)

¼ cup (25 g) thinly sliced green onions (cut on the bias)

BAKED SHRIMP, CHÈVRE, CHILE OIL, AND OREGANO

SERVES 2

½ cup (120 ml) extra virgin olive oil

½ teaspoon sweet paprika

¼ teaspoon cayenne

⅛ teaspoon smoked paprika

8 jumbo (U15) shrimp, deveined

Kosher salt and ground black pepper

6 ounces (170 g) chèvre

2 tablespoons coarsely chopped
fresh oregano

Lemon wedges, for serving

Warm crusty bread, for serving

This dish was an early OP favorite of Michelle's and mine. No wonder, as it is a riff on a classic Greek dish called *garides saganaki*, in which shrimp are baked with feta cheese and tomatoes. In this version, we add chile oil for a little heat. Serve it with lots of crusty bread to soak up the shrimp-flavored sauce at the bottom.

1   In a small bowl or a glass jar, combine the olive oil with the sweet paprika, cayenne, and smoked paprika and stir to combine. Cover and set in a warm place for at least 12 hours.

2   Preheat the oven to 400°F (204°C). Season the shrimp with kosher salt and black pepper.

3   Pour the chile oil into a baking dish just large enough to accommodate the shrimp more or less in a single layer. Add the shrimp to the dish, making sure the largest parts of their bodies are flush against the bottom of the dish. If their tails stick up or overlap, this is okay.

4   Crumble the chèvre over the shrimp, leaving some pieces the size of large marbles, and breaking others into smaller bits. Bake until the shrimp are fully cooked and the cheese is beginning to bubble and brown, about 20 minutes. Sprinkle the oregano evenly over the shrimp and serve with lemon wedges and bread.

STEAMED MANILA CLAMS WITH CHORIZO

As strange as it might seem for a city with a direct and relatively safe passage to the open ocean, Portland fights—and often loses—the battle to get our due portion of the 285-million-pound yield of Oregon's fisheries. The purchasing power of California, Seattle, and especially Asia simply trump Portland's. This has (happily) contributed to the porcine dynasty's rise and reign over the Portland food scene and, for that, we would like to shout out a big thank you to the invisible guiding hand of the economy. But still, we do get some of the good seafood. This OP version of surf and turf is refined by the quality and freshness of the ingredients: Oregon clams, California extra virgin olive oil, and our own Navarre, the spiciest of our chorizos. Be sure to have good, crusty bread on hand, as this broth begs for dunking.

SERVES 4

¼ cup (60 ml) good-quality
    extra virgin olive oil

5 ounces (140 g) OP Chorizo Navarre
    or other spicy chorizo, cut into
    matchsticks

½ teaspoon crushed red pepepr flakes

1 tablespoon minced garlic

¼ cup (60 ml) dry white wine

1 cup (240 ml) chicken stock

2 pounds (910 g) Manila clams,
    scrubbed and purged

4 tablespoons (60 g) unsalted butter,
    cut into cubes

Fine sea salt and ground black pepper

Lemon juice

4 green onions, sliced thinly
    on the bias

1 tablespoon coarsely chopped fresh
    flat-leaf parsley

Warm crusty bread, for serving

1. Set a pan large enough to accommodate the clams over medium heat. Heat 2 tablespoons of the olive oil and sauté the chorizo pieces in it. Soon you will begin to see the paprika and garlic-scented fat render out of the sausage. When the chorizo pieces have begun to crisp, but are not crisped all the way, remove the pan from the heat. Let cool for 30 seconds.

2. Add the red pepper flakes and garlic, return the pan to heat, and stir. The idea is to cook the garlic but not to let it brown in the slightest. After a minute or so, add the white wine and stock, and then the clams. Raise the heat to medium-high. Once the liquid is at a boil, the clams will start to open up. Swirl the pan a bit so that the clams cook more evenly.

3. When almost all of the clams are open, add the butter and continue to swirl the pan until it is melted. Taste and add sea salt, black pepper, and lemon juice as needed. Off the heat, add the green onion and parsley. Divide among four bowls. Finish with remaining 2 tablespoons of olive oil and serve with bread.

CHERRY, BASIL, AND CHÈVRE CROSTINI

This crostini and the two that follow evoke summer at OP—when the sun is setting, the sliding doors are open, and Portland is at its most beguiling.

1   In a nonstick sauté pan over low heat, heat ¼ cup (60 ml) of olive oil and toast all four slices of baguette until golden brown on one side, about 7 minutes. Flip the slices and cook a few seconds more before transferring to a cutting board to cool. Once the toasts are room temperature, spread each one evenly with chèvre.

2   In a medium bowl, combine the cherries with the balsamic vinegar and basil. Season to taste with kosher salt and black pepper. Divide this mixture evenly among the four toasts. Drizzle with olive oil.

WINE NOTE FROM JESS: This crostini and that ones that follow are shockingly good with a glass of manzanilla or fino sherry.

SERVES 4

Extra virgin olive oil

4 slices of baguette, cut on the bias so they are 4 inches (10 cm) long

6 ounces (170 g) chèvre, at room temperature

16 Bing cherries, pitted and halved

¼ cup (60 ml) excellent-quality balsamic vinegar, such as 30-year aged

4 large fresh basil leaves, julienned

Kosher salt and ground black pepper

CHÈVRE CROSTINI

SERVES 4

DRIED FRUIT CHUTNEY

1 cup (170 g) dried cranberries

½ cup (85 g) dark raisins

½ cup (85 g) golden raisins

1 cup (170 g) chopped dried apricots

1 cup (200 g) brown sugar

¾ cup (180 ml) apple cider

½ cup (120 ml) late harvest Sauvignon
Blanc vinegar, or substitute apple
cider vinegar

½ cup (120 ml) water

¾ teaspoon ground ginger

¾ teaspoon mustard powder

2 teaspoons yellow mustard seeds

1 cinnamon stick

½ teaspoon crushed red pepper flakes

Kosher salt and ground black pepper

CROSTINI

Extra virgin olive oil

4 slices of baguette, cut on the bias
so they are 4 inches (10 cm) long

4 ounce (115 g) chèvre, at room
temperature

4 slices Lomo (page 124),
or substitute prosciutto

Ground black pepper

This recipe makes about 3 cups (700 g) of dried fruit chutney, some of which you'll use on the crostini and most of which you'll keep for another use. We like to serve it with cheese.

1   To make the chutney, combine all of the ingredients in a medium pot and simmer over medium-hight heat until the liquid is reduced and thickened to the point that it looks like room temperature honey, about 15 minutes.

2   Pour the mixture into a shallow dish and let it cool until warm. Transfer half of the mixture to a mortar and pound with a pestle until thick and gooey. Return the contents of the mortar to the dish and stir to combine. Measure out ¼ cup (50 g) of chutney for the crostini and set aside. Transfer the remainder to an airtight container and refrigerate for up to 1 month. (Bring to room temperature before using.)

3   To make the crostini, heat ¼ cup (60 ml) of olive oil in a nonstick sauté pan over low heat, and toast all four slices of baguette until golden brown on one side, about 7 minutes. Flip them and cook for a few seconds more, then remove to a cutting board to let cool. Once the toasts are room temperature, spread each one evenly with chèvre. Follow this with 1 tablespoon of chutney, and top each toast with a slice of lomo. Season with black pepper and drizzle with olive oil.

SMOKED TROUT CROSTINI

When I eat smoked fish on any type of toast with sour cream, capers, and dill, I always ask myself, "Why don't I do this more often?" You, dear reader, deserve this snack more often, too.

NOTE: THIS IS A 2-DAY RECIPE.

Special Equipment: You will need a grill or smoker, 2 pounds (910 g) of applewood chips, 1 pound (455 g) of hickory wood ships, and a bag of charcoal.

1 To make the brine for the trout, in a small pot, combine the kosher salt, sugar, lemon slices, bay leaves, and peppercorns with water. Bring to a boil over high heat and let boil for 1 minute, then cool to room temperature.

2 Lay the trout in a small baking dish and pour the brine over the trout; the fish should be completely submerged. Refrigerate for 12 hours.

3 Line a baking sheet with parchment paper. Remove the trout from the brine and discard the brine. Lay the trout on the prepared baking sheet, skin side down, and refrigerate, uncovered, for 12 hours to allow the trout to dry. This step is essential for bold smoke flavor.

4 Soak a handful of apple wood chips in water to cover for 30 minutes; drain. Prepare your grill or smoker for smoking and, when it is ready, smoke the trout until it is fully cooked through, about 45 minutes. When the trout is done, the flesh should be firm and flaky, not mushy. Let cool to room temperature.

5 Preheat the oven to 350°F (176°C). Slice the baguette as thinly as possible until you have at least 24 slices. Discard any slices with large holes that would prevent the bread from holding a topping. Lay the slices in a single layer on a baking sheet. Drizzle the olive oil over them as evenly as possible. Sprinkle with sea salt and black pepper and bake until golden brown and completely crispy, about 8 minutes.

6 Peel the skin off the trout—it will come off easily—and flake the flesh into bite-size pieces. In a bowl, combine the flaked trout, sour cream, dill, green onion, and capers and stir to blend. Season to taste with sea salt and pepper.

7 To assemble the crostini, place 1 tablespoon of the trout mixture on each toasted baguette slice.

SERVES 8

BRINE

¼ cup (36 g) kosher salt

1 tablespoon sugar

1 lemon, sliced into rounds

3 bay leaves

5 black peppercorns

2 cups (480 ml) water

1 (10 ounce/280 g) cleaned and boned trout

1 day-old baguette

2 tablespoons extra virgin olive oil

Fine sea salt and ground black pepper

¼ cup (60 ml) sour cream

1 teaspoon chopped fresh dill

3 tablespoons thinly sliced green onion

1 teaspoon minced capers

SKORDALIA AND WHITE ANCHOVIES ON TOAST

SERVES 4 TO 6

SKORDALIA

2 large Yukon gold potatoes

1 bay leaf

6 black peppercorns

2 large cloves garlic, degermed and
    smashed to a paste in a mortar
    and pestle

1 egg yolk

¼ cup (60 ml) olive oil

Pinch of fine sea salt

16 thin (¼-inch/6-mm) baguette slices,
    cut on a slight bias to be the same
    length as the anchovies

16 white anchovies packed in oil
    and vinegar

Coarsely chopped fresh
    flat-leaf parsley

Ground black pepper

My mom always made skordalia—the Greek man's aïoli—out of the left-over mashed potatoes from my dad's restaurant. Michelle and I would fanatically spread it on everything: stale bread, vegetables, lamb, and goat. This is Mom's recipe. You'll need a ricer or food mill to make it.

1   To make the skordalia, peel the potatoes and cut each into eighths. Add the potatoes, bay leaf, and peppercorns to a medium saucepan filled about halfway with salted water. Bring to a boil over medium-high heat, turn down the heat to maintain a gentle simmer, and cook until the potatoes are tender when pierced with a fork, about 8 minutes.

2   Using a slotted spoon, transfer the potatoes to a bowl or plate, being careful to leave the peppercorns and bay leaf in the pan. Discard the cooking water and return the potatoes to the pan. Set the pan over low heat and stir the potatoes continuously, until they are very dry, about 3 minutes. Put the hot potatoes through a ricer or food mill set over a bowl. Let cool until warm.

3   Add the garlic, egg yolk, 4 tablespoons olive oil, and a pinch of sea salt to the cooled potatoes and stir with a wooden spoon until well combined. The skordalia should be creamy and spreadable. If necessary, thin it with a little water.

4   In a large nonstick sauté pan, warm about 2 tablespoons of olive oil over medium heat. Working in batches, toast the baguette slices until golden brown on only one side, about 3 minutes. Transfer the slices to paper towels to drain.

5   Spread each toast with a generous layer of skordalia and top each with a white anchovy. Once assembled on a platter, sprinkle all the toasts with chopped parsley and black pepper and drizzle with the remaining olive oil.

WINE NOTE FROM JESS: This dish begs for a briny coastal white wine or rosé. The garlicky skordalia and vinegary fish take well to acidic wines. You could stay classic and pretend you're in Greece by drinking a fine, crisp Assyrtiko, or you could surf the Euro coasts with a Spanish Albariño from a quality-focused producer like Do Ferreiro, a waxy Italian Pigato from Enoteca Bisson or Punta Crena, or the finest Provençal rosé you can find. Extra props if you can find rosé from Clos Sainte Magdeleine or Domaine du Bagnol. These producers make rosé in Cassis and, *mon Dieu*, that's where it's at!

PERSIMMON SALAD

This salad is a refreshing choice alongside a charcuterie board, or it can be served on its own as a light snack.

1 To make the dressing, in a small pot over medium heat, heat the honey, stirring occasionally until the color becomes darker, about 10 minutes. Remove from the heat and let cool for 10 minutes. Whisk in the vinegar, adding it in a steady stream until the dressing is emulsified. Season to taste with salt.

2 Using a sharp knife, trim off the stem and leaves from the persimmons and cut them into wedges ¼ inch (6 mm) thick. Arrange the wedges on four plates, dividing them evenly. Drizzle each plate with a portion of the dressing and scatter over hazelnuts and cheese. Twist and pinch the coppa slices to form them into rosette-like shapes and put five on each plate. Drizzle 1½ teaspoons of olive oil over each salad, top with equal portions of watercress, and finish with a pinch of sea salt.

WINE NOTE FROM JESS: This dish is complex and it took me awhile to find the wine that tastes best with it. Persimmon is not a weak fruit, and it calls for something equally robust in style and flavor. It's also sweet, which presents a challenge when you're trying to stick to the dry wine spectrum as we do at OP. Eventually, I gave up on a dry wine and went for the gold: Jurançon. Jurançon is a tiny region in Southwest France that produces stunning late-harvest dessert wines with no shyness of acidity. They are not as weighty and thick as the nearby dessert wines of Sauternes, but they are bright, fresh, and juicy. They also happen to be quite rare, so fortunately off-dry Gewürztraminer also tastes pretty epic with this salad.

SERVES 4

DRESSING

⅓ cup (90 ml) honey

2 tablespoons sherry vinegar

Fine sea salt

4 Fuyu persimmons

1 cup (130 g) toasted hazelnuts

4 ounces (115 g) chèvre, crumbled

20 thin slices Coppa (page 123)

2 tablespoons extra virgin olive oil

20 sprigs watercress

Fine sea salt

OCTOPUS TERRINE WITH DILL

At OP, we embrace octopods of all sizes, and we like to think that they've wrapped their tentacles around our cooking and embraced us as well. While our customer favorite is the octo-snack (see page 227), this terrine's spare prep and fantastical presentation makes it number one on the staff hit list.

1. Preheat the oven to 350°F (176°C). In the smallest baking dish that will accommodate the octopus in a single layer, combine the octopus with the canola oil, white wine, and 1 bay leaf. The octopus should be mostly covered with oil. Cover the dish with its lid or aluminum foil and bake for about 12 minutes or until the skin is easily pierced with a fork. Remove from the oil and let drain and cool.

2. Line a 9 by 12-inch (23 by 30-cm) loaf pan with plastic wrap and set the octopus parts inside. Push them down so they create an even layer of octopus flesh against the bottom and sides of the loaf pan. Wrap the plastic wrap over the top and weight down with an identical loaf pan or 2 cans of tomatoes. Place in the refrigerator.

3. Boil the potatoes in salted water with the remaining bay leaf and the black peppercorns until they are very tender, about 10 minutes. Drain and let cool. Once the potatoes are very cool, combine in a bowl with the crème fraîche, green onion, half the dill, and salt and pepper to taste. Keep in mind that octopus itself is inherently salty, so don't overdo it.

4. Carefully, with a sharp-as-all-hell knife, slice the terrine thinly and divide the slices among four plates. Gingerly dollop potato salad next to each portion of terrine. Garnish both the terrine and the potato salad with the remaining dill. Finish with a drizzle of olive oil and a squeeze of lemon.

WINE NOTE FROM JESS: I'm semi-obsessed with the deliciousness of this dish and often find myself devouring it so quickly that I forget all about my wine. However, when I manage enough restraint to stop for a sip, I hope to find a crisp and silky Loire Valley Sauvignon Blanc in my glass. The subtle grassiness in the wine with the fresh, herbaceous dill in the dish are two peas in a pod, and the salty octopus fits the minerally Sauvignon like a glove. If you're feeling earthy and natural, get yourself some Clos Roche Blanche Touraine Sauvignon No. 2, but if you want to peer into the gates of heaven, find a bottle of Thomas-Labaille Sancerre. You will not regret it.

SERVES 10

2 cleaned octopuses, weighing a total of 4 to 6 pounds (1.8–2.7 kg)

1 quart (1 liter) canola oil

¼ cup (60 ml) dry white wine

2 bay leaves

10 Yukon gold potatoes

6 black peppercorns

¼ cup (60 ml) crème fraîche

1 green onion, thinly sliced on the bias

2 tablespoons chopped fresh dill

Fine sea salt and ground black pepper

¼ cup (60 ml) extra virgin olive oil

½ lemon

Transcontinental Telepathy: The Dressner Tour Visits OP

In March 2014, the wine importer Louis/Dressner took a two-night diversion through Portland while on their "False Prophets of Doom" tour, a circuit for European wine growers led by Dressner captains Denyse Louis, Jules Dressner, Kevin McKenna, and Josefa Concannon. The reason for the diversion (or, let's say, ninety percent of the reason) was to put on an industry tasting with the good people at PDX Wine. (The other ten percent was to come to a party that we threw for them.)

Why would we plan a party for sixty-five wine folks that involved making two 25-pound (11-kg) Porchettas (page 62) and a charcuterie board big enough to feed an army, as well as filling five refrigerators with wine? The short answer: it was an excuse to eat, drink, and dance with amazing winemakers. The longer answer: because Eli's charcuterie makes us thirsty for the kinds of wines our guests make. There is a kind of symbiosis between the winemaking and charcuterie. Let me explain.

There is no denying Eli's love affair with Old-World European charcuterie. It's at the heart of what he does. How I feel about wine is similar: I have adoration for a very old place and process. Europe is the homeland of both wine and charcuterie; in various pockets and precincts of the continent, artisans and farmers have always been cultivating grapes, raising or hunting animals, and making wine and charcuterie as part of their daily sustenance. Over time, these two kinds of products interacted and shaped each other in many ways, the most important of which was the birth of cultures where wine and charcuterie were consumed together without fashion or fancy, but as part of the good old-fashioned everyday.

Conveniently, the same regions that make magnificent charcuterie also happen to make amazing wines. Choucroute Garnie (page 211) with Alsatian or German Riesling, Saucisson Sec (page 140) and Rillettes (page 27) with Cabernet Franc from the Loire, Mortadella (page 88) with Lambrusco from Emilia Romagna—the list of natural matches goes on and on. The possibilities in pairing Old-World meats and wines not only forces me to spend a lot of time digging deep into the food and wine traditions of Europe, but it also provides an endlessly inspiring direction for the OP wine list.

For the OP charcuterie program and the food served in our restaurants, I gravitate toward a certain fresh vibrancy in wines. The wildness of Pic Saint-Loup in the wines of Zélige-Caravent, the taut structure of Luca Roagna's Barolo, the smoked earth notes of Olga Raffault Chinon, or the exuberant crunchiness of Jean Paul Brun's

THERE IS NO DENYING ELI'S LOVE AFFAIR WITH OLD-WORLD EUROPEAN CHARCUTERIE. IT'S AT THE HEART OF WHAT HE DOES AND IS HIS TRUE INSPIRATION. HOW I FEEL ABOUT WINE IS SIMILAR: I HAVE ADORATION FOR A VERY OLD PLACE AND PROCESS.

Beaujolais—these wines all share a sense of aliveness. The winemakers (both New- and Old-World) at our party make these fresher types of wines that keep you coming back for more. This doesn't mean they lack complexity; on the contrary, many are so nuanced that their layers exceed the most bombastic styles. Take the elegant and ethereal wines of Koehler-Ruprecht from Germany. Are they tropical, heady, and full of fruit and spice with in-your-face floral aromatics? Perhaps not. Do they whisper secrets to you while you drink them? Most certainly.

Beyond the drinkability and pairability of their wines, these producers are making wine in ways we want to support. They are stewards of the land, making products of their environments, not products based on brand portfolios and marketing research. They are making wines in ways that generations before them did: without chemicals and inputs, with little modification and manipulation. Much like we approach charcuterie, they make a product that is meant to be consumed regularly and that elevates the quality of life.

Old-World winemakers are not the only ones working at this level of craft, and although we at OP feel a sort of transcontinental telepathy with Old-World wine and charcuterie methods, we are in no way dogmatic or geographically limited. New-World producers are knocking our socks off—Barnaby and Olga Tuttle at Teutonic Wine Company, John Paul at Cameron, and Scott and Dana Frank at Bow & Arrow are spirited local winemakers unafraid to work with lesser-known grapes, challenging vineyards, and the difficulties of a cool growing climate. I work with their wines because, beyond the fact that they are making really delicious juice that pairs with the dishes in our restaurants, they match Eli's unbridled dedication to craft. They don't take shortcuts or make concessions. They are self-starters who began with next to nothing except a whole lot of passion. They are also a good complement to our Old-World focus: both French Muscadet and Bow & Arrow Melon de Bourgogne pair with our oyster and seafood selections; Alsatian and German Rieslings and Teutonic Riesling marry perfectly with Choucroute Garnie (page 211). And a glass of Cameron Giuliano with our Rotisserie Chicken (see page 253) makes for a life well lived.

The mix and match of American and European winemakers was the highlight of our party. There was Barnaby Tuttle talking with Gernot Kollman about the myths of the "Mosel mafia"; Eric Texier, Scott Frank, and Josefa Concannon discussing how to make wine without fear; Franck Peillot, Jules Dressner, and Sasa Radikon rooting around the white wine and Champagne buckets like kids in a candy store; Arianna Occhipinti and Olivier Rivière cutting a rug. It was a simple night of talk and food and wine and music, offered in thanks for the work these winemakers, and many others like them, do every day.

JESS HERETH, OP WINE DIRECTOR

ARUGULA, GRAPEFRUIT, PISTACHIOS, AND RICOTTA SALATA

SERVES 4

8 ruby grapefruit

2 tablespoons lemon juice

¼ cup (60 ml) honey

8 cups (240 g) mature arugula
(not baby arugula)

½ cup (60 g) toasted shelled pistachios

Kosher salt

½ cup (70 g) grated ricotta salata

Extra virgin olive oil

Ground black pepper

When you eat as much charcuterie as we do, you need a soldier of a salad to give you a one-two punch of acidity and vitamin C. This is the one.

1   Cut the peels off the grapefruit and cut in between each membrane to free the segments. Divide the segments equally among four plates, arranged in a single layer. In a small bowl, stir together the lemon juice and honey until fully incorporated.

2   In a large mixing bowl, combine the arugula and the pistachios. Dress with as much honey-lemon mixture as you like and season to taste with kosher salt; toss to combine. Divide the arugula and pistachios evenly among the plates of grapefruit, and do the same with the ricotta salata. Finish each salad with a drizzle of olive oil and a sprinkle of black pepper.

WINE NOTE FROM JESS: The first time I tried this dish, I tasted several wines to see what worked. After many mediocre moments, I got to a Vouvray by François Pinon and stopped dead in my tracks. Now this is what food and wine pairing is about! The texture and flavors of Chenin Blanc echo those in the dish in an almost indescribable way: earthy, waxy nuttiness counterbalanced by bitter, sweet, and sour. Plus, I'm fanatical about how much quality and value the Loire Valley can deliver if you're paying attention to the good producers. That said, a just barely off-dry German Riesling is mighty tempting with this, too.

CAPONATA SICILIANA

Up here in the Northwest, when the eggplants hit, they hit in the tons. Caponata is one of the best and most classic ways to utilize a surplus. It's also the perfect vegetable condiment to serve with a charcuterie board.

1   Line a baking sheet with a clean kitchen towel and distribute the eggplant cubes in an even layer on the towel. Mix eggplant cubes with 1½ tablespoons salt. Let sit for 1 hour to allow the eggplant to expel some of its moisture. Meanwhile, preheat the oven to 400°F (204°C).

2   When the eggplant has been salted for 1 hour, pat the cubes dry with another kitchen towel or with paper towels. Drizzle with 4 tablespoons (60 ml) of the olive oil and toss to combine. Roast the eggplant until golden brown, about 20 minutes. Set aside.

3   In a medium pan over medium-low heat, heat the remaining 2 tablespoons of olive oil and sauté the onion, celery, and garlic until softened but not browned, about 5 minutes. Raise the heat to medium, stir in the tomato paste, and cook for 1 minute. Add the sugar and the vinegars and cook until the liquid reduces to a syrup, about 2 minutes. Add the raisins, pine nuts, capers, and olives and stir to incorporate. Remove from the heat and let cool.

4   In a medium bowl, combine the cooled vegetable-nut-raisin mixture, the cooked eggplant, and the basil and mix thoroughly. Season to taste with black pepper, red pepper flakes, salt, and olive oil. Serve with grilled baguette slices.

WINE NOTE FROM JESS: Eggplant loves tannins—a rarity in the vegetable world—so my first thought for this dish was red wine! But then I had to face the sweetness of the raisins, the sourness of the vinegar and capers, and the earthy flavor of the olives, which made my job much more difficult. I perused the wine library in my brain and kept going back to Grenache. That's good, but I needed to go deeper. Then I remembered the aromatic Frappatos of Sicily. Could this be the wine? A Sicilian dish with a Sicilian wine, just waiting to meet and fall in love? I popped a bottle of my favorite Frappato from Arianna Occhipinti and served myself a generous portion of Caponata Siciliana. *Amore*!

SERVES 4

1 (16-ounce/455-g) eggplant, cut into 1-inch (2.5-cm) cubes

Kosher salt

6 tablespoons (90 ml) extra virgin olive oil, plus extra for finishing

½ red onion, julienned

2 stalks celery, thinly sliced crosswise

3 cloves garlic, thinly sliced crosswise

2 tablespoons tomato paste

1½ tablespoons sugar

2 tablespoons sherry vinegar

2 tablespoons red wine vinegar

½ cup (45 g) golden raisins

½ cup (45 g) toasted pine nuts

2 tablespoons capers, rinsed

¼ cup (35 g) coarsely chopped oil-cured olives

4 large fresh leaves basil, julienned

Ground black pepper

Crushed red pepper flakes

Grilled baguette slices, for serving

CHAPTER 10

Dinner

STEAK TARTARE

Customers often tell us that our steak tartare is the best they've ever had. Now that could be the booze talking, but it could also be that we get the ideal texture by hand chopping rather than using a grinder. Since the egg yolks are raw, make sure they are impeccably fresh and tasty.

1. Massage the beef, pressing it as flat as possible—and wrap it tightly in plastic wrap. Freeze until fully frozen, at least 40 minutes. This is a very important step, as it makes the beef easier to work with. When you're ready to make the tartare—that is, right before you serve it—let the meat defrost for 30 minutes.

2. Cut the piece of beef horizontally and then vertically in order to create four equal quarters. Using a very sharp chef's knife, shave off a very thin layer from the top of each quarter (the layer that has been exposed to air while the beef defrosted).

3. Switch to a new, immaculately clean cutting board, and wash your hands and knife really well. Cut the meat into ¼-inch (6 mm) strips and then dice those strips. In a bowl, combine the meat, olives, shallot, parsley, and the olive oil. Mix together with a soupspoon until the mixture has a spreadable consistency. Season to taste with kosher salt and black pepper. Put four (or eight) plates in the refrigerator to chill, along with the meat mixture.

4. In a nonstick sauté pan over medium heat, heat the remaining ⅓ cup of olive oil and, working in batches if necessary, toast the baguette slices until golden brown on just one side, about 3 minutes. Set aside to cool.

5. Divide the steak tartare among the chilled plates. Press the back of a spoon down into each portion of tartare to make a small indentation. Add an egg yolk to each tartare, in the indentation, and season to taste with Maldon salt and black pepper. Serve with the toasted baguette slices.

SERVES 8 AS A STARTER, 4 AS A MAIN DISH

13 ounces (370 g) very lean eye of round steak or beef filet

2 Cerignola olives, pitted and minced

1 tablespoon minced shallot

1 tablespoon minced fresh flat-leaf parsley

⅔ cup (150 ml) extra virgin olive oil

Kosher salt and ground black pepper

4 to 8 baguette slices, cut on an extreme bias so they are at least 4 inches (10 cm) long

4 or 8 egg yolks (1 per person)

Maldon salt, to finish

ROASTED RADICCHIO WITH CRUCOLO

SERVES 4

2 heads radicchio

Good-quality olive oil

Fine sea salt and ground black pepper

6 ounces (170 g) Crucolo cheese
(or substitute fontina), grated on
the large holes of a box grater

8 Cerignola olives, pitted and torn
in half

Aged balsamic vinegar, for drizzling

Our Oregon farmers supply us with radicchio all winter long, both the elongated Treviso and the round Chioggia varieties. The inspiration for this dish is *radicchio al forno* from the Veneto region of Italy. Alex Yoder, the chef at OP Southeast, said about this dish: "I knew the pairing of bitter radicchio with melted Crucolo would be a winner, but the frico (cheese crisp) that formed in the bottom of the cast-iron skillet when I produced the first version was a happy surprise. I like this with an inexpensive Italian white, something from the Piedmont, like Favorita, or a simple Venetian Soave—or really, whatever Jess, our wine director, tells me to drink."

1   Preheat the oven to 400°F (204°C). Examine the radicchio and peel away any damaged outer leaves. Trim any discoloration from the base. Quarter each head lengthwise to create eight wedges. Rub each wedge with olive oil and sprinkle with sea salt and pepper.

2   Place the radicchio wedges core side up on a baking sheet and roast until you notice the edges becoming brown and crispy, about 8 minutes. Remove from the oven and let cool. Leave the oven on.

3   Once the radicchio wedges are cool enough to handle, gently separate the now-pliable leaves so the wedge opens like a fan. Place two thin layers of grated Crucolo in between several of the leaves in each wedge, and then place the wedges core side up in a large cast-iron skillet. Sprinkle the remaining grated Crucolo over the top, allowing some to fall into the skillet.

4   Drizzle the wedges with olive oil and bake until the Crucolo has melted and the cheese in the bottom of the pan has crisped up, about 4 minutes. Divide the wedges among four plates, allowing any oozing cheese to drape over the tops. Scatter the olives over the radicchio. Finish each plate with a drizzle of balsamic vinegar and a little olive oil.

OP NORTHWEST'S ROTISSERIE CHICKEN

Before opening our Northwest location, we were looking for something special in the design to set it apart. OP co-owner Tyler, being the resourceful restaurateur he is, found a bright red rotisserie oven owned by a guy who used it to roast chickens at carnivals in Los Angeles. Not only was the price right, but the lovable carnie drove it up to Portland himself. Today it sits behind the meat counter, roasting birds perfectly day after day. The most important part of cooking this dish is the brine, Colin's (the chef de cuisine at OP Northwest) gift to you. Each OP rotisserie chicken is served with chicken jus and schmaltz potatoes. These are by no means necessary, but we've included both recipes as well as a nonrotisserie recipe for the home cook.

NOTE: GO TO A GOOD BUTCHER OR YOUR FARMERS' MARKET FOR A BIRD THAT IS NICE AND PLUMP AND FULLY COVERED IN THICK SKIN WITH A YELLOW TINT.

1. To make the brine, combine all of the brine ingredients in a pot that's big enough to also hold the chicken fully submerged but small enough to fit in your fridge. Set the pot over medium-high heat and bring the brine to a boil, stirring occasionally to help dissolve the salt. As soon it reaches a boil, transfer the pot to the refrigerator and let sit for about 30 minutes.

2. Carefully add the chicken to the brine, making sure it's submerged and refrigerate for 24 hours.

3. Preheat the oven to 400°F (204°C). Remove the chicken from the brine using clean hands. Discard the brine. Pat the chicken dry and, using a 3-foot (1-meter) piece of butcher's twine, truss the chicken: Place the chicken on its back and wrap the middle of the twine around the chicken's neck (there should be enough of the neck still on the chicken to do this on either side). You should have two even lengths of twine. Slide them under the chicken toward the legs and criss-cross them around the ends of the legs twice for good measure. Tighten them up by pulling on each end of the twine, so that the legs are trussed in tight to the chicken's body, over the opening of the cavity. Then take the twine back over the breast toward the neck, wrap it around the neck again, and make a nice bow knot. Tuck the wing-tips into the twine where it passes close to them. Remember that all you are trying to do is to keep the legs and wings snug to the bird so they do not overcook while the rest of the bird roasts. Season the chicken with sea salt and pepper,

CONTINUED

SERVES 3 OR 4

BRINE

4 quarts (4 liters) water

1 cup plus 2 tablespoons (300 g) kosher salt

⅓ cup (90 ml) honey

2 lemons, halved

½ bunch fresh thyme

1 head garlic, halved crosswise

2 tablespoons black peppercorns

1 (3-pound/1.4-kg) whole chicken

Fine sea salt and ground black pepper

TO SERVE (OPTIONAL)

Chicken Jus (page 255)

Schmaltz Potatoes (page 254)

being sure that you cover all of the skin. Place the bird breast side up in a rack set in a roasting pan and roast for 25 minutes. Rotate the pan 180 degrees so that the skin turns golden on all sides and roast for another 25 minutes. Using a roasting fork, tilt the chicken so that the juices run out of the cavity. If the juices are clear, the chicken is done; if they're pink or bloody, return the chicken to the oven and continue to roast for 10 minutes.

4   Transfer the chicken from the roasting pan to a carving board and let it rest for about 5 minutes. Serve the bird whole with jus and potatoes, if you like.

5   To get the schmaltz for later use, pour the liquid from the roasting pan through a fine-mesh strainer into a container. Cover and refrigerate the strained liquid until the fat has solidified on top. Scoop the fat into a separate container and keep it, tightly covered, in the fridge for up to 7 days. Discard the liquid.

SCHMALTZ POTATOES

SERVES 4

2 cups (480 ml) schmaltz (see above) or substitute duck fat

1½ pounds (680 kg) fingerling potatoes

1 bunch green onions, both green and white parts, sliced on a bias

Fleur de sel

When you make the Rotisserie Chicken (page 253), you can capture the fat from the roasting juices—that's your schmaltz, a.k.a. pure culinary gold. If you don't have schmaltz, or if you don't have enough from the chicken, you can use duck fat, but you'll have to call these potatoes something different.

1   Preheat the oven to 375°F (191°C). In a pot over medium heat melt the schmaltz until it is liquid, 3 to 5 minutes. Put the potatoes in a small roasting pan and pour the warm fat over them. Roast for 1 hour, or until there's no resistance when you poke the potatoes with a fork or sharp knife.

2   Using a slotted spoon, remove the potatoes from the roasting pan; reserve the schmaltz in the pan. Slice each potato in half lengthwise. Place a sauté pan over high heat for 2 to 3 minutes. Add a bit of the reserved fat to the pan—just enough to coat the bottom—and add the potatoes cut side down. Fry for 3 to 5 minutes, or until the cut surfaces are golden. Sprinkle the green onions on top and season with fleur de sel.

CHICKEN JUS

If you are going to serve this jus with the roasted chicken, begin this recipe 3½ hours before you start cooking the chicken. When you buy the whole bird for the chicken recipe, ask the butcher or the farmer if she has a couple of extra chicken carcasses. If none are available, use wings, legs, necks, or backs.

1   Preheat the oven to 400°F (204°C).

2   Place the chicken parts in a roasting pan and roast for 15 minutes, or until they develop a nice, brown color. Set aside.

3   Heat a small sauté pan over medium heat and place the onion cut side down in it. Cook the onion until the cut surface is blackened, about 5 minutes. The burnt onion will bring color to the jus. Set aside.

4   In a large pot over high heat, combine the canola oil, carrots, and tomato paste and cook until you see some browning, about 10 minutes, stirring often to prevent burning. Add the chicken and the blackened onion to the pot; then add the water, leeks, peppercorns, thyme, and bay leaves. Lower the heat to medium and bring to a simmer, not a boil. Simmer for 3 hours, checking every 20 to 30 minutes and skimming off any scum that may bubble to the top.

5   At the 3-hour mark, set a cheesecloth-lined strainer over another, smaller pot and very carefully strain the stock into the new pot. Place the pot over medium heat and cook until the liquid reduces to about 2 cups (480 ml). This should take 30 to 40 minutes.

6   Remove from the heat and season to taste with salt. Keep the jus refrigerated until ready to serve, then reheat to serve. The jus will keep refrigerated for 1 week.

MAKES 2 CUPS (480 ML)

2 pounds (910 g) chicken wings, legs, necks, backs, or carcasses

½ onion, halved

1 tablespoon canola oil

2 large carrots, coarsely chopped

¼ cup (60 ml) tomato paste

7 quarts (7 liters) water

2 leeks, washed and coarsely chopped

1 tablespoon peppercorns

6 sprigs fresh thyme

2 bay leaves

Fine sea salt

WHOLE ROASTED ASTORIA SARDINES

For two weeks in late spring, Portland enjoys the benefit of the Astoria sardine season. Blue and silver in color, relatively mild in flavor, and large in size, these sardines are best roasted whole. The cauliflower accompaniment in this dish adds sweet and sour flavors that go well with the oily fish. The garlic sauce is really a very thin aïoli, which, once you've made it, you'll want to put on everything.

NOTE: IT'S TOUGH TO FIND ASTORIA SARDINES OUTSIDE OF THE PACIFIC NORTHWEST. MONTEREY SARDINES ARE THE CLOSEST SUBSTITUTE.

1   Preheat the oven to 400°F (204°C). Using a mortar and pestle, pound the garlic with a pinch of sea salt until pureed. Scrape the pureed garlic into a bowl and add the egg yolk and a squeeze of lemon juice. Working very slowly (drop by drop at first), add the canola oil and ½ cup (120 ml) of the olive oil to the egg yolk, whisking continuously to create an emulsion. When the mixture gets thick and shiny, add a little water to it to make it smooth and creamy, and then continue whisking in the oil. Season with salt and lemon juice to taste. Thin the sauce with water to the consistency of heavy cream. Set aside.

2   Cut the cauliflower into 1-inch (2.5-cm) florets; discard the stem. Toss in a bowl with ¼ cup olive oil, sea salt, and pepper and roast until tender. Combine the roasted cauliflower in a bowl with the capers, raisins, and pine nuts. Add more olive oil and lemon juice to taste. Keep the oven on.

3   Heat a medium cast-iron skillet over high heat until very hot. Add ¼ cup of olive oil. Season the fish all over with sea salt and pepper and sear in the hot skillet for about 2 minutes on each side. Transfer the skillet to the oven and roast until the meat is an even color, 6 to 8 minutes.

4   To serve, make a pool of about 2 tablespoons of garlic sauce in the center of each of four plates (you will have some sauce left over—you're welcome). Divide the cauliflower salad evenly among the plates and top each pile with one whole sardine. Finish with a drizzle of olive oil.

SERVES 4

1 medium clove garlic, degermed

Fine sea salt

1 egg yolk

Lemon juice

½ cup (120 ml) canola oil

1 cup (240 ml) extra-virgin olive oil

1 large head cauliflower

Ground black pepper

2 tablespoons capers

¼ cup (43 g) golden raisins

2 tablespoons toasted pine nuts

4 very fresh whole Astoria sardines, cleaned (about 3 ounces/85 g each)

CREPINETTE

SERVES 6

CREPINETTE

3 pounds (1.4 kg) boneless lamb
    shoulder, cut in four pieces

2 tablespoons fine sea salt

¼ cup (60 ml) extra-virgin olive oil

1 onion, quartered

1 carrot, chopped in large rounds

1 head garlic, cloves separated, peeled,
    and chopped

5 cups (1.2 liters) chicken stock

3 (14-ounce / 397-g) cans plum
    tomatoes, drained, with juices
    reserved

6 sprigs fresh thyme

2 bay leaves

2 bunches fresh chives, chopped

6 sheets caul fat, each 12 inches by 12
    inches (30 cm by 30 cm)

RATATOUILLE

¼ cup (300 ml) olive oil

2 onions, diced

2 heads garlic, cloves separated,
    peeled, and minced

3 pounds (1.4 kg) canned Roma
    tomatoes, drained, with juices
    reserved

1 eggplant, cut into ½-inch
    (1.3-cm) cubes

Fine sea salt

4 zucchini, cut into ½-inch
    (1.3-cm) cubes

3 yellow squash, cut into ½-inch
    (1.3-cm) cubes

1 bunch fresh oregano, chopped

OP Northwest chef Colin Stafford created this dish, and it's absolutely one of his best ideas: lamb braised slowly until tender enough to pull apart; then shaped, and wrapped in a delicate pouch of caul fat; and finally browned and served with a deep, rich ratatouille. This is as technically complex as the OP kitchen gets. Serve this with a bottle of something fabulously untrendy, like a mellow Bordeaux.

1   To make the crepinette, position a rack in the lower half of the oven. Preheat the oven to 375°F (191°C). Sprinkle the lamb shoulder with the fine sea salt. In a large Dutch oven over high heat, heat the olive oil, and add the lamb. Brown the pieces on all sides, turning them with tongs every 3 to 4 minutes. Transfer the lamb to a large plate. Pour out the oil in the pot and return the pot to high heat. Add the onion, carrot, and garlic and stir for 3 minutes until the vegetables are lightly toasted. Add the chicken stock and drained tomatoes and bring to a simmer. Then add the browned lamb; the pieces should be fully covered with liquid. If not, cover using the reserved tomato juice. Add the thyme and bay leaves and return the liquid to a simmer. Cover the pot with its lid and transfer to the oven. After 1 hour, start checking for doneness by inserting a meat fork or skewer into the lamb; the fork will easily slide in and out when the lamb is done.

2   Remove the pot from the oven and let cool for 15 minutes. Using your trusty tongs, transfer the four pieces of lamb to a plate. Discard the cooking liquid. Transfer the plate to the fridge and let cool for another 15 minutes. Put the lamb on a cutting board and begin pulling it apart with your hands. You're looking for the same texture as pulled pork. Transfer the pulled lamb to a 4 by 12-inch (10 by 30-cm) pâté mold. Press it down firmly with your hands: you want it packed tight. Cover with plastic wrap and refrigerate overnight.

3   Set the pâté mold on a cutting board. Run a sharp knife around the inside of the mold to loosen the terrine. Flip the mold onto the cutting board; the terrine should come out. Slice the terrine into six equal portions and transfer to a plate.

4   Lay out one sheet of caul fat on the cutting board. Place one slice of the terrine at the top center of the sheet. Fold in the caul fat sides over the terrine, and then fully wrap the slice by folding it toward you until you get to the bottom of the sheet of caul fat. Repeat with the remaining sheets of caul fat and terrine slices. Place in the refrigerator.

CONTINUED

5   To make the ratatouille, preheat the oven to 375°F (191°C). In a large pan over medium heat, warm the 1 tablespoon of olive oil. Add the onions and garlic and cook for 3 to 4 minutes, until translucent. Add the drained tomatoes and simmer for 30 minutes, or until the mixture has reduced by half; this is the tomato jus. Meanwhile, in a large bowl, toss the eggplant with ½ cup (120 ml) of the olive oil and a liberal amount of sea salt. Transfer the eggplant to a baking sheet and roast for 10 minutes, until soft. Transfer the eggplant to a bowl. In another bowl, toss the zucchini and squash together with the remaining ½ cup (120 ml) of olive oil and some sea salt. Now transfer these to the baking sheet and roast for 10 minutes, until fragrant. Keep the oven on.

6   By now the tomato jus should be ready. Transfer the roasted vegetables to the tomato jus, put a lid on the pot, and place it in the oven. Cook for 30 minutes, or until the vegetables are very tender but not falling apart. Taste for seasoning and add more salt, if needed. Keep the oven on.

7   Place a large ovenproof nonstick pan—big enough to hold all six of your terrine packages—on high heat and add the remaining 3 tablespoons olive oil. Sprinkle a pinch of sea salt on each terrine slice and, once the oil is very hot, add the terrine slices. Let them sizzle away and render fat for 5 minutes on the first side, until golden. Flip the slices and immediately transfer the pan to the oven. Cook for 5 minutes, then remove from the oven.

8   Fold the fresh oregano into the ratatouille. Set out six serving plates and place two heaping spoonfuls of ratatouille on each, and then place one terrine slice on top. If you want to, spoon on a bit more ratatouille to finish.

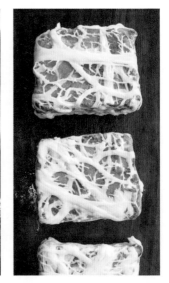

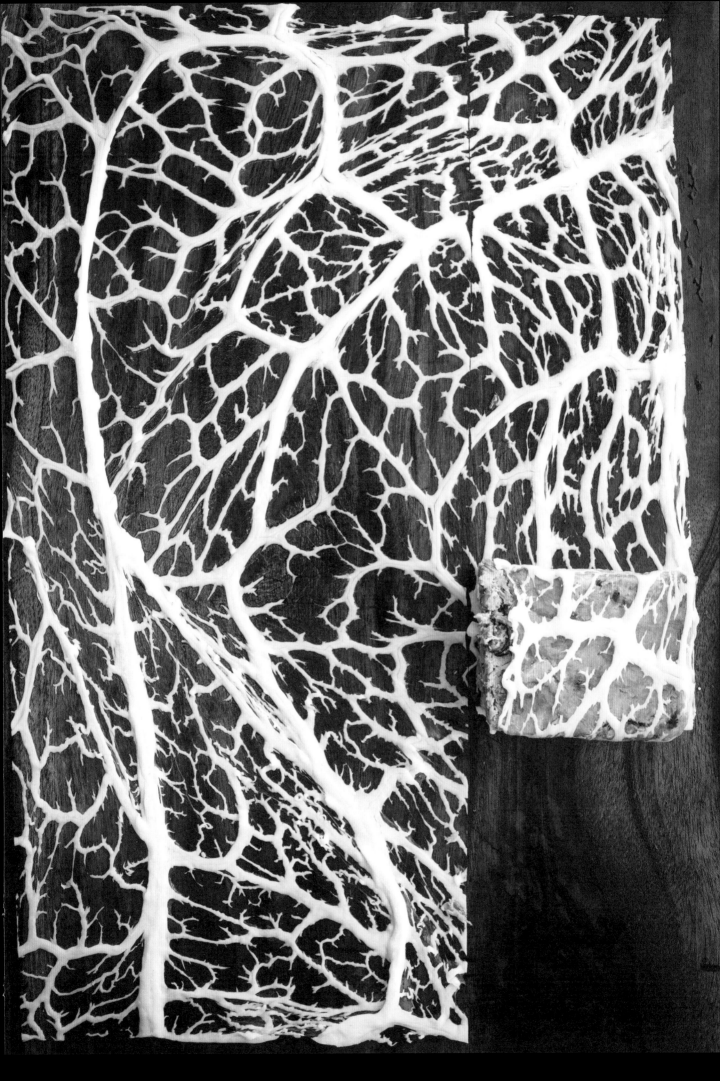

BRAISED BEEF SHORT RIBS

SERVES 8

3 onions, quartered

1 carrot, peeled and halved

3 cups (720 ml) dry red wine (good enough that you'd be willing to drink it)

1 cup (240 ml) balsamic vinegar

⅓ cup (90 ml) tomato paste

2 ounces (60 g) dried porcini mushrooms

4 anchovy fillets

2 tablespoons sugar

1 bay leaf

Fine sea salt

8 bone-in beef short ribs

Ground black pepper

¼ cup (60 ml) vegetable oil

2 quarts (2 liters) chicken stock

3 (¼-inch/6-mm) thick slices of bacon, cut into lardons

6 medium Yukon gold potatoes, cut into quarters lengthwise

3 tablespoons olive oil

12 oil-cured olives, pitted and torn in half

16 Gaeta olives, pitted and torn in half

2 tablespoons unsalted butter, cubed

3 tablespoons coarsely chopped fresh flat-leaf parsley

These short ribs have become a signature dish for us, an OP winter staple. The lardons taste fantastic coated in the rich braising liquid, and the olives provide enough brine and complexity to keep the whole thing from insulting your intelligence.

NOTE: THIS IS A 2-DAY RECIPE.

1 Preheat the oven to 350°F (176°C). In a Dutch oven, combine the onions, carrot, wine, balsamic vinegar, tomato paste, porcini, anchovies, sugar, bay leaf, and 2 tablespoons of sea salt and cook over medium heat, stirring from time to time to prevent sticking, until the liquid has thickened to a consistency just looser than ketchup, about 30 minutes.

2 Meanwhile, season the short ribs with sea salt and pepper. In a large sauté pan over medium heat, heat the vegetable oil and brown the ribs evenly on all sides, about 4 minutes per side, working in batches, if necessary. Set aside.

3 When the wine mixture has the right consistency, add the ribs to the Dutch oven and cover with chicken stock, making sure they are submerged. Cover and braise in the oven until the ribs are tender when pierced with a fork, about 3 hours. Let the ribs cool completely in their braising liquid, then refrigerate overnight.

4 Preheat the oven to 400°F (204°C). Remove the Dutch oven from the refrigerator. The fat on the surface of the braising liquid will be about ¼ inch (6 mm) thick and hard as plastic; remove it by peeling it off, or if needed, don gloves and crack it into pieces, then fish out the pieces and discard them. Using a slotted spoon or tongs, remove the ribs from the braising liquid and transfer to a medium baking dish.

5 Return the Dutch oven with the defatted braising liquid to the oven and heat until it is fully liquid again, about 10 minutes. Keep the oven on. Pour the liquid through a strainer set over a bowl and discard the solids; set the liquid aside. Place the bacon lardons on a baking sheet and bake them until they are crisped, about 15 minutes. Remove from the oven and set aside; keep the oven on.

6 Add enough strained braising liquid to the baking dish holding the ribs to film the bottom, about 1 cup (240 ml) or so. In a bowl, toss the potatoes with the olive oil and season with sea salt. Place on a baking sheet, and roast along with the ribs until the potatoes are golden brown, and the ribs are warmed through, about 25 minutes.

7   While the potatoes and ribs are roasting, add the oil-cured and
    Gaeta olives, the bacon lardons, and the remaining strained braising
    liquid to the Dutch oven. Bring to a simmer over medium-high
    heat and reduce the liquid to 2 cups (480 ml), about 20 minutes;
    it should be thick enough to coat a spoon. Add the butter and stir
    continuously until the butter is melted and combined into the
    sauce. Stir in the parsley and season with black pepper to taste.

8   Arrange three potato wedges on each of the eight plates and top
    with a rib. Spoon sauce over each rib, taking care to distribute
    lardons, olives, and sauce evenly over the meat.

CHERRY TOMATO, CABBAGE, AND CHOWCHOW SALAD

SERVES 2

CHOWCHOW

1 green tomato, cut into ¼-inch (6-mm) cubes

Kernels from 1 ear of yellow corn

⅛ head green cabbage, cut into ¼-inch (6-mm) squares

¼ head cauliflower, cut into ¼-inch (6-mm) florets

1 red bell pepper, stemmed, seeded, and cut into ¼-inch (6-mm) squares

1 Anaheim chile, stemmed, seeded, and cut into ¼-inch (6-mm) squares

1 small zucchini, cut into ¼-inch (6-mm) cubes

2 cups (480 ml) water

1 cup (240 ml) white wine vinegar

2 tablespoons kosher salt

⅓ cup (90 g) sugar

2 tablespoons yellow mustard seeds

1 tablespoon sweet paprika

Pinch of ground turmeric

20 cherry tomatoes, halved

4 ounces (115 g) buffalo mozzarella, cut into ¼ inch (6-mm) slices

4 fresh basil leaves, julienned

Extra virgin olive oil

Fine sea salt and ground black pepper

Fresh buffalo mozzarella and tomatoes have been a natural pairing since the Italians mustered enough courage to eat the strange New World fruits. In this dish, the classic combination takes on new dimensions with the addition of chowchow, a quick pickle of Southern origins. This salad is perfect served alongside the Roasted Halibut, Ham, and Mussel Salad (page 266).

1   To make the chowchow, combine the green tomato, corn, cabbage, cauliflower, red pepper, Anaheim chile, and zucchini in a shallow bowl and stir to mix. Combine the water, vinegar, kosher salt, sugar, mustard seeds, paprika, and turmeric in a small saucepan and bring to a boil. Once the mixture boils, pour it over the vegetables. Let cool to room temperature.

2   Divide the cherry tomatoes between two plates, arranging them in a single layer. Divide the mozzarella between the plates, laying the slices flat on top of the tomatoes. Sprinkle with the basil. Using a slotted spoon, add as much of the chowchow as you desire to each plate. Spoon a tablespoon or so of the pickling liquid evenly over each salad. Finish with extra virgin olive oil, fine sea salt, and black pepper to taste. Leftover chowchow will keep in an airtight container in the refrigerator for up to 4 days.

ROASTED HALIBUT, HAM, AND MUSSEL SALAD

SERVES 4

4 pounds (1.8 kg) rock salt

12 medium fingerling potatoes

2 pounds (910 g) mussels, purged and beards removed

½ cup (120 ml) dry white wine

1 egg yolk

1½ cups (360 ml) extra virgin olive oil

2 teaspoons sherry vinegar

¼ cup (60 ml) Dijon mustard

Kosher salt

8 ounces (227 g) Sweetheart Ham (page 111) or good-quality smoked ham, minced,

¼ cup minced sweet pickles

2 green onions, sliced thinly on the bias

1 stalk celery, sliced thinly crosswise

½ cup (120 ml) canola oil

4 (5-ounce/140 g) halibut fillets

Ground black pepper

½ lemon

Growing up, I always had an unfulfilled yearning for ham salad; I wished someone would make a quality ham salad that didn't resemble dog food. In this dish, OP Southwest chef Alex Yoder grants my wish, elevating the pedestrian ham salad with the addition of tender steamed mussels. Add a nicely cooked piece of halibut and roasted fingerling potatoes, and you have the perfect summer dinner.

NOTE: THE ROCK SALT CAN BE REUSED TO PREPARE MULTIPLE BATCHES OF SALT-ROASTED POTATOES. AFTER A FEW USES, IT WILL BEGIN TO DISCOLOR AS THE MOISTURE IT PULLS OUT OF THE POTATOES BEGINS TO CARAMELIZE. WE USUALLY USE OURS FOUR OR FIVE TIMES. THE SALT SHOULD BE REFRIGERATED BETWEEN USES.

1   Preheat the oven to 350°F (176°C). Create a layer of rock salt in a shallow 8 by 8-inch (20 by 20-cm) baking dish. Place the fingerling potatoes on top of the rock salt so that they are not touching, then add the remaining rock salt to cover the potatoes completely. Cover the dish with aluminum foil and bake until the potatoes are tender when pierced with a fork, about 35 minutes. Leave the oven on. Remove the potatoes from the salt and set aside to cool.

2   Combine the mussels and white wine in a pan large enough to accommodate the mussels. Cover, place over medium-high heat, and cook until the mussels open, 5 minutes. Drain the mussels, discarding the wine. Spread the mussels out on a baking sheet to cool, discarding any that didn't open. Once the mussels are cool enough to handle, gently pull them out of their shells and set aside. Discard the shells.

3   Put the egg yolk in a heavy ceramic bowl and, starting a drop at a time, whisk in 1 cup (240 ml) of the olive oil. When the emulsion forms and the mixture thickens, begin adding the oil in a thin, steady stream, whisking continuously. When the mixture becomes very thick, thin it with water, a few drops at a time, until it has the consistency of runny mayonnaise. Whisk in the sherry vinegar and mustard and season to taste with kosher salt. Transfer the mixture to a medium bowl and add the shelled mussels, the ham, pickles, green onions, and celery. Stir gently to combine and season to taste with black pepper.

4   Turn up the oven to 400°F (204°C). With the side of a broad knife, flatten each roasted fingerling potato against a cutting board so that it is still in one piece but has two flat sides. Heat the remaining

CONTINUED

½ cup (120 ml) of olive oil in a large nonstick skillet over medium heat and fry the fingerling potatoes on both sides until golden and crisped, about 4 minutes per side. Remove to paper towels to drain.

5 Heat the canola oil over medium-high heat in a heavy ovenproof sauté pan large enough to accommodate the four halibut fillets. Season the fillets with kosher salt and pepper. Sear the halibut fillets until they begin to develop a golden crust, about 3 minutes per side. Transfer the pan to the oven. After 3 minutes, remove the pan from the oven and flip the fillets. Return the pan to the oven and cook until a skewer slides in and out easily without resistance, 1 to 6 minutes depending on the thickness of the fillets.

6 Divide the potatoes evenly among four plates and top each portion with a halibut fillet. Squeeze some lemon juice over the fish and divide the mussel salad evenly among the plates.

CHOCOLATE SALAMI

This may come across as gimmicky—a ploy to keep the salami train rolling through to dessert—but it's actually a classic, something Italian *nonnas* and German *grossmutters* bake over holidays. It's also a fun recipe to make with kids.

1   Preheat the oven to 350°F (176°C).

2   Spread the pumpkin seeds, hazelnuts, and almonds in a single layer on a baking sheet and bake until lightly toasted, 12 to 15 minutes. Set aside.

3   Place the butter and chocolate in a heatproof medium bowl over a pan of barely simmering water, and whisk together until melted and smooth. Set aside.

4   In a large bowl, whisk together the egg yolks and brown sugar until thickened and uniformly tan in color, then whisk in the cocoa powder, orange zest, wine, cinnamon, cloves and nutmeg until fully incorporated. Using a rubber spatula, scrape in the melted chocolate mixture. Add the toasted nuts, candied ginger, and potato chips and fold together until completely incorporated. Snuggle the mixture in the prepared baking dish. Cover with plastic wrap and refrigerate for 30 minutes, until firm. Line a baking sheet with waxed paper.

5   Using a spatula or knife, divide the mixture into six equal pieces and then form each into a ball. Dust your work surface with confectioners' sugar, and embrace your inner kindergartener as you roll each piece back and fourth to form a log 1¼ inches (3 cm) in diameter, salami-length, and coated with confectioners' sugar.

6   Transfer the salamis to the prepared baking sheet and chill in the freezer for at least 5 minutes. Serve just slightly thawed, cut into thin slices.

SERVES 5 OR 6

½ cup (75 g) hulled pumpkin seeds

½ cup (65 g) chopped hazelnuts

¼ cup (35 g) slivered almonds

4 tablespoons (60 g) unsalted butter

8 ounces (227 g) dark chocolate (above 70 percent cocoa solids), broken into small pieces

4 egg yolks

½ cup (100 g) brown sugar

¼ cup (50 g) cocoa powder

1 teaspoon orange zest

¼ cup red wine, preferably a mellow Cabernet or Merlot

1 teaspoon ground cinnamon

Pinch of ground cloves

Pinch of freshly grated nutmeg

½ cup (80 g) diced candied ginger

½ cup (42 g) finely crushed potato chips

Confectioners' sugar, for dusting

Acknowledgments

From Meredith Erickson:

First and foremost thank you to Eli Cairo for being an incredible sausage maker and teacher, and an even better friend. Working with you was a complete joy. On to Greece!

To Michelle Cairo for being up for anything, agreeing to it all, and being a sister in what seems to be an endless sausage party.

To Tyler Gaston for the aid of words, dishwashing, cooking, driving, jokes, booze, de-feathering, reminiscing, building, and more booze.

To Marty for the good times, endless support, and laughs. You smell great.

To Nate Tilden for building something worth writing about.

To the OP partners for giving me one of the best trips in my life: the trip to Switzerland.

Big thank you to Jess Hereth for your words and thoughts on wine. And for throwing the best wine party imaginable.

To Alex Yoder, Colin Stafford, Victor Deras, and Melissa McKinney for recipes and endless patience.

To Wolfy and Alison for bringing great travel vibes, intense hangovers, and even better photos.

To the best Swiss guide a girl can ask for: Fabian Brunner.

To Karen Brooks for making the introduction.

To Kim Witherspoon and the entire Inkwell team, as always.

To Aaron Wehner and Julie Bennett for always believing. And to Kelly Snowden and Kara Plikaitis for being so easy to work with and so diligent about the details.

Thank you to our world-class testers, namely: Jane Rabinowicz, Patrick McEntyre, David McEntyre, David Levine, Jackie Dahlquist, David Briggs, Bonnie Crocker, Dana Drutz, Benjamin Culpepper, Micah Corcoran-Eller, Johnny Phompadith, Aron Adams, Jeff Linsing, Margaret Zynda, Amanda Grooms, Kimberly Patton, Jacob Lydamore, Catherine Coleman, Amy Maetzold-Hill, Jon Vaught, and Zach Eidem.

As always, thank you to my family and friends. These books are not always easy, and neither am I.

From Elias Cairo:

Thank you to Mom and Dad for showing me that working hard at something you love is the only way.

To Meredith Erickson, how in the hell did you keep all of these scattered ideas together and never let us settle on the easy way? You are one of the most talented people I have ever met. My favorite part of this is that we became pals.

To Eric Wolfinger, what a pleasure it has been to work with you. I thought I was getting a great photographer, but what I actually got was so much more. Your good eye, design, and willingness to be down for whatever was amazing. Honestly, thank you so much for being so invested in this project. With all the work we did, you made it a blast the whole time. You make it look so easy.

To Alex Yoder, Colin Stafford, Victor Deras, Melissa McKinney, and Amelia Lane, for all of the real recipes that are in this book. I am not worthy.

To Michelle Cairo, Mom likes me more. FACT. But thank you for risking it all on us.

To Tyler Gaston, we aren't tasting. We are drinking!

To Martin Schwartz, I want to be you.

To Nate Tilden, honestly for everything.

To Jessica Rose Hereth, you are cuter than a kitten. Also, thanks for having great taste.

To Alison Christiana, move here.

To Fabian Brunner, checking shit out since 1998.

To Famillia Stump, *danke für wirklich alles*.

To the Louis/Dressner Team and for everyone who attended our dinner, one of my favorite times ever.

To the amazingly talented and hardest working folks that actually make Olympia Provisions work.

To Josh Graves, Paul Oppliger, and Handsome Joe Brennan, for making the best damn product day in and day out.

To Karen Brooks, for the introduction and all you do for Portland.

To Julie Bennett, Aaron Wehner, and Emma Campion, for giving a guy whose nickname is "spell check" a chance to write a book.

To Kelly Snowden and Kara Plikaitis, for all of the endless hours you spent catching all of my mistakes, and keeping me calm by saying we will get through this.

To Clancy Drake, Dawn Yanagihara, and Andrea Chesman, for catching and fixing every last thing.

And to Kim Witherspoon, Stump's Alpenrose, Berggasthaus Aescher, Metzgerei Fässler, Adolph Fässler, Berggasthaus Forelle, Jakob Knaus, Berggasthaus Rotsteinpass, Jann Marugg, Brugger Jorg, Deep Canyon Preserve, Beau Culpepper, The Oregon Culinary Institute, K.M.S., Le Creuset, and to everyone who has supported this small business.

Index

Copyright © 2015 by Olympia Meats, LLC and Meredith Erickson

Photographs copyright © 2015 by Eric Wolfinger

All rights reserved.

Published in the United States by Ten Speed Press, an imprint of the
Crown Publishing Group, a division of Penguin Random House LLC, New York.

www.crownpublishing.com

www.tenspeed.com

Ten Speed Press and the Ten Speed Press colophon are registered
trademarks of Penguin Random House LLC.

Cairo, Elias.

Olympia Provisions : cured meats and tall tales from an American
charcuterie / Elias Cairo and Meredith Erickson; photography by Eric Wolfinger.

pages cm

Includes bibliographical references and index.

1. Cooking (Meat) 2. Meat—Preservation. I. Erickson, Meredith, 1980—II. Wolfinger, Eric.
III. Olympia Provisions (Firm) IV. Title. V. Title: Cured meats and tall tales
from an American charcuterie.

TX749.C335 2015

641.6'6—dc23

2015012027

Hardcover ISBN: 978-1-60774-701-7

eBook ISBN: 978-1-60774-702-4

Printed in China

Design by Kara Plikaitis

10 9 8 7 6 5 4 3 2 1

First Edition